Steck-Vaughn

English ASAP™

Connecting English to the Workplace

SCANS Consultant

Shirley Brod
Workforce ESL Consultant
Boulder, Colorado

Program Consultants

Judith Dean-Griffin
ESL Teacher
Windham Independent School District
Texas Department of Criminal Justice
Huntsville, Texas

Marilyn K. Spence
Workforce Education Coordinator
Orange Technical Education Centers
Mid-Florida Tech
Orlando, Florida

Brigitte Marshall
English Language Training
for Employment Participation
Albany, California

Christine Kay Williams
ESL Specialist
Towson University
Baltimore, Maryland

Marcia L. Taylor
ESL Basic Skills Instructor
JobLink 2000
Employee Learning Center
ISPAT Inland Steel Company
East Chicago, Indiana

STECK-VAUGHN
C O M P A N Y

A Division of Harcourt Brace & Company

www.steck-vaughn.com

Acknowledgments

Executive Editor:	Ellen Northcutt
Supervising Editor:	Tim Collins
Assistant Art Director:	Richard Balsam
Interior Design:	Richard Balsam, Jill Klinger, Paul Durick
Electronic Production:	Rebecca Gonzales, Katie Keenan
Assets Manager:	Margie Foster

Photo Credits

Randal Alhadeff–p.3a, 3b, 3c, 15a, 15b, 34-35, 39a, 39b, 46-47, 58-59, 63d, 66, 75c, 77, 87b, 87c, 88a, 94-95, 99b, 102, 106-107, 111b, 111d, 118-119; Don Couch–p.63b, 114; Chris Cunningham–p.27b, 75a; Christine Galida–p.4c, 15d, 27c, 27d, 39c, 51b, 53, 75d, 87d, 88c, 118 (all); Ken Lax–p.88b, 111a; James Minor–p.96; David Omer–p22-23, 82-83; Park Street–p.3d, 4b, 6, 10-11, 15c, 30, 39d, 51a, 70-71, 75b, 80, 99a, 99d, 111c; Ken Walker–p.4a, 18, 32, 51d, 63a, 63c, 107; Rick Williams–p.27a, 42, 51c, 87a, 99c.

Additional photography: P. 41 ©FoodPix; p.108 ©PhotoDisc.

Illustration Credits

Cover: Tim Dove, D Childress

Cindy Aarvig, Barbara Beck/Integrity Graphics, David Griffin, Chuck Joseph, Linda Kelen, Michael Krone, Gordon Ricke, Joel Snyder/Publishers' Graphics, Danielle Szabo/kreativ design, Victoria Vebell.

Contents

Units	SCANS Competencies	Workforce Skills
Unit 1 **Communication**	Serve customers Communicate information Understand technological systems Apply technology to tasks Organize and maintain information	Transfer a call Deal with a wrong number Keep a phone log Use voice mail
Unit 2 **Your Workplace**	Communicate information Monitor and correct performance Improve systems Allocate resources	Report progress on work Ask for and understand feedback Report job completion Create a status report
Unit 3 **Technology**	Apply technology to specific tasks Design or improve systems Maintain and troubleshoot technologies Communicate information	Report problems Create solutions Troubleshoot Make recommendations for improvement
Unit 4 **Time** **Management**	Allocate time Monitor performance Organize and interpret information	Build a schedule Organize tasks efficiently Meet deadlines
Unit 5 **Customer** **Service**	Serve customers Solve problems Communicate information Understand social systems	Understand your customers' needs Explain your product Use telephone skills for customer service Write a customer service letter
Unit 6 **Culture of Work**	Communicate information Work on teams Understand social systems Understand organizational systems	Make suggestions Build on team members' strengths Ask for help Be an effective team member
Unit 7 **Finances**	Allocate money Acquire and evaluate data Interpret information Monitor and correct performance	Understand a budget Use a budget Complete work on budget Keep budget records
Unit 8 **Health and** **Safety**	Evaluate and interpret information Understand organizational systems Communicate information	Understand health benefits Read and compare benefit plans Understand your rights Complete a claim form
Unit 9 **Working with** **People**	Work well with people from culturally diverse backgrounds Understand social systems Negotiate Interpret information	Avoid discriminatory language Respect cultural differences Resolve differences Understand policies
Unit 10 **Career** **Development**	Interpret and communicate information Acquire and evaluate data Organize and maintain files Understand social systems	Decide what you want from a job Analyze a job description Compare jobs Evaluate career choices

Each unit of *English ASAP* systematically presents one or more SCANS Competencies.
The SCANS Foundation Skills are integrated throughout the instruction.

Units	Grammar
Unit 1 **Communication**	**and/or/but** Gerunds and infinitives
Unit 2 **Your Workplace**	**Should/shouldn't** (review) Object pronouns with **for** and **to** **Make/do**
Unit 3 **Technology**	Adverbs with **-ly** Future with **going to** (review)
Unit 4 **Time** **Management**	Present perfect tense with **for** and **since** (statements, negatives, **yes/no** questions, short answers) Irregular past participles Reporting speech in the present tense
Unit 5 **Customer** **Service**	Comparative adjectives with **-er/more than** (review) Superlative adjectives with **-est/the most**
Unit 6 **Culture of Work**	Linking verbs Conditional sentences with **will**
Unit 7 **Finances**	Present perfect with **already** and **yet** Simple past tense with **ago**
Unit 8 **Health and** **Safety**	Nouns used as adjectives Sequence of modification Reflexive pronouns
Unit 9 **Working with** **People**	Clauses with **when/while** and the simple past/past progressive tenses Clauses with **before/after** and the simple past tense **as...as**
Unit 10 **Career** **Development**	Future with **going to** (review) Conditional sentences with **will** (review) Present perfect with **ever** and **never**

English ASAP is a complete, communicative, SCANS-based, four-skill ESL program for teaching adult and young adult learners the skills they need to succeed at work.

FEATURES

♦ *English ASAP is SCANS-based. English ASAP*'s SCANS-based syllabus teaches skills learners need to succeed in the workplace. The syllabus is correlated with the SCANS competencies, a taxonomy of work skills recognized by the U.S. Department of Labor as essential to every job. Additionally, the syllabus is compatible with the work skills and competencies in the Comprehensive Adult Student Assessment System (CASAS) Competencies, the Mainstream English Language Training Project (MELT), the National Institute for Literacy's Equipped for the Future Framework for Adult Literacy, and state curriculums for adult ESL from Texas and California.

 The *On Your Job* symbol appears on the Student Book page and corresponding page in the Teacher's Edition each time learners apply a SCANS-based skill to their jobs or career interests.

♦ *English ASAP is about the world of work.* All of the conversations, reading selections, listening activities, and realia are drawn from authentic workplace situations. *English ASAP* presents settings and workers from major career clusters, including transportation, health care, service occupations, office occupations, construction, hospitality, and industrial occupations.

♦ *English ASAP* **teaches the skills required in all job descriptions.** Learners gain valuable experience working in teams; teaching others; serving customers; organizing, evaluating, and communicating information; understanding and using technology; negotiating; allocating resources; and completing projects.

♦ *English ASAP* **is communicative.** Numerous conversational models and communicative activities in the Student Books and Teacher's Editions—including problem-solving activities, surveys, and cooperative learning projects—get learners talking from the start.

♦ **English ASAP is appropriate for adults and young adults.** The language and situations presented in *English ASAP* are ones adults and young adults are likely to encounter. The abundance of attractive, true-to-life photographs, illustrations, and realia will interest and motivate adult and young adult learners.

◆ *English ASAP* **addresses all four language skills.** Each level of *English ASAP* addresses listening, speaking, reading, and writing. Starting in Level 1, a two-page grammar spread in each Student Book unit plus corresponding Workbook reinforcement and supplementary grammar worksheets in the Teacher's Editions ensure that learners get appropriate grammar practice.

◆ *English ASAP* **starts at the true beginner level.** *English ASAP* begins at the Literacy Level, designed for learners who have no prior knowledge of English and have few or no literacy skills in their native language(s) or are literate in a language with a non-Roman alphabet. Learners master foundation literacy skills in tandem with listening and speaking skills. The next level, Level 1, is intended for learners with little or no prior knowledge of English. As learners continue through the program, they master progressively higher levels of language and work skills. The Placement Tests help teachers place learners in the appropriate level of the program. For information on placement, see page v of this Teacher's Edition.

◆ *English ASAP* **is appropriate for multilevel classes.** Because unit topics carry over from level to level with increasing sophistication, the series is ideal for use in multilevel classes. For example, a Literacy Level skill in the technology unit is naming machines. A Level 2 skill in the technology unit is completing machine maintenance reports. Units are situational and nonsequential, making *English ASAP* appropriate for open-entry/open-exit situations.

◆ *English ASAP* **meets the needs of individual workplaces and learners.** Because the demands of each workplace and each individual's job are unique, the abundance of *On Your Job* activities allows learners to relate their new skills to their workplaces and career interests. In addition, the Personal Dictionary feature in each unit lets learners focus only on the vocabulary they need to do their jobs. Finally, with Steck-Vaughn's *Workforce Writing Dictionary,* learners can create a complete custom dictionary of all the vocabulary they need to know to succeed.

COMPONENTS

English ASAP consists of:

♦ Student Books

♦ Workbooks starting at Level 1

♦ Teacher's Editions

♦ Audiocassettes

♦ Steck-Vaughn *Workforce Writing Dictionary*

♦ Placement Tests, Form A and Form B

Student Books

Each four-color Student Book consists of ten 12-page units, providing learners with ample time on task to acquire the target SCANS competencies and language.

♦ **The Student Books follow a consistent format for easy teaching and learning.** Each unit is consistently organized and can be taught in approximately eight to twelve classroom sessions.

♦ **Complete front matter offers valuable teaching suggestions.** Ideas on how to teach each type of activity in the Student Book units and suggested teaching techniques give teachers valuable information on how to use *English ASAP* with maximum success.

♦ **Clear directions and abundant examples ensure that learners always know exactly what to do.** Examples for each activity make tasks apparent to learners and teachers. Clear exercise titles and directions tell teachers and learners exactly what learners are to do.

♦ **Performance Check pages provide a complete evaluation program.** Teachers can use these pages to evaluate learners' progress and to track the program's learner verification needs. Success is built in because work skills are always checked in familiar formats.

Workbooks

The Workbooks contain ten eight-page units plus a complete Answer Key. Each Workbook unit always contains at least one exercise for each section of the Student Book. To allow for additional reinforcement of grammar, there are multiple exercises for the Grammar section. The exercises for each section of the Student Book are indicated on the corresponding page of the Teacher's Edition and in a chart at the front of each Workbook. Because the Answer Keys are removable, the Workbooks can be used both in the classroom and for self-study.

Teacher's Editions

The complete Teacher's Editions help both new and experienced teachers organize their teaching, motivate their learners, and successfully use a variety of individual, partner, and teamwork activities.

◆ **Unit Overviews provide valuable information on how to motivate learners and organize teaching.** Each opener contains a complete list of the SCANS and workplace skills in the unit to help teachers organize their teaching. The Unit Warm-Up on each unit opener page helps teachers build learners' interest and gets them ready for the unit. The openers also contain a list of materials—including pictures, flash cards, and realia—teachers can use to enliven instruction throughout the unit.

◆ **The Teacher's Editions contain complete suggested preparation and teaching procedures for each section of the Student Book.** Each section of a unit begins with a list of the workplace skills developed on the Student Book page(s). Teachers can use the list when planning lessons. The teaching notes give suggestions for a recommended three-part lesson format:

Preparation: Suggestions for preteaching the new language, SCANS skills, and concepts on the Student Book page(s) before learners open their books.

Presentation: Suggested procedures for working with the Student Book page(s) in class.

Follow-Up: An optional activity to provide reinforcement or to enrich and extend the new language and competencies. The Follow-Ups include a variety of interactive partner and team activities. Each activity has a suggested variant, marked with ◆ for use with learners who require activities at a slightly more sophisticated level. For teaching ease, the corresponding Workbook exercise(s) for each page or section of the Student Book are indicated on the Teacher's Edition page starting at Level 1.

◆ **The Teacher's Editions contain SCANS Notes, Teaching Notes, Culture Notes, and Language Notes.** Teachers can share this wealth of information with learners or use it in lesson planning.

◆ **Each Teacher's Edition unit contains an additional suggested Informal Workplace-Specific Assessment.** Teachers will find these suggestions invaluable in evaluating learners' success in relating their new skills to their workplaces or career interests. Designed to supplement the Performance Check pages in each unit of the Student

Books, these brief speaking activities include having learners state their workplace's customer service policies, their workplace's policies on lateness and absence, and the procedures they use at work to maintain equipment.

♦ **Blackline Masters.** In the Literacy Level, the Blackline Masters help teachers present or reinforce many basic literacy skills. Starting at Level 1, the Blackline Masters reinforce the grammar in each unit.

♦ **Additional features in the Teacher's Editions.** The Teacher's Editions contain Individual Competency Charts for each unit and a Class Cumulative Competency Chart for recording learners' progress and tracking the program's learner verification needs. A Certificate of Completion is included for teachers to copy and award to learners upon successful completion of that level of *English ASAP*. In addition, each unit of the Literacy Level Teacher's Edition contains an ASAP Project, an optional holistic cooperative learning project. Learners will find these to be valuable and stimulating culminating activities. Starting at Level 1, the ASAP Project appears directly on the Student Book pages.

Audiocassettes

The audiocassettes contain all the dialogs and listening activities marked with this cassette symbol. The audiocassettes provide experience in listening to a variety of native speakers in the workplace. The Listening Transcript at the back of each Student Book and Teacher's Edition contains the scripts of all the listening selections not appearing directly on the pages of the Student Books.

Workforce Writing Dictionary

The Steck-Vaughn *Workforce Writing Dictionary* is a 96-page custom dictionary that lets learners create a personalized, alphabetical list of words and expressions related to their own workplaces and career interests. Each letter of the alphabet is allocated two to four pages and is illustrated with several workforce-related words. Learners can use the dictionary to record all of the relevant language they need to succeed on their jobs.

Placement Tests

The Placement Tests, Form A and Form B, help teachers place learners in the appropriate level of *English ASAP*. For more information see page v of this Teacher's Edition.

About SCANS

Each unit of *English ASAP* systematically presents one or more SCANS Competencies. The Foundation Skills are integrated through all the instruction.

WORKPLACE KNOW-HOW

The know-how identified by SCANS is made up of five competencies and a three-part foundation of skills and personal qualities needed for solid job performance. These include:

COMPETENCIES—effective workers can productively use:

- **Resources**—allocating time, money, materials, space, staff;

- **Interpersonal Skills**—working on teams, teaching others, serving customers, leading, negotiating, and working well with people from culturally diverse backgrounds;

- **Information**—acquiring and evaluating data, organizing and maintaining files, interpreting and communicating, and using computers to process information;

- **Systems**—understanding social, organizational, and technological systems, monitoring and correcting performance, and designing or improving systems;

- **Technology**—selecting equipment and tools, applying technology to specific tasks, and maintaining and troubleshooting technologies.

THE FOUNDATION—competence requires:

- **Basic Skills**—reading, writing, arithmetic and mathematics, speaking and listening;

- **Thinking Skills**—thinking creatively, making decisions, solving problems, seeing things in the mind's eye, knowing how to learn, and reasoning;

- **Personal Qualities**—individual responsibility, self-esteem, sociability, self-management, and integrity.

Reprinted from *What Work Requires of Schools—A SCANS Report for America 2000,* Secretary's Commission on Achieving Necessary Skills, U.S. Department of Labor.

For Additional Information

For more information on SCANS, CASAS, adult literacy, and the workforce, visit these websites.

For more information about Steck-Vaughn, visit our website.

www.steckvaughn.com

CASAS Information

www.casas.org

Center for Applied Linguistics

www.cal.org

Education Information

www.ed.gov

Literacy Link

www.pbs.org/learn/literacy

National Center on Adult Literacy

www.literacyonline.org/ncal/index.html

National Institute for Literacy

novel.nifl.gov

School-to-Work Information

www.stw.ed.gov

Workforce Information

www.doleta.gov

Workforce Investment Act

www.usworkforce.org

www.icesa.org

Steck-Vaughn

English ASAP™

Connecting English to the Workplace

SCANS Consultant

Shirley Brod
Workforce ESL Consultant
Boulder, Colorado

Program Consultants

Judith Dean-Griffin
ESL Teacher
Windham Independent School District
Texas Department of Criminal Justice
Huntsville, Texas

Marilyn K. Spence
Workforce Education Coordinator
Orange Technical Education Centers
Mid-Florida Tech
Orlando, Florida

Brigitte Marshall
English Language Training
for Employment Participation
Albany, California

Christine Kay Williams
ESL Specialist
Towson University
Baltimore, Maryland

Marcia L. Taylor
ESL Basic Skills Instructor
JobLink 2000
Employee Learning Center
ISPAT Inland Steel Company
East Chicago, Indiana

STECK-VAUGHN®
C O M P A N Y
A Division of Harcourt Brace & Company

www.steck-vaughn.com

Introduction to Student Book 3

About SCANS, the Workforce, and *English ASAP: Connecting English to the Workplace*

SCANS and the Workforce

The Secretary's Commission on Achieving Necessary Skills (SCANS) was established by the U.S. Department of Labor in 1990. Its mission was to study the demands of workplace environments and determine whether people entering the workforce are capable of meeting those demands. The commission identified skills for employment, suggested ways for assessing proficiency, and devised strategies to implement the identified skills. The commission's first report, entitled *What Work Requires of Schools—SCANS Report for America 2000*, was published in June 1991. The report is designed for use by educators (curriculum developers, job counselors, training directors, and teachers) to prepare the modern workforce for the workplace with viable, up-to-date skills.

The report identified two types of skills: Competencies and Foundations. There are five SCANS Competencies: (1) Resources, (2) Interpersonal, (3) Information, (4) Systems, and (5) Technology. There are three parts contained in SCANS Foundations: (1) Basic Skills (including reading, writing, arithmetic, mathematics, listening, and speaking); (2) Thinking Skills (including creative thinking, decision making, problem solving, seeing things in the mind's eye, knowing how to learn, and reasoning); and (3) Personal Qualities (including responsibility, self-esteem, sociability, self-management, and integrity/honesty).

Steck-Vaughn's *English ASAP: Connecting English to the Workplace*

English ASAP is a complete SCANS-based, four-skills program for teaching ESL and SCANS skills to adults and young adults. *English ASAP* follows a work skills-based syllabus that is compatible with the CASAS and MELT competencies.

English ASAP is designed for learners enrolled in public or private schools, in corporate training environments, in learning centers, or in institutes, and for individuals working with tutors. *English ASAP* has these components:

Student Books

The Student Books are designed to allow from 125 to 235 hours of instruction. Each Student Book contains 10 units of SCANS-based instruction. A Listening Transcript of material appearing on the Audiocassettes and a Vocabulary list, organized by unit, of core workforce-based words and phrases appear at the back of each Student Book. Because unit topics carry over from level to level, *English ASAP* is ideal for multi-level classes.

The *On Your Job* symbol appears on the Student Book page each time learners apply a work skill to their own jobs or career interests.

Tip An abundance of tips throughout each unit provides information and strategies that learners can use to be more effective workers and language learners.

Teacher's Editions

Teacher's Editions provide reduced Student Book pages with answers inserted and wraparound teacher notes that give detailed suggestions on how to present each page of the Student Book in class. Starting at Level 1, the Teacher's Editions also provide blackline masters to reinforce the grammar in each unit. The Literacy Level Teacher's Edition contains blackline masters that provide practice with many basic literacy skills. The complete Listening Transcript, Vocabulary, and charts for tracking individual and class success appear at the back of each Teacher's Edition.

Workbooks

The Workbooks, starting at Level 1, provide reinforcement for each section of the Student Books.

Audiocassettes

The Audiocassettes contain all the dialogs and listening activities in the Student Books.

 This symbol appears on the Student Book page and corresponding Teacher's Edition page each time material for that page is recorded on the Audiocassettes. A Listening Transcript of all material recorded on the tapes but not appearing directly on the Student Book pages is at the back of each Student Book and Teacher's Edition.

Workforce Writing Dictionary

Steck-Vaughn's *Workforce Writing Dictionary*, is a 96-page custom dictionary that allows learners to create a personalized, alphabetical list of the key words and phrases they need to know for their jobs. Each letter of the alphabet is allocated two to four pages for learners to record the language they need. In addition, each letter is illustrated with several workforce-related words.

Placement Tests

The Placement Tests, Form A and Form B, can be used as entry and exit tests and to assist in placing learners in the appropriate level of *English ASAP*.

To the Teacher

Placement

In addition to the Placement Tests, the following table indicates placement based on the CASAS and new MELT student performance level standards.

Placement

New MELT SPL	CASAS Achievement Score	English ASAP
0–1	179 or under	Literacy
2–3	180–200	Level 1
4–5	201–220	Level 2
6	221–235	Level 3
7	236 and above	Level 4

About Student Book 3

Organization of a Unit

Each twelve-page unit contains these nine sections: Unit Opener, Getting Started, Talk About It, Keep Talking, Listening, Grammar, Reading and Writing, Extension, and Performance Check.

Unit Opener

Each Unit Opener includes photos and several related, work-focused questions. The photos and questions activate learners' prior knowledge by getting them to think and talk about the unit topic. The **Performance Preview**, which gives an overview of all the skills in the unit, helps teachers set goals and purposes for the unit. Optionally, teachers may want to examine the Performance Preview with learners before they begin the unit.

Getting Started

An initial **Team Work** activity presents key work skills, concepts, and language introduced in the unit. It consists of active critical thinking and peer teaching to activate the use of the new language and to preview the content of the unit. A **Partner Work** or **Practice** the **Dialog** activity encourages learners to use the new language in communicative ways. A culminating class or group **Survey** encourages learners to relate the new language to themselves and their workplaces or career interests.

Talk About It

This page provides opportunities for spoken communication. **Practice the Dialog** provides a model for conversation. **Partner Work** presents a personalized **On Your Job** activity that allows learners to use the model in Practice the Dialog to talk about their own workplace experiences.

Useful Language The **Useful Language** box contains related words, phrases, and expressions for learners to use as they complete Partner Work.

ASAP
PROJECT The **ASAP Project** is a long-term project learners complete over the course of the unit. Learners create items such as files of human resources forms, lists of interview questions, and work schedules that they can use outside of the classroom.

Keep Talking

The Keep Talking page contains additional conversation models and speaking tasks. It also includes the **Personal Dictionary** feature. This feature allows learners to record the language relevant to the unit topic that they need to do their jobs. Because each learner's job is different, this personalized resource enables learners to focus on the language that is most useful to them. In addition, learners can use this feature in conjunction with Steck-Vaughn's *Workforce Writing Dictionary* to create a completely customized lexicon of key words and phrases they need to know.

Listening

The Listening page develops SCANS-based listening skills. Tasks include listening for greetings, names of places, directions, instructions, and times.

All the activities develop the skill of **focused listening.** Learners learn to recognize the information they need and to listen selectively for only that information. They do not have to understand every word; rather, they have to filter out everything except the relevant information. This essential skill is used by native speakers of all languages.

Many of the activities involve **multi-task listening**. In these activities, called **Listen Again** and **Listen Once More**, learners listen to the same selection several times and complete a different task each time. First they might listen for the main idea. They might listen again for specific information. They might listen a third time in order to draw conclusions or make inferences.

Culminating discussion questions allow learners to relate the information they have heard to their own needs and interests.

A complete Listening Transcript for all dialogs recorded on the Audiocassettes but not appearing directly on the Student Book pages is at the back of the Student Book and Teacher's Edition. All the selections are recorded on the Audiocassettes.

Grammar

Grammar, a two-page spread, presents key grammatical structures that complement the unit competencies. Language boxes show the new language in a clear, simple format that allows learners to make generalizations about the new language. Oral and written exercises provide contextualized reinforcement relevant to the workplace.

Reading and Writing

Reading selections, such as excerpts from instruction manuals, job evaluations, and

To the Teacher

timecards, focus on items learners encounter at work. Exercises and discussion questions develop reading skills and help learners relate the content of the selections to their workplaces or career interests.

The writing tasks, often related to the reading selection, help learners develop writing skills, such as completing job applications, writing to-do lists, and writing schedules.

Extension

The Extension page enriches the previous instruction. As in other sections, realia is used extensively. Oral and written exercises help learners master the additional skills, language, and concepts, and relate them to their workplaces and career interests.

CultureNotes **Culture Notes**, a feature that appears on each Extension page, sparks lively, engaging discussion. Topics include asking for directions, using machines, using employee handbooks, and exchanging greetings.

Performance Check

The two-page Performance Check allows teachers and learners to track learners' progress and to meet the learner verification needs of schools, companies, or programs. All work skills are tested in the same manner they are presented in the units; so, formats are familiar and non-threatening, and success is built in. The **Performance Review** at the end of each test alerts teachers and learners to the work skills that are being evaluated. The check-off boxes allow learners to track their success and gain a sense of accomplishment and satisfaction. Finally, a culminating discussion allows learners to relate their new skills to their development as effective workers.

Teaching Techniques

Make Your Classroom Mirror the Workplace

Help learners develop workplace skills

by setting up your classroom to mirror a workplace. Use any of these suggestions.

◆ Establish policies on lateness and absence similar to those a business might have.

◆ Provide learners with a daily agenda of the activities they will complete that day, including partner work and small group assignments. Go over the agenda with learners at the beginning and end of class.

◆ With learner input, establish a list of goals for the class. Goals can include speaking, reading, and writing English every day; using effective teamwork skills; or learning ten new vocabulary words each day. Go over the goals with learners at regular intervals.

◆ Assign students regular jobs and responsibilities, such as arranging the chairs in a circle, setting up the overhead projector, or making copies for the class.

Presenting a Unit Opener

The unit opener sets the stage for the unit. Use the photos and questions to encourage learners to:

◆ Speculate about what the unit might cover.

◆ Activate prior knowledge.

◆ Relate what they see in the photos to their own work environments.

Peer Teaching

Because each adult learner brings rich life experience to the classroom, *English ASAP* is designed to help you use each learner's expertise as a resource for peer teaching.

Here are some practical strategies for peer teaching:

◆ Have learners work in pairs/small groups to clarify new language concepts for each other.

◆ If a learner possesses a particular work skill, appoint that learner as "class consultant" in that area and have learners direct queries to that individual.

◆ Set up a reference area in a corner of your classroom. Include dictionaries, career books, and other books your learners will find useful.

Partner Work and Team Work

The abundance of Partner Work and Team Work activities in *English ASAP* serves the dual purposes of developing learners' communicative competence and providing learners with experience using key SCANS interpersonal skills, such as working in teams, teaching others, leading, negotiating, and working well with people from culturally diverse backgrounds. To take full advantage of these activities, follow these suggestions.

◆ Whenever students work in groups, appoint, or have students select, a leader.

◆ Use multiple groupings. Have learners work with different partners and teams, just as workers do in the workplace. For different activities, you might group learners according to language ability, skill, or learner interest.

◆ Make sure learners understand that everyone on the team is responsible for the team's work.

◆ At the end of each activity, have teams report the results to the class.

◆ Discuss with learners their teamwork skills and talk about ways teams can work together effectively. They can discuss how to clarify roles and responsibilities, resolve disagreements effectively, communicate openly, and make decisions together.

Purpose Statement

Each page after the unit opener begins with a brief purpose statement that summarizes the work skills presented on that page. When learners first begin working on a page, focus their attention on the purpose statement and help them read it. Ask them what the page will be about. Discuss with the class why the skill is important. Ask learners to talk about their prior knowledge of the skill. Finally, show learners how using the skill will help them become more effective on their jobs.

Survey

The **Survey** on each **Getting Started** page helps learners relate the new language and skills to their own lives. Before learners begin the activity, help them create questions they'll need to ask. Assist them in deciding how they'll record their answers. You may need to model taking notes, using tally marks, and other simple ways to record information. Assist learners in setting a time limit before they begin. Remember to allow learners to move about the room as they complete the activity.

Many Survey results can be summarized in a bar graph or pie chart.

◆ A bar graph uses bars to represent numbers. Bar graphs have two scales, a vertical scale and a horizontal scale. For example, to graph the number of learners who get paid by check versus those paid by direct deposit, the vertical scale can represent numbers of students, such as 2, 4, 6, 8, etc. The horizontal scale can consist of two bars. One bar represents the number of learners paid by check. The other bar represents the number of learners paid by direct deposit. The two bars can be different colors to set them apart. Bars should be the same width.

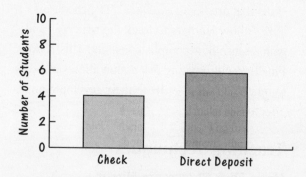

◆ A pie chart shows the parts that make up a whole set of facts. Each part of the pie is a percentage of the whole. For example, a pie chart might show 40% of learners are paid by check and 60% are paid by direct deposit.

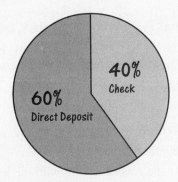

Presenting a Dialog

To present a dialog, follow these suggested steps:

◆ Play the tape or say the dialog aloud two or more times. Ask one or two simple questions to make sure learners understand.

◆ Say the dialog aloud line-by-line for learners to repeat chorally, by rows, and then individually.

◆ Have learners say or read the dialog together in pairs.

◆ Have several pairs say or read the dialog aloud for the class.

Presenting the Personal Dictionary

The Personal Dictionary enables learners to focus on the vocabulary in each unit that is relevant to their particular jobs. To use this feature, have learners work in teams to brainstorm vocabulary words they might put in their dictionaries. Have team reporters share their ideas with the class. Then allow learners a few minutes to add to their dictionaries. Remind students to continue adding words throughout the unit.

For further vocabulary development, learners can enter the words from their Personal Dictionary into their *Workforce Writing Dictionaries.*

To the Teacher

Presenting a Listening Activity

Use any of these suggestions:

◆ To activate learners' prior knowledge, have them look at the illustrations, if any, and say as much as they can about them. Encourage them to make inferences about the content of the listening selection.

◆ Have learners read the directions. To encourage them to focus their listening, have them read the questions before they listen so that they know exactly what to listen for.

◆ Play the tape or read the Listening Transcript aloud as learners complete the activity. Rewind the tape and play it again as necessary.

◆ Help learners check their work.

In multi-task listening, remind learners that they will listen to the same passage several times and answer different questions each time. After learners complete a section, have them check their own or each others' work before you rewind the tape and proceed to the next questions.

Presenting a Tip

Tip A variety of tips throughout each unit present valuable advice on how to be a successful employee and/or language learner. To present a tip, help learners read the tip. Discuss it with them. Ask them how it will help them. For certain tips, such as those in which learners make lists, you may want to allow learners time to start the activity.

Presenting a Discussion

English ASAP provides a variety of whole-class and team discussions. Always encourage students to state their ideas and respond appropriately to other learners' comments. At the end of each discussion, have team reporters summarize their team's ideas and/or help the class come to a consensus about the topic.

Prereading

To help learners read the selections with ease and success, establish a purpose for reading and call on learners' prior knowledge to make inferences about the reading. Use any of these techniques:

◆ Have learners look over and describe any photographs, realia, and/or illustrations. Ask them to use the illustrations to say what they think the selection might be about.

◆ Have learners read the title and any heads or sub-heads. Ask them what kind of information they think is in the selection and how it might be organized. Ask them where they might encounter such information outside of class and why they would want to read it.

◆ To help learners focus their reading, have them review the comprehension activities before they read the selection. Ask them what kind of information they think they will find out when they read. Restate their ideas and/or write them on the board in acceptable English.

◆ Remind learners that they do not have to know all the words in order to understand the selection.

Evaluation

To use the Performance Check pages successfully, follow these suggested procedures:
Before and during each evaluation, create a relaxed, affirming atmosphere. Chat with the learners for a few minutes and review the material. When you and the learners are ready, have learners read the directions and look over each exercise before they complete it. If at any time you sense that learners are becoming frustrated, stop to provide additional review. Resume when learners are ready. The evaluation formats follow two basic patterns:

1. **Speaking** competencies are checked in the format used to present them in the unit. Have learners read the instructions. Make sure learners know what to do. Then have learners complete the evaluation in one of these ways:

Self- and Peer Evaluation: Have learners complete the spoken activity in pairs. Learners in each pair evaluate themselves and/or each other and report the results to you.

Teacher/Pair Evaluation: Have pairs complete the activity as you observe and evaluate their work. Begin with the most proficient learners. As other learners who are ready to be evaluated wait, have them practice in pairs. Learners who complete the evaluation successfully can peer-teach those who are waiting or those who need additional review.

Teacher/Individual Evaluation: Have individuals complete the activity with you as their partner. Follow the procedures in Teacher/Pair Evaluation.

2. **Listening, reading,** and **writing** competencies are also all checked in the same format used to present them in the unit. When learners are ready to begin, have them read the instructions. Demonstrate the first item and have learners complete the activity. In Listening activities, play the tape or read the listening transcript aloud two or more times. Then have learners check their work. Provide any review needed, and have learners try the activity again.

When learners demonstrate mastery of a skill to your satisfaction, have them record their success by checking the appropriate box in the Performance Review. The Teacher's Edition also contains charts for you to reproduce to keep track of individual and class progress.

Steck-Vaughn

English ASAP

Connecting English to the Workplace

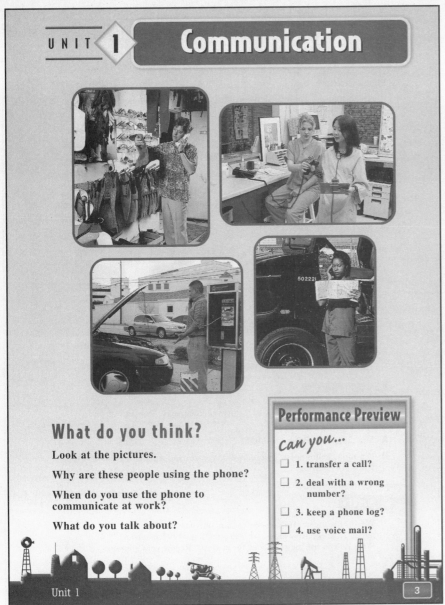

★ Serve customers
★ Communicate information
★ Understand technological systems
★ Apply technology to tasks
★ Organize and maintain information

Workforce Skills

• Transfer a call
• Deal with a wrong number
• Keep a phone log
• Use voice mail

Materials

• Picture cards of employees on the telephone and of a telephone
• Clock, calendar
• Phone log pages
• Picture cards or realia of receptionist, plant manager, cellular phone, dentist, and prescription

Unit Warm-Up

To stimulate discussion about the unit topic (using the telephone to communicate at work), show pictures of employees using the phone on the job. Ask learners to talk about times they use the telephone at work. What problems do they have using the phone?

★   ★   ★   ★   ★

WORKFORCE SKILLS (page 3)

Transfer a call

★   ★   ★   ★   ★

PREPARATION

Display the picture cards. Have learners brainstorm a list of words and phrases people can use on the telephone.

PRESENTATION

1. Focus attention on the photographs. Ask learners what the unit might be about. Write their ideas on the board and/or restate them in acceptable English.

2. Have learners talk about the photos. Ask them to describe what is going on in each picture and who is talking on the phone. Have learners speculate about who the callers are.

3. Help learners read the questions. Discuss the questions with the class.

4. You may want to use the Performance Preview to provide learners with an overview of the skills in the unit. Have learners read the list of skills and discuss what they will learn in this unit.

FOLLOW-UP

Role-Play: Go around the room and have each learner role-play answering the telephone at work. Discuss what these phone greetings have in common. Are they polite? Do they tell who is answering the phone?

♦ Have partners role-play short telephone calls of the sort that might take place where they work. Ask a few pairs to present their role-plays to the class.

WORKBOOK

Unit 1, Exercises 1A–1B

Getting Started .... Using the telephone

TEAM WORK

The people are talking to callers. What does each person say next? Complete their statements. Write the letter.

> **a.** Please hold a moment and I'll transfer you.
>
> **b.** Would you like to leave a voice mail message?
>
> **c.** You have the wrong number.

Sorry, there's no one here by that name. _c_

Elena Montoya is in another department. _a_

Tom isn't here now. He's at lunch. _b_

PARTNER WORK

Take turns asking to speak to learners in your class. Your partner answers your request.

A May I speak to Pedro Guardia?

B I'm sorry. Pedro doesn't work on Fridays. Do you want to leave a voice mail message?

SURVEY

Work with a team. How many learners on your team use the phone at work? How many use voice mail at work? at school? What do you use the telephone for at work? Report your answers to the class.

4 Unit 1

Teaching Note

Use this page to introduce the new language in the unit. Whenever possible, encourage peer teaching. Supply any new language the learners need.

PREPARATION

1. Preteach or review **voice mail** and **transfer a call.** Show a picture card and act out leaving a voice mail message and transferring a call.

2. Ask learners if they have ever received a call meant for someone else, either at home or at work. Discuss what they do in these situations.

PRESENTATION

1. Have learners read and discuss the Purpose Statement. For more information see "Purpose Statement" on page viii.

2. Focus attention on the photographs. Encourage learners to say as much as they can about them. Write their ideas on the board and/or restate them in acceptable English.

3. Have teams read the Team Work instructions. Make sure each team knows what to do. Remind the teams that they are responsible for making sure that each member understands the new language. Then have teams complete the activity. Have team reporters share their answers with the class.

4. Have partners read the Partner Work instructions. Make sure each pair knows what to do. If necessary, model the activity. Then have partners complete the activity. Have learners switch partners and repeat the activity. Have pairs perform their conversations for the class. For more information, see "Partner Work and Team Work" on page viii.

 5. Have teams read the Survey instructions. Make sure everyone knows what to do. Then have teams complete the activity.

Have team reporters share their answers with the class. For more information, see "Survey" on page viii.

FOLLOW-UP

Chart: Use the information from the Survey to make a three-column table on the board. Label columns *Name, Telephone,* and *Voice Mail.* Have learners write their names and put check-marks in the appropriate columns.

♦ Help learners use the information in the chart to create a bar graph. The horizontal axis should show the second and third column labels; the vertical axis, the number of learners.

WORKBOOK

Unit 1, Exercises 2A–2C

Talk About It
Transferring a call

 PRACTICE THE DIALOG

1. **A** Hi, my name's Ted Morgan. Is this customer service?

   B Yes, it is. How may I help you?

   A I don't think the ground beef that I bought yesterday is fresh.

2. **B** I'm sorry. I'll transfer you to the meat department, sir.

   C Meat department, Yolanda speaking.

   B Yolanda, this is Sam. A customer has a complaint about the ground beef he bought. Can you talk to him?

   C Sure, Sam. I'd be happy to talk to him.

   B Thanks, Yolanda. I'll transfer him now.

3. **C** Meat department, Yolanda speaking.

   A Yes, I think the ground beef I bought at your store smells bad.

With two classmates, practice transferring calls. Use the dialog above and the Useful Language.

> ### Useful Language
>
> I'll connect you now.
>
> That number's busy.
>
> Can you hold, please?

ASAP PROJECT

Work with a team. Make a book of phrases to use on the phone at work. Record phrases in the following categories: answering the phone, introducing yourself, transferring a call, dealing with wrong numbers, and saying good-bye. Complete this project as you work through the unit.

Unit 1

`5`

WORKFORCE SKILLS (page 5)

Transfer a call

★　　★　　★　　★　　★

ASAP PROJECT

Have learners read the instructions. Discuss the project and its purpose with learners. Make sure that everyone understands. Help learners assign themselves to teams depending upon their skills, knowledge, interests, or other personal strengths. Have each team select a leader. Throughout the rest of the unit, allow time for learners to work on the project. Have the teams agree on a deadline when the project will be finished. For more information see "ASAP Project" on page vi.

PREPARATION

Teach or review the new language in the lesson. Show a picture card of a telephone. Act out transferring a call. Identify what you're doing. Say, "I'm transferring a call." Explain that many telephones have hold and transfer buttons.

PRESENTATION

1. Have learners read and discuss the Purpose Statement. For more information see "Purpose Statement" on page viii.

 2. Focus attention on the illustrations. Encourage learners to say as much as they can about them. Have learners say what the people are doing. Then present the dialog. See "Presenting a Dialog" on page ix.

3. Have teams read the instructions under the dialog. Focus attention on the Useful Language box. Help learners read the expressions. If necessary, model pronunciation. Then have learners work in teams of three to complete the activity. Have learners change teams and repeat the activity. Have several teams present their dialogs to the class.

FOLLOW-UP

Dialogs: Present this situation. A customer phones *Bargain Tires and Brakes* to complain that an employee put the wrong tire on his/her car. The customer wants to speak to the manager. Have teams of three role-play the phone call. Ask several teams to present their dialogs to the class.

♦ Have team members talk about problems they've had transferring calls or having their calls transferred. Have them discuss ways to handle each problem. Ask team reporters to share ideas with the class.

WORKBOOK

Unit 1, Exercise 3

WORKFORCE SKILLS (page 6)

Deal with a wrong number

★   ★   ★   ★   ★

Culture Note

Tell learners that if they receive a call for someone else in their workplace, they should try to transfer the call, rather than ask the caller to call the company again. Discuss why customers might appreciate this.

Personal Dictionary

Have learners add the words in their Personal Dictionary to their *Workforce Writing Dictionary*. For more information see "Workforce Writing Dictionary" on page v.

Keep Talking — Dealing with a wrong number

 PRACTICE THE DIALOG

A Hello. Speedy Plumbing Service. This is Christina. May I help you?

B May I speak with Paul?

A I'm sorry. There's no Paul here. You have the wrong number.

B Is this 555-1278?

A No, it isn't.

B Oh, I'm sorry.

A No problem. Have a nice day.

Take turns dealing with wrong numbers. Use the dialog and the Useful Language above.

Useful Language

What number are you trying to reach?

No one with that name works here.

 Tip Don't give your name or number to callers who dial the wrong number. Ask the caller the number he or she wanted. **What number did you want?**

Personal Dictionary ▸ Communicating on the Phone

Write the words and phrases that you need to know.

_____

_____

_____

6   Unit 1

PREPARATION

Act out answering a phone call and dealing with a wrong number. Have learners point out key phrases. Write them on the board.

PRESENTATION

1. Have learners read and discuss the Purpose Statement. For more information see "Purpose Statement" on page viii.

2. Focus attention on the photograph. Encourage learners to say as much as they can about it. Have them identify the workplace and speculate about what the employee is saying. Present the dialog. See "Presenting a Dialog" on page ix.

 3. Have pairs read the instructions under the dialog. Focus attention on the Useful

Language box. Help learners read the expressions. If necessary, model pronunciation. Then have partners complete the activity. Have learners switch partners and repeat the activity. Ask several pairs to present their dialogs to the class.

4. Have learners read the Personal Dictionary instructions. Then use the Personal Dictionary procedures on page ix. Remind learners to add words to their dictionaries throughout the unit.

Tip Have learners read the Tip independently. Have learners discuss how the advice will help them. For more information see "Presenting a Tip" on page ix.

FOLLOW-UP

Hello . . . Good-bye! Have learners work in pairs to role-play dealing with a

wrong number. Provide each pair a slip of paper with information such as the following: You are Kevin. You work for *Sunset Auto.* You receive a call that is a wrong number. The caller is looking for Lee at 555-9876. Ask one learner to role-play the employee; the other, the caller. Then have them swap slips with another pair and reverse roles. Have several partners present their role-plays.

♦ Have learners use the language from the role-plays to write a telephone script for dealing with a wrong number. Check pairs' scripts.

WORKBOOK

Unit 1, Exercises 4A–4B

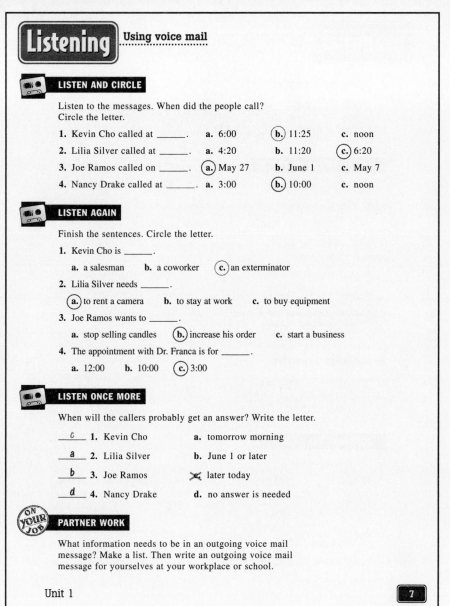

Listening — Using voice mail

LISTEN AND CIRCLE

Listen to the messages. When did the people call?
Circle the letter.

1. Kevin Cho called at _____.   **a.** 6:00   **(b.)** 11:25   **c.** noon
2. Lilia Silver called at _____.   **a.** 4:20   **b.** 11:20   **(c.)** 6:20
3. Joe Ramos called on _____.   **(a.)** May 27   **b.** June 1   **c.** May 7
4. Nancy Drake called at _____.   **a.** 3:00   **(b.)** 10:00   **c.** noon

LISTEN AGAIN

Finish the sentences. Circle the letter.

1. Kevin Cho is _____.
   a. a salesman   **b.** a coworker   **(c.)** an exterminator
2. Lilia Silver needs _____.
   (a.) to rent a camera   **b.** to stay at work   **c.** to buy equipment
3. Joe Ramos wants to _____.
   a. stop selling candles   **(b.)** increase his order   **c.** start a business
4. The appointment with Dr. Franca is for _____.
   a. 12:00   **b.** 10:00   **(c.)** 3:00

LISTEN ONCE MORE

When will the callers probably get an answer? Write the letter.

___c___ 1. Kevin Cho   **a.** tomorrow morning
___a___ 2. Lilia Silver   **b.** June 1 or later
___b___ 3. Joe Ramos   ~~**c.**~~ later today
___d___ 4. Nancy Drake   **d.** no answer is needed

PARTNER WORK

What information needs to be in an outgoing voice mail message? Make a list. Then write an outgoing voice mail message for yourselves at your workplace or school.

Unit 1   **7**

PREPARATION

1. To present or review **voice mail** follow the procedure in Preparation, page 4. Use a clock and a calendar to review times of day, months, **tomorrow morning,** and **later today,** if necessary.

2. Explain that many companies have voice mail systems to let callers record messages for employees who are away from their phones. Write a voice mail message on the board. Help learners identify the caller's name and telephone number, the time, the date, and the reason for the call.

PRESENTATION

1. Have learners read and discuss the Purpose Statement. For more information see "Purpose Statement" on page viii.

 2. Have learners read the Listen and Circle instructions. Then have them read the items and answer choices. Make sure that everyone understands the instructions. If necessary, model the first item. Then play the tape or read the Listening Transcript aloud two or more times as learners complete the activity. Have learners check their work. For more information see "Presenting a Listening Activity" on page ix.

 3. Have learners read the Listen Again instructions. Then follow the procedures in 2.

 4. Have learners read the Listen Once More instructions. Then follow the procedures in 2.

5. Have partners read the Partner Work instructions and complete the activity.

Ask partners to share their messages with the class.

FOLLOW-UP

More Messages: Have small teams write an outgoing message for a workplace. Then have teams pass their message around to all the other teams. Each team adds an incoming message. Ask the teams to read aloud their outgoing message and the incoming messages they received.

♦ For each message teams received, have them identify the caller's name, phone number, and reason for calling, as well as the time and date of the call. Have one or two teams present the information to the class.

WORKBOOK

Unit 1, Exercise 5

WORKFORCE SKILLS
(pages 8–9)

Transfer a call

Deal with a wrong number

Use voice mail

Keep a phone log

Language Note

*Point out that **and, but,** and **or** are used to join words, groups of words, or complete sentences.*

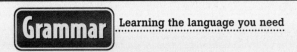

A. Study the Examples

She answers the phone	and	does the bookkeeping.
	or	
	but	never makes phone calls.

COMPLETE THE SENTENCES

Use the language in A.

1. Alice is a receptionist. She answers phone calls all day for her department
_____ *and* _____ (**and, but**) helps people who visit the office.

2. Sometimes she handles customer complaints _____ *but* _____ (**or, but**) never gets upset.

3. She likes talking to people _____ *and* _____ (**and, but**) enjoys her job.

4. Alice transfers calls _____ *or* _____ (**or, but**) takes messages.

5. Alice helps the people who call _____ *and* _____ (**or, and**) handles wrong numbers.

B. Study the Examples

I	enjoy	working outdoors.
	spend time	
	stopped	

COMPLETE THE SENTENCES

Use the language in B.

1. Andy _____ *enjoys using* _____ (**enjoy/use**) his cellular phone.

2. Carl _____ *spends time updating* _____ (**spend time/update**) the phone log every afternoon.

3. Juliette _____ *stopped working* _____ (**stop/work**) in customer service last year.

4. Al usually _____ *enjoys helping* _____ (**enjoy/help**) customers.

`8`

Unit 1

PREPARATION

Preteach or review the language in the grammar boxes with learners before they open their books, if necessary. Use pantomime or picture cards to teach or review **bookkeeping** and **working outdoors.** To review **voice mail,** see page 4.

2. Use picture cards or realia to teach or review **receptionist, cellular phone,** and **plant manager.**

PRESENTATION

1. Have learners read and discuss the Purpose Statement. For more information see "Purpose Statement" on page viii.

2. Have learners read the grammar box in A. Have learners use the language in the box to say as many sentences as

possible. Tell learners that they can use the grammar boxes throughout the unit to review or check sentence structures.

3. Have learners read the instructions for Complete the Sentences. If necessary, model the first item. Allow learners to complete the activity. Have learners check each other's work in pairs. Ask several learners to read their completed sentences aloud while the rest of the class checks their work.

4. Focus attention on the grammar box in B. Follow the procedures in 2.

5. Focus attention on Complete the Sentences and follow the procedures in 3.

English ASAP

C. Study the Examples

He	wants	to transfer the call to the plant manager.
	plans	
	knows how	

COMPLETE THE SENTENCES

Write the correct form of the word. Use the language in C.

1. Claudette _____plans to work_____ (**plan/work**) late this evening.

2. Carlos and Chen _____want to finish_____ (**want/finish**) a project that is due tomorrow.

3. Ed _____does not know how to manage_____ (**not know how/manage**) his time efficiently.

4. We _____plan to return_____ (**plan/return**) less important phone calls tomorrow.

5. Tim _____wants to get_____ (**want/get**) to work early on Friday.

6. Ana and Henry _____plan to start_____ (**plan/start**) cleaning the supply room this afternoon.

7. Richard _____knows how to make_____ (**know how/make**) project schedules.

PARTNER WORK

Talk about how you plan your time at your workplace or school. Use the language in B and C.

D. Study the Examples

They	like	using voice mail.
	can't stand	to use voice mail.
	began	

They	started	using voice mail.
	love	to use voice mail.
	continued	

TEAM WORK

Work with a small group. Tell what you like about using the phone at work. Tell what you don't like. Use the language in D.

A I like **helping customers**. I don't like **to transfer calls.**

Unit 1

9

---

6. Focus attention on the grammar box in C. Follow the procedures in 2.

7. Focus attention on Complete the Sentences and follow the procedures in 3.

 8. Have partners read the Partner Work instructions. Make sure each pair knows what to do. If necessary, model the activity. Have learners switch partners and repeat the activity. Ask several pairs to present their dialogs to the class.

9. Focus attention on the grammar box in D. Follow the procedures in 2.

 10. Have teams read the Team Work instructions. Make sure each team knows what to do. If necessary, model the activity. Then have teams complete the activity. Have learners change teams and repeat the

activity. Ask teams to present their conversations to the class.

FOLLOW-UP

Adding Information: Have learners work in teams. Give each team a picture card of people at work. Have one team member start by describing what a person in the picture is doing ("She's answering the phone."). Have each team member add to the sentence, using *and, but,* or *or* ("She's answering the phone, but she's not taking a message."). Have teams show their pictures and say some sentences aloud.

♦ Have learners write a few sentences about what they do at school or their workplace. Have them use *and, but,* and *or.* Have several learners read their sentences aloud.

WORKBOOK

Unit 1, Exercises 6A–6D

BLACKLINE MASTERS

Blackline Master: Unit 1

★　　★　　★　　★　　★

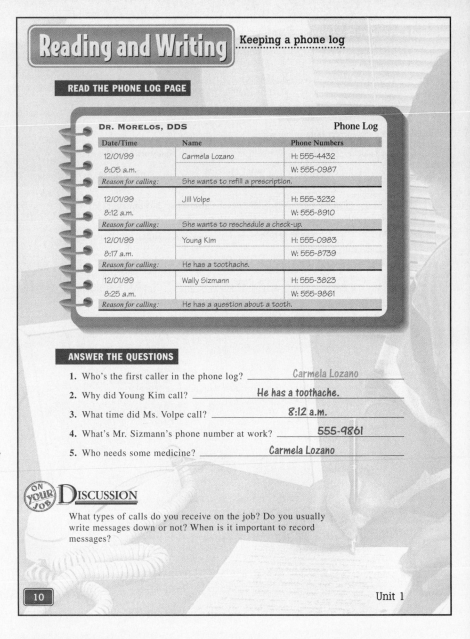

Reading and Writing   Keeping a phone log

READ THE PHONE LOG PAGE

DR. MORELOS, DDS		Phone Log
Date/Time	Name	Phone Numbers
12/01/99	Carmela Lozano	H: 555-4432
8:05 a.m.		W: 555-0987
Reason for calling:	She wants to refill a prescription.	
12/01/99	Jill Volpe	H: 555-3232
8:12 a.m.		W: 555-8910
Reason for calling:	She wants to reschedule a check-up.	
12/01/99	Young Kim	H: 555-0983
8:17 a.m.		W: 555-8739
Reason for calling:	He has a toothache.	
12/01/99	Wally Sizmann	H: 555-3823
8:25 a.m.		W: 555-9861
Reason for calling:	He has a question about a tooth.	

ANSWER THE QUESTIONS

1. Who's the first caller in the phone log? _____ Carmela Lozano
2. Why did Young Kim call? _____ He has a toothache.
3. What time did Ms. Volpe call? _____ 8:12 a.m.
4. What's Mr. Sizmann's phone number at work? _____ 555-9861
5. Who needs some medicine? _____ Carmela Lozano

DISCUSSION

What types of calls do you receive on the job? Do you usually write messages down or not? When is it important to record messages?

10   Unit 1

SCANS Note

Tell learners that taking detailed and accurate phone messages is an important part of working on a team, helping customers, and supporting coworkers. Discuss ways learners can make sure their phone messages are accurate.

PREPARATION

1. Present or review **phone log** by displaying a phone log. Identify the categories on the individual pages. Write a phone message on the board. Give each learner a phone log page and help them log in the information on the board.

2. Use pantomime, realia, and pictures to teach or review **dentist, toothache,** and **prescription.**

PRESENTATION

1. Have learners read and discuss the Purpose Statement. For more information see "Purpose Statement" on page viii.

2. Have learners preview the phone log page before they read. Encourage learners to say everything they can about the page. Write their ideas on the board and/or restate them in acceptable English. Then have them read the page independently.

3. Have learners read the questions in Answer the Questions. Make sure everyone knows what to do. Then have learners complete the activity independently. Have learners review each other's work in pairs. Ask several learners to share their answers with the class while the rest of the class checks their work.

 4. Have learners read the Discussion questions. Make sure everyone knows what to do. Then have learners work in teams to discuss calls they receive on the job, whether they record messages, and when it's important to take messages. Have team reporters share their team's ideas with the class. Have teams compare ideas.

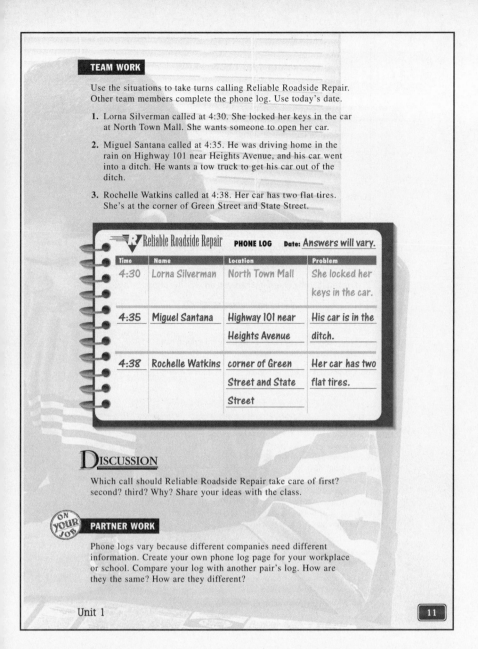

TEAM WORK

Use the situations to take turns calling Reliable Roadside Repair. Other team members complete the phone log. Use today's date.

1. Lorna Silverman called at 4:30. She locked her keys in the car at North Town Mall. She wants someone to open her car.

2. Miguel Santana called at 4:35. He was driving home in the rain on Highway 101 near Heights Avenue, and his car went into a ditch. He wants a tow truck to get his car out of the ditch.

3. Rochelle Watkins called at 4:38. Her car has two flat tires. She's at the corner of Green Street and State Street.

Reliable Roadside Repair PHONE LOG **Date:** Answers will vary.

Time	Name	Location	Problem
4:30	Lorna Silverman	North Town Mall	She locked her keys in the car.
4:35	Miguel Santana	Highway 101 near Heights Avenue	His car is in the ditch.
4:38	Rochelle Watkins	corner of Green Street and State Street	Her car has two flat tires.

DISCUSSION

Which call should Reliable Roadside Repair take care of first? second? third? Why? Share your ideas with the class.

ON YOUR JOB **PARTNER WORK**

Phone logs vary because different companies need different information. Create your own phone log page for your workplace or school. Compare your log with another pair's log. How are they the same? How are they different?

Unit 1

11

5. Have teams read the Team Work instructions and look over the phone log. Make sure each team knows what to do. If necessary, model the activity. Then have teams complete the activity. See "Partner Work and Team Work" on page viii. Have team reporters share their completed phone logs with the class.

6. Have learners read the Discussion questions. Make sure everyone knows what to do. Then have learners work in teams to discuss which calls Reliable Roadside Repair should take care of first, second, and third. Have team reporters share and explain their team's answers to the class.

ON YOUR JOB **7.** Have partners read the Partner Work instructions. Make sure each pair knows what to do. If necessary, model the

activity on the board. Then have pairs complete the activity. Have several pairs present their phone log pages to the class. Have learners compare the pages.

FOLLOW-UP

Message Logs: Have learners work in teams. Have one learner in each team use the phone log page he or she created in Partner Work to record incoming messages from other team members. Have teams discuss how well the phone log page works and recommend changes, if necessary. Ask team reporters to summarize discussions for the class.

♦ Have teams write a list of questions to ask when taking a message to ensure that all the blanks on the phone log will be complete. Help the class make a

master list of questions. Post the list in the classroom.

WORKBOOK

Unit 1, Exercises 7A–7B

WORKFORCE SKILLS (page 12)

Evaluate your phone skills

★　　★　　★　　★　　★

Culture Note

Tell learners that some jobs and workplaces rely heavily on phone communication. Others rely on person-to-person communication. Ask which type of communication is most important at learners' workplaces.

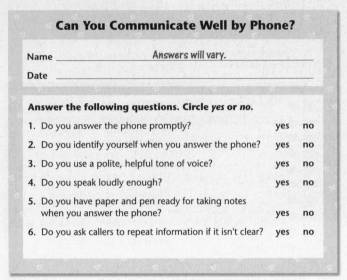

Extension — Evaluating your phone skills

COMPLETE THE EVALUATION FORM

Evaluate your workplace phone skills.

Can You Communicate Well by Phone?

Name _____ Answers will vary. _____

Date _____

Answer the following questions. Circle *yes* or *no*.

1. Do you answer the phone promptly?　　yes　no
2. Do you identify yourself when you answer the phone?　　yes　no
3. Do you use a polite, helpful tone of voice?　　yes　no
4. Do you speak loudly enough?　　yes　no
5. Do you have paper and pen ready for taking notes when you answer the phone?　　yes　no
6. Do you ask callers to repeat information if it isn't clear?　　yes　no

DISCUSSION

Talk with your team members about how you answered the questions. What do you already do well when you use the phone? What phone skill do you need to improve the most? What's one thing you can do to improve your telephone skills? Which questions on the list would have different answers if you were talking from your home? Make notes of your answers and share them with the class.

Culture Notes

What information should you give when you leave someone a voice mail message at work? How do you politely say that a message is important?

12　　　　　　　　　　　　　　　　Unit 1

PREPARATION

If necessary, use pantomime and modeling to review or teach **promptly, loudly, polite tone of voice, identify yourself,** and **repeat.** Ask learners why each of these behaviors are important when communicating by phone.

PRESENTATION

1. Have learners read and discuss the Purpose Statement. For more information see "Purpose Statement" on page viii.

2. Have learners read the instructions for Complete the Evaluation Form. If necessary, model the first item. Make sure everyone understands the activity. Then have learners complete the evaluation form independently. Check learners' answers.

3. Have teams read the Discussion questions. Make sure each team knows what to do. Then have teams complete the activity. Have team reporters share the teams' ideas about ways to improve telephone skills.

 5. Have learners read Culture Notes and talk over their responses in teams. Have team reporters share their ideas with the class. For more information see "Culture Notes" on page vii.

FOLLOW-UP

Table: Help the class use the information from the evaluation forms to create a table that shows how many learners in the class answered each question affirmatively. Have learners discuss the table.

♦ Have teams talk about what they do when a telephone call is cut off. Have team reporters share ideas with the class.

WORKBOOK

Unit 1, Exercise 8

Performance Check

How well can you use the skills in this unit?
....

Complete the activities. Go over your work with a partner or your teacher. Then complete the Performance Review on page 14.

| SKILL 1 | TRANSFER A CALL |

Work with two other students. You're a clerk at Best Auto Repair. A customer would like to speak with Jason Ramsey. He's working on her car. Have a partner or your teacher be the caller. You transfer the call to your other partner.

| SKILL 2 | DEAL WITH A WRONG NUMBER |

Your partner or your teacher dialed a wrong number. You respond.

| SKILL 3 | KEEP A PHONE LOG |

You work at Reliable Roadside Repair and got these phone calls. Write the information in the phone log. Use today's date.

1. Billy Goodwin called at 4:45. His car has two flat tires. He is at the corner of Brown Street and Park Street.

2. Carol Justin called at 5:00. She's at Village Center Mall, and her car won't start. She wants someone to come and start her car.

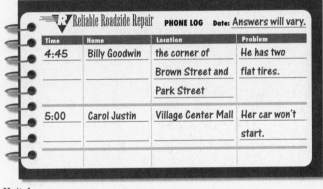

Reliable Roadside Repair PHONE LOG Date: Answers will vary.

Time	Name	Location	Problem
4:45	Billy Goodwin	the corner of Brown Street and Park Street	He has two flat tires.
5:00	Carol Justin	Village Center Mall	Her car won't start.

Unit 1

13

PRESENTATION

Use any of the procedures in "Evaluation," page x, with pages 13 and 14. Record individuals' results on the Unit 1 Individual Competency Chart. Record the class's results on the Class Cumulative Competency Chart.

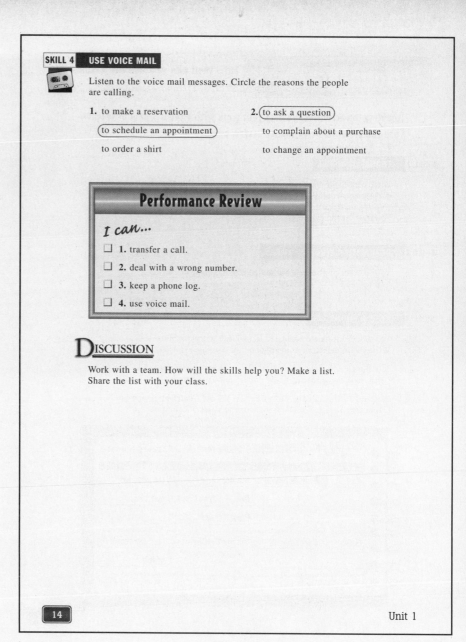

SKILL 4 USE VOICE MAIL

Listen to the voice mail messages. Circle the reasons the people are calling.

1. to make a reservation

   (to schedule an appointment)

   to order a shirt

2. (to ask a question)

   to complain about a purchase

   to change an appointment

Performance Review

I can...

☐ **1.** transfer a call.

☐ **2.** deal with a wrong number.

☐ **3.** keep a phone log.

☐ **4.** use voice mail.

Discussion

Work with a team. How will the skills help you? Make a list. Share the list with your class.

Unit 1

PRESENTATION

Follow the instructions on page 13.

INFORMAL WORKPLACE-SPECIFIC ASSESSMENT

Ask learners to role-play calling a company of their choice and leaving a voice mail message.

WORKBOOK

Unit 1, Exercise 9

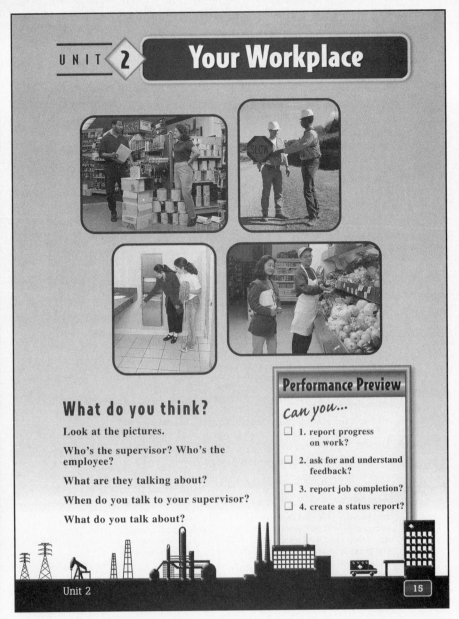

Unit 2 Overview
—SCANS Competencies—

★ Communicate information
★ Monitor and correct performance
★ Improve systems
★ Allocate resources

Workforce Skills

● Report progress on work
● Ask for and understand feedback
● Report job completion
● Create a status report

Materials

● Picture cards of people talking to supervisors and writing reports, specific workplaces, and employees making or doing something
● Status reports, if possible, from learners' workplaces
● Picture cards, or realia or pictures of salad bar items, a cashier, and soap
● Pictures or realia of auto parts including brakes, oil, and oil filter

Unit Warm-Up

To stimulate discussion about the unit topic (reporting project status), show pictures of people talking with supervisors at work. Create a class chart to show how often learners talk with their supervisors: *Frequently, Sometimes, Almost Never.* Have each learner write his or her name on the chart and place a check-mark in the appropriate column.

★　　★　　★　　★　　★

WORKFORCE SKILLS (page 15)

Report progress on work

Ask for and understand feedback

Report job completion

★　　★　　★　　★　　★

PREPARATION

1. Teach or review **supervisor, status report,** and **feedback** by using picture cards, realia, and role-play. Encourage learners to use peer teaching to clarify unfamiliar vocabulary.

2. Discuss times learners received feedback. Ask how the experience was helpful.

PRESENTATION

1. Focus attention on the photographs. Ask learners what the unit might be about. Write their ideas on the board and/or restate them in acceptable English.

2. Have learners talk about the photos. Ask them to identify the types of jobs, name the objects they see, and describe what is going on in each picture. Help learners imagine what the people in the pictures are saying.

3. Focus attention on the questions. Have learners discuss them in teams. Have team reporters share their answers with the class.

4. You may want to use the Performance Preview to provide learners with an overview of the skills in the unit. Have learners read the list of skills and discuss what they will learn in this unit.

FOLLOW-UP

Talking to The Boss: Have learners work in teams to brainstorm and write a list of reasons employees talk to their supervisors. Ask team reporters to read the lists to the class.

◆ Help the class make a master list of reasons employees talk to their supervisors. Then read the items aloud one at a time and ask learners to indicate by a show of hands if they've talked to a supervisor for that reason.

WORKBOOK

Unit 2, Exercises 1A–1B

WORKFORCE SKILLS (page 16)

Report progress on work

★   ★   ★   ★   ★

Getting Started

Reporting problems at work

TEAM WORK

Look at the pictures. Match the problem with the situation.
Discuss other problems that stop the people from doing their jobs.

a. We need another cashier.

b. We're out of soap.

c. The ground is really wet.

PARTNER WORK

Student A presents a problem. Student B provides a solution.

A The supplier didn't leave any soap for us.

B We should tell Mr. Johnson about the problem.

 SURVEY

Some people give spoken status reports to their supervisors.
Others give written reports. Find out how your classmates report
progress at their workplace or school. Make a graph that shows
how many learners give spoken status reports and how many give
written status reports.

16

Unit 2

Teaching Note

*Use this page to introduce the new
language in the unit. Whenever possible,
encourage peer teaching. Supply any
new language the learners need.*

PREPARATION

1. Display and identify a **status report.**
Use picture cards and realia to teach or
review **cashier** and **soap.**

2. To teach **problem** and **solution,**
create a problem, such as lack of chalk
for the chalkboard, and a solution, such
as borrowing chalk from another room.
Ask learners to describe a problem they
have had to report at work.

PRESENTATION

1. Have learners read and discuss the
Purpose Statement. For more information
see "Purpose Statement" on page viii.

2. Focus attention on the illustrations.
Encourage learners to say as much as
they can about them. Write their ideas
on the board and/or restate them in
acceptable English.

3. Have teams read the Team Work
instructions. Make sure each team
knows what to do. Remind the teams
that they are responsible for making
sure that each member understands the
new language. Then have teams complete
the activity. Have team reporters share
their answers with the class.

4. Have partners read the Partner Work
instructions. Make sure each pair knows
what to do. If necessary, model the
activity. Then have partners complete
the activity. Have learners switch partners
and repeat the activity. Have one or two
pairs perform their conversations for the
class. For more information, see "Partner
Work and Team Work" on page viii.

5. Have teams read the
Survey instructions. Make
sure everyone knows what
to do. Then have teams complete the
activity. Post the graphs and have teams
compare them. For more information,
see "Survey" on page viii.

FOLLOW-UP

Good News/Bad News: Have partners
create dialogs in which a worker presents
bad news to a supervisor. Encourage use
of examples from learners' workplaces.
Have several pairs present their dialogs
to the class.

♦ Have teams brainstorm language for
presenting bad news, such as, "I'm
afraid there's a problem." Have several
teams read their lists aloud.

WORKBOOK

Unit 2, Exercises 2A–2B

Talk About It — Reporting progress on work

PRACTICE THE DIALOG

A How's your work coming along?

B I'm getting ready to start chopping the tomatoes. Everything else is already on the salad bar.

A It looks like you're almost ready for the dinner rush.

B I think so. Is there anything else I can do?

A No, I think that's everything.

PARTNER WORK

Your partner asks how your work is coming. Report your progress on a task from your workplace or school to your partner. Use the dialog above and the Useful Language.

Useful Language

I've completed. . .

I'm working on. . .

I still need to. . .

ASAP PROJECT

As a team create an oral status report on your work in class this week. Present your report to the class. At the end of the unit, create a written status report on your work during the unit. Share your report with the class. Complete these reports as you work though the unit.

Unit 2

17

ASAP PROJECT

Have learners read the instructions. Discuss the project and its purpose with learners. Make sure that everyone understands. Help learners assign themselves to teams depending upon their skills, knowledge, interests, or other personal strengths. Have each team select a leader. Throughout the rest of the unit, allow time for learners to work on the project. Have the teams agree on a deadline when the project will be finished. For more information see "ASAP Project" on page vi.

PREPARATION

1. To teach or review **status report,** see Preparation on page 16. Review that status reports can be oral or written. Use realia, pictures, and explanation to clarify **tomatoes, salad bar,** and **dinner rush.**

2. Present or review **completed, working on,** and **still need to** by acting out stages of a task, such as erasing the board.

PRESENTATION

1. Have learners read and discuss the Purpose Statement. For more information see "Purpose Statement" on page viii.

 2. Focus attention on the illustration. Encourage learners to say as much as they can about it. Have them say what they think the people are talking about. Write learners' ideas on the board and/or

restate them in acceptable English. Then present the dialog. See "Presenting a Dialog" on page ix.

 3. Have partners read the Partner Work instructions. Focus attention on the Useful Language box. Help learners read the expressions. If necessary, model pronunciation. Then have learners complete the activity. Have learners switch partners and repeat the activity. Have one or two pairs present their dialogs to the class.

FOLLOW-UP

Keeping Track: Ask partners to create lists of tasks each of them might do at work to complete a job. Circle one task on each list and explain that this is the task they are working on now. Have them tell their partner what they've

completed and what they still need to do. Ask a few pairs to present their status reports to the class.

♦ Have teams discuss different ways of keeping track of progress on a project, such as a checklist or dates on a schedule. Have teams share ideas with the class.

WORKBOOK

Unit 2, Exercises 3A–3B

WORKFORCE SKILLS (page 18)

Report job completion

★   ★   ★   ★   ★

Culture Note

Point out that some supervisors prefer daily, weekly, or even hourly status reports while others only want to know when a task is completed. Do learners know what their supervisors prefer? If not, ask how they think they can find out.

Personal Dictionary

Have learners add the words in their Personal Dictionary to their *Workforce Writing Dictionary*. For more information see "Workforce Writing Dictionary" on page v.

Keep Talking — Reporting job completion

PRACTICE THE DIALOG

A Can we go over the work I did on this car?

B Sure, do you have the work order?

A Yes, the owner wanted me to check the brakes and change the oil. I also had to put on new brake shoes.

B How did it go?

A Well, the job took a little longer than usual because the car needed a special oil filter.

B That's OK. Thanks for letting me know.

ON YOUR JOB — PARTNER WORK

Take turns with your partner reporting the completion of a job. Tell what job you completed. Report any problems you had, and tell what you did about the problems. Use the dialog above.

Personal Dictionary ▸ Reporting Progress

Write the words and phrases that you need to know.

_____

_____

_____

18   Unit 2

PREPARATION

1. To present or review **brakes, oil, oil filter,** and **car,** use realia or pictures.

2. To present or review **completing a task,** follow the procedures on page 17.

PRESENTATION

1. Have learners read and discuss the Purpose Statement. For more information see "Purpose Statement" on page viii.

 2. Focus attention on the photograph. Encourage learners to say as much as they can about it. Have them speculate about what the people are doing and talking about. Then present the dialog. See "Presenting a Dialog" on page ix.

3. Have partners read the Partner Work instructions. Make sure each pair knows what to do. Then have partners complete the activity. Have learners switch partners and repeat the activity. Have one or two pairs present their dialogs to the class.

4. Have learners read the Personal Dictionary instructions. Then use the Personal Dictionary procedures on page ix. Remind learners to add words to their dictionaries throughout the unit.

FOLLOW-UP

It's Done! Have partners role-play reporting job completion. Give each pair a slip of paper with a specific work task on it, such as setting a table, organizing files, or clearing a yard. Have one partner report completion of the task, while the other asks questions. Have several pairs present their role-plays to the class.

♦ Have pairs write their dialogs. Post them in the classroom.

WORKBOOK

Unit 2, Exercise 4

Listening — Asking for and understanding feedback

 LISTEN AND CIRCLE

What type of feedback is the employee asking for? Circle the letter.

1. **a.** How can I get organized?
   b. How can I talk to my supervisor?
   c. How can I do two jobs at the same time?

2. **a.** Why do we have an express service?
   b. Why does dry cleaning take three days?
   c. Why are customers getting upset?

3. **a.** How can I be neater?
   b. How can I work faster?
   c. How can I give someone feedback?

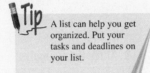

Tip
A list can help you get organized. Put your tasks and deadlines on your list.

 LISTEN AGAIN

What does the supervisor recommend? Circle the letter.

1. **a.** make a list of tasks　　**b.** work late
   c. buy a notebook　　**d.** work on two tasks at once

2. **a.** smile at customers　　**b.** give everyone express service
   c. hire more employees　　**d.** ask customers what they need

3. **a.** talk to customers　　**b.** take a training class
   c. be more friendly　　**d.** pay more attention to the groceries

Unit 2 　 **19**

SCANS Note

Suggest that understanding feedback is important. Ask learners if they always understand the feedback they get. Discuss what learners can do if they don't understand the feedback someone is giving them.

PREPARATION

To present or review **cleaners, cleaning,** and **express service,** role-play a customer taking clothes into a dry cleaning shop. To present or review **checkout lane** and **checker,** show a picture of the checkout area in a supermarket.

PRESENTATION

1. Have learners read and discuss the Purpose Statement. For more information see "Purpose Statement" on page viii.

2. Focus attention on the illustration. Encourage learners to say as much as they can about it.

 3. Have learners read the Listen and Circle instructions. Then have them read the items.

Make sure that everyone understands the instructions. If necessary, model the first item. Then play the tape or read the Listening Transcript aloud two or more times as learners complete the activity. Have learners check their work. For more information see "Presenting a Listening Activity" on page ix.

 4. Have learners read the Listen Again instructions. Then follow the procedures in 3.

Tip Have learners read the Tip. Have learners discuss how the advice will help them. For more information, see "Presenting a Tip" on page ix.

FOLLOW-UP

More Feedback: Have learners work in teams. Give each a picture of a specific workplace, such as a bakery, auto shop, or receptionist's office. Ask teams to brainstorm questions that employees at the site might ask when seeking feedback. Have teams present their pictures and questions to the class.

♦ Have teams use their questions to write a dialog between an employee and a supervisor at the workplace. Have pairs present their dialogs to the class.

WORKBOOK

Unit 2, Exercise 5

Report progress on work

Report job completion

★   ★   ★   ★   ★

Language Note

Point out that subject pronouns are often used at the beginning of a sentence, and object pronouns are used after the verb and after prepositions, such as **for** *and* **to.** *Help learners identify other prepositions these pronouns follow, such as* **near, with,** *and* **about.**

Grammar	Learning the language you need

A. Study the Examples

I	me
he	him
she	her
you	you
we	us
they	them

I'll give the message to her.

COMPLETE THE DIALOG

A   Did the supplier write to ___us___ (us, them) about the mistakes on our bill?

B   Yes, the company sent a letter to ___me___ (me, them).

I made a copy to give to ___you___ (me, you).

A   Oh, I didn't get it.

B   Well, Paula was here, and I gave the copy to ___her___ (her, me).

I guess Paula forgot to give the copy to ___you___ (them, you).

I'll bring another copy to ___you___ (her, you) in a minute.

B. Study the Example

She took a message for me.

COMPLETE THE SENTENCES

Use the language in A and B.

1.   This message is for Mr. Dell. Please give it to ___him___ (him, them).

2.   I need some help. Please clean the restrooms for ___me___ (her, me).

3.   We don't understand the problem. Please explain it to ___us___ (you, us).

4.   Mrs. Williams needs some paper. Please go to the supply room and get some paper for ___her___ (her, them).

5.   Paulina called Mrs. Lee, but she didn't leave a message for ___her___ (her, them).

20   Unit 2

PREPARATION

Review the language in the grammar boxes with learners before they open their books, if necessary. Use pictures or realia to present or review **message, repairs,** and **laundry.** Present and identify a **copy** of a letter.

PRESENTATION

1. Have learners read and discuss the Purpose Statement. For more information see "Purpose Statement" on page viii.

2. Have learners read the grammar boxes in A. Have learners use the language in the boxes to say as many sentences as possible. Tell learners that they can use the grammar boxes throughout the unit to review or check sentence structures.

3. Have learners read Complete the Dialog. If necessary, model the first item. Allow learners to complete the activity. Have learners check each other's work in pairs. Have them say the dialog aloud in pairs. Ask several pairs to read the dialog aloud while the rest of the class checks their work.

4. Focus attention on the grammar box in B. Follow the procedures in 2.

5. Have learners read the instructions for Complete the Sentences. If necessary, model the first item. Allow learners to complete the activity. Have learners check each other's work in pairs. Ask several learners to read their sentences aloud while the rest of the class checks their work.

C. Study the Examples

I	should	call the front desk.
She	shouldn't	
They		

COMPLETE THE SENTENCES

Write *should* or *shouldn't*. Use the language in C.

1. Yolanda doesn't have a truck driver's license. She _____shouldn't_____ drive the company truck.

2. She wants to get her truck driver's license. She _____should_____ call the Department of Motor Vehicles.

3. She wants to learn to drive a delivery truck. She _____should_____ take driving lessons.

4. She doesn't have a lot of money. She _____shouldn't_____ go to Ace Driving School. It's very expensive. She _____should_____ go to City Community College. It's much cheaper.

PARTNER WORK

Take turns describing the skills you would like to learn. Follow the dialog below. Use the language in C.

A I want to learn to use a computer.

B You should take a class at the Adult Learning Center.

D. Study the Examples

He makes	bread.
	some repairs.
	the beds.

He does	the dishes.
	the laundry.
	the cleaning.

COMPLETE THE SENTENCES

Use the language in D.

At the restaurant, everyone has specific jobs. Tim always _____makes_____ the salads. Sylvia _____does_____ the dishes and _____makes_____ bread. Ricardo _____makes_____ the cakes. Lin and I both _____do_____ the cleaning. Together we make a great team.

Unit 2   **21**

---

6. Focus attention on the grammar box in C. Follow the procedures in 2.

7. Focus attention on Complete the Sentences. Follow the procedures in 5.

 8. Have partners read the Partner Work instructions. Make sure each pair knows what to do. If necessary, model the activity. Then have partners complete the activity. Have learners switch partners and repeat the activity. Ask several pairs to present their dialogs to the class.

9. Focus attention on the grammar boxes in D. Follow the procedures in 2.

10. Focus attention on Complete the Sentences. Follow the procedures in 5.

FOLLOW-UP

Make/Do: Have learners work as partners and give each pair a picture card of employees doing or making something at work. Ask them to talk about what the people are doing or making. Encourage them to say as much as they can about the pictures. Have several pairs present their descriptions to the class.

♦ Have partners talk about what they make or do at work. Have pairs present their conversations to the class.

WORKBOOK

Unit 2, Exercises 6A–6D

BLACKLINE MASTERS

Blackline Master: Unit 2

WORKFORCE SKILLS
(pages 22–23)

Create a status report

Report progress on work

★   ★   ★   ★   ★

Teaching Note

Tell learners that when creating status reports, they should first write a list of all the things they are supposed to do on a project. Then, they can easily see what they have already finished doing and what they still need to finish.

Reading and Writing
Creating a status report

READ THE STATUS REPORT

A status report tells your supervisor how much work you've completed and what you still need to finish.

> **PRO PAINT SHOP**
>
> **TO:** Leticia Ramos
> **FROM:** Eric Montoya
> **DATE:** April 18, 2000
> **SUBJECT:** Status Report
>
> Leticia,
> Here is the status of the painting job at 1621 Dodge Street.
> This week:
> 1. I spoke with the clients to verify the work order.
> 2. I assigned four people to do the painting.
> 3. I created work assignments and timetables.
> 4. The workers started preparing the rooms for painting.
> Next week:
> 1. We will finish preparing all the rooms for painting.
> 2. We will paint the upstairs rooms in the house by Wednesday.
> 3. We will paint the downstairs rooms by Friday.
>
> As you can see, we are still on schedule. We should be ready to begin painting by next Tuesday.

ANSWER THE QUESTIONS

Use the memo.

1. Who is the status report for? _____ Leticia Ramos

2. Who did Eric speak with? _____ the clients

3. How many people are working with Eric? _____ four

4. Did they finish preparing the rooms for painting this week? _____ no

5. When will they start painting? _____ Tuesday

 DISCUSSION

How will the status report help Eric's boss? How will it help Eric? How do your status reports help you and your teacher or boss?

22

Unit 2

PREPARATION

1. If necessary, explain that a memo is a written message. Explain or review what a status report is by writing a sample status report on the board about a project you are working on at home or at work. Point out tasks you've already completed and tasks you still need to finish.

2. Use the picture on page 23 to present or review **nature center, trails, sign posts,** and **ranger station.**

PRESENTATION

1. Have learners read and discuss the Purpose Statement. For more information see "Purpose Statement" on page viii.

2. Have learners preview the status report before they read. Encourage learners to say everything they can about the report.

Write their ideas on the board and/or restate them in acceptable English.

3. Have learners read the instructions for Read the Status Report. Then have them read the report independently.

4. Have partners read the Answer the Questions instructions. Make sure each pair knows what to do. Then have learners complete the activity in pairs. Ask several learners to share their answers with the class while the rest of the class checks their work.

 5. Have learners read the Discussion questions. Make sure everyone knows what to do. Then have learners work in teams to discuss their ideas. Have team reporters share their ideas with the class.

English ASAP

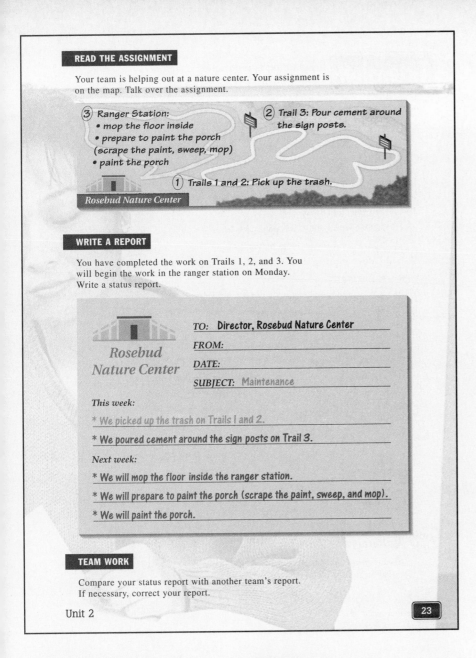

READ THE ASSIGNMENT

Your team is helping out at a nature center. Your assignment is on the map. Talk over the assignment.

(3) **Ranger Station:**
• mop the floor inside
• prepare to paint the porch (scrape the paint, sweep, mop)
• paint the porch

(2) **Trail 3:** Pour cement around the sign posts.

(1) **Trails 1 and 2:** Pick up the trash.

Rosebud Nature Center

WRITE A REPORT

You have completed the work on Trails 1, 2, and 3. You will begin the work in the ranger station on Monday. Write a status report.

Rosebud Nature Center

TO: Director, Rosebud Nature Center

FROM:

DATE:

SUBJECT: Maintenance

This week:

* We picked up the trash on Trails 1 and 2.

* We poured cement around the sign posts on Trail 3.

Next week:

* We will mop the floor inside the ranger station.

* We will prepare to paint the porch (scrape the paint, sweep, and mop).

* We will paint the porch.

TEAM WORK

Compare your status report with another team's report. If necessary, correct your report.

Unit 2

23

---

6. Have learners work in teams to preview the map. Encourage learners to say everything they can about it. Clarify vocabulary as needed. Write learners' ideas on the board and/or restate them in acceptable English. Then have teams read the assignment on the map.

7. Have teams read the Write a Report instructions. Make sure each team knows what to do. If necessary, model the activity. Then have teams complete the activity.

8. Have teams read the Team Work instructions. Then have teams complete the activity. Have team reporters share their completed status reports with the class, and ask teams to say how the feedback was helpful.

FOLLOW-UP

Priority Job: Have individual learners list tasks they need to perform at work or school. Have learners work in pairs to prioritize their lists from most important to least important. Ask several learners to explain how a prioritized list can help them at work.

♦ Give teams sample status reports of projects that are not yet completed. Have teams say as much as they can about the reports, including which tasks employees have already finished and which they still need to complete. Ask teams to present their discussions to the class.

WORKBOOK

Unit 2, Exercises 7A–7B

WORKFORCE SKILLS (page 24)

Report progress on work

Report job completion

★　　★　　★　　★　　★

Culture Note

Remind learners that sometimes supervisors or customers unexpectedly phone or stop by to check on the status of work. Ask learners to discuss ways to deal with this situation. What should they do if they are not sure of the status?

Extension Responding appropriately about your performance

READ AND CIRCLE

Read each supervisor's question. Circle the best response. Share your answers with the class.

1. Were you able to finish the tire rotation on Mr. Wu's car?

 (a.) I've done all but one tire. It will be about ten more minutes.

 b. I'm not finished yet. I don't care when I finish.

2. Did you clean Room 204?

 a. Of course I did. It was on my job list, wasn't it?

 (b.) Yes, I did all the things on the list.

3. Carlos, we have a staff meeting at 1:00. Can you make it?

 a. Yes, maybe.

 (b.) I'm in the middle of a big project, but I'll be there.

4. Marta is new and needs help finding the supplies. Can you help her?

 a. Why do I have to do it? I have other things I need to finish.

 (b.) Sure. Let me finish this work. Then I'll be happy to help her.

5. Samantha, what are you doing?

 (a.) I finished the painting. I'm taking a break before I clean up.

 b. I'm on break.

6. Hilda needs help finishing her job. Can you stay late?

 (a.) I have an appointment this evening. But I can stay for an hour.

 b. One hour is all I can stay. I have better things to do.

TEAM WORK

Think of other ways to answer these questions. Share them with your team. Respond in a positive tone of voice.

 **Culture Notes**

You're behind in your work. What do you do? Who do you tell? What do you say? Why?

24   Unit 2

PREPARATION

If necessary, present or review **reporting progress** and **completion of a job** by following the procedures in Preparation on page 17. Review the Useful Language for responding to questions about work status on page 17.

PRESENTATION

1. Have learners read and discuss the Purpose Statement. For more information see "Purpose Statement" on page viii.

2. Have learners read the instructions for Read and Circle. If necessary, model the first item. Make sure everyone understands the activity. Then have learners complete the activity independently. Ask several learners to read their answers aloud.

3. Have teams read the Team Work instructions. Make sure each team knows what to do. Then have teams complete the activity. Have team reporters share their teams' responses with the class.

 4. Have learners read Culture Notes and talk over their ideas in teams. Have team reporters share their ideas with the class. For more information see "Culture Notes" on page vii.

FOLLOW-UP

How's It Going? Have pairs role-play situations in which supervisors check on the status of a work project. Have one partner role-play the supervisor and the other, the employee. Have several pairs perform their role-plays for the class.

◆ Have partners create written status reports based on their role-plays. Remind them to list tasks they have already completed and tasks they haven't finished yet. Have several pairs present the reports to the class.

WORKBOOK

Unit 2, Exercise 8

---

24   English ASAP

Performance Check
How well can you use the skills in this unit?
....

**Complete the activities. Go over your work with a partner or your teacher.
Then complete the Performance Review on page 26.**

SKILL 1   **REPORT PROGRESS ON WORK**

Your supervisor has asked how you are doing on your work.
Report your progress to a partner or your teacher. Include what is
completed and what you still need to finish.

SKILL 2   **ASK FOR AND UNDERSTAND FEEDBACK**

 The employees are asking for feedback. What problems are they
asking about? Listen and circle the letter.

1. (a.) She keeps forgetting things.
   b. She keeps getting lost.

2. (a.) Her work takes too long.
   b. She makes mistakes.

What feedback does the supervisor give? Listen again and circle
the letter.

1. a. Use your gloves.
   b. Use the right shovel.
   (c.) Use a list.

2. a. Don't line up any of the cans.
   (b.) Just line up the cans in the front row.
   c. Line up all the cans.

SKILL 3   **REPORT JOB COMPLETION**

You have just finished a task at your workplace or school. Tell
your partner or teacher about the job you completed. Talk about
any trouble you had. Tell what you did about the problems.

Unit 2   `25`

PRESENTATION

Use any of the procedures in
"Evaluation," page x, with pages 25 and
26. Record individuals' results on the
Unit 2 Individual Competency Chart.
Record the class's results on the Class
Cumulative Competency Chart.

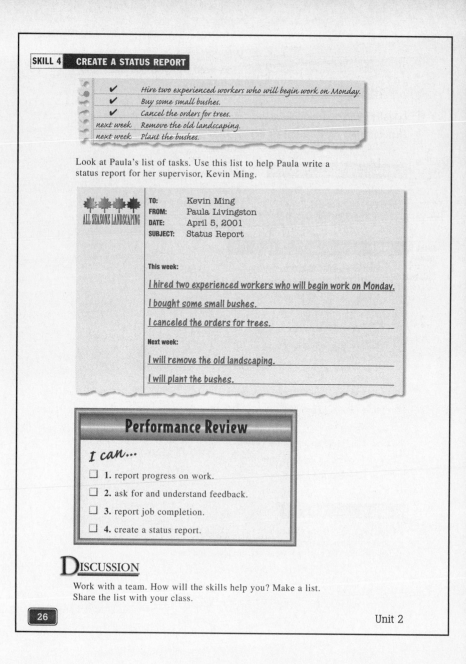

✔	Hire two experienced workers who will begin work on Monday.
✔	Buy some small bushes.
✔	Cancel the orders for trees.
next week	Remove the old landscaping.
next week	Plant the bushes.

Look at Paula's list of tasks. Use this list to help Paula write a status report for her supervisor, Kevin Ming.

ALL SEASONS LANDSCAPING

TO:	Kevin Ming
FROM:	Paula Livingston
DATE:	April 5, 2001
SUBJECT:	Status Report

This week:

I hired two experienced workers who will begin work on Monday.

I bought some small bushes.

I canceled the orders for trees.

Next week:

I will remove the old landscaping.

I will plant the bushes.

Performance Review

I can...

☐ **1.** report progress on work.

☐ **2.** ask for and understand feedback.

☐ **3.** report job completion.

☐ **4.** create a status report.

DISCUSSION

Work with a team. How will the skills help you? Make a list. Share the list with your class.

26

Unit 2

PRESENTATION

Follow the instructions on page 25.

INFORMAL WORKPLACE-SPECIFIC ASSESSMENT

Ask learners to say how they decide when to ask for feedback on their work, how often they ask, and who they ask.

WORKBOOK

Unit 2, Exercise 9

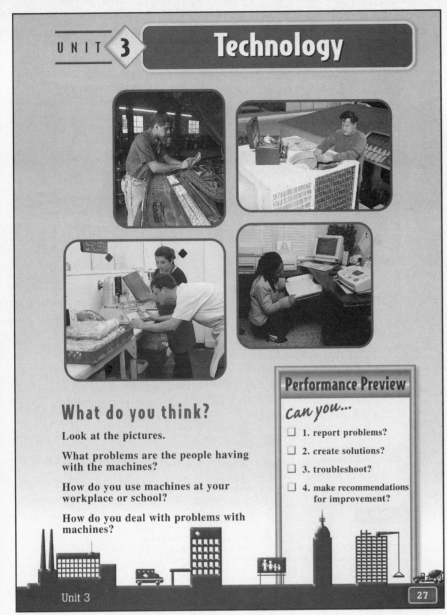

UNIT 3 — Technology

What do you think?

Look at the pictures.

What problems are the people having with the machines?

How do you use machines at your workplace or school?

How do you deal with problems with machines?

Performance Preview

can you...

- ☐ 1. report problems?
- ☐ 2. create solutions?
- ☐ 3. troubleshoot?
- ☐ 4. make recommendations for improvement?

Unit 3 | 27

Unit 3 Overview
—SCANS Competencies—

★ Apply technology to specific tasks
★ Design or improve systems
★ Maintain and troubleshoot technologies
★ Communicate information

Workforce Skills

- Report problems
- Create solutions
- Troubleshoot
- Make recommendations for improvement

Materials

- Picture cards, diagrams, and/or real items in this unit (copier, scanner, cash register, VCR, clothes dryer, brake pedals, electronic scales, debit card and reader, car engine, car battery, repair person, quarter, suggestion cards, electric pencil sharpener, tape player, toner cartridge, baggage, and baggage tags)
- Ads for machine repair services
- A product with a bar code label

Unit Warm-Up

To stimulate discussion about the unit topic (identifying and solving problems with machines), point out classroom machines, such as a projector or computer. Have a few learners describe problems they've had with machines.

★   ★   ★   ★   ★

WORKFORCE SKILLS (page 27)

Report problems
Create solutions

★   ★   ★   ★   ★

PREPARATION

Display picture cards of machines in this unit. Identify them and have learners say as much about them as they can. Encourage peer teaching to clarify vocabulary.

PRESENTATION

1. Focus attention on the photographs. Ask learners what the unit might be about. Write their ideas on the board and/or restate them in acceptable English.

2. Have learners talk about the photos. Ask them to describe what is going on in each picture. Help learners identify the types of jobs depicted and the machines that the employees are working on.

3. Help learners read the questions. Discuss the questions with the class.

4. You may want to use the Performance Preview to provide learners with an overview of the skills in the unit. Have learners read the list of skills and discuss what they will learn in this unit.

FOLLOW-UP

More Machines: Have teams discuss the machines they use that need repairs most frequently (either at work or at home). Ask them to make a top-ten list of machines that have problems often.

♦ Have teams discuss what they do when a machine needs repairs. How do they know when it is appropriate to repair the machine themselves and when they need to call an expert? Have team reporters share their teams' ideas with the class.

WORKBOOK

Unit 3, Exercises 1A–1B

WORKFORCE SKILLS (page 28)

Report problems

Create solutions

★　　★　　★　　★　　★

Teaching Note

Use this page to introduce the new language in the unit. Whenever possible, encourage peer teaching. Supply any language the learners need.

PREPARATION

1. Use picture cards or real objects to present or review **copier, scanner, cash register, VCR,** and **car battery.** To teach **delayed,** write on the board: *Meeting: 9:00.* Cross out 9:00, replace it with 9:15, and say, "The meeting was delayed."

2. Display an ad for machine repair. Ask learners where they've seen such an ad and what the ad is for.

PRESENTATION

1. Have learners read and discuss the Purpose Statement. For more information see "Purpose Statement" on page viii.

2. Focus attention on the ads. Encourage learners to say as much as they can about them. Write their ideas on the board and/or restate them in acceptable English.

3. Have teams read the Team Work instructions. Make sure each team knows what to do. Then have teams complete the activity. Have team reporters share their answers with the class.

4. Have partners read the Partner Work instructions. Make sure each pair knows what to do. If necessary, model the activity. Then have partners complete the activity. Have learners switch partners and repeat the activity. Have one or two pairs present their answers to the class. See "Partner Work and Team Work" on page viii.

5. Have teams read the Survey instructions. Make sure everyone knows what to do. Then have teams complete the activity, writing machine names along the horizontal axis and number of learners along the vertical axis. Have teams share their graphs with the class.

FOLLOW-UP

Broken Machines: Have teams discuss times a broken machine caused problems at work. What happened? Who took care of the problem? Have team reporters summarize discussions for the class.

♦ Have pairs role-play employees. One explains a problem with a machine and the other suggests calling one of the companies in the ads. Have several pairs perform their dialogs for the class.

WORKBOOK

Unit 3, Exercises 2A–2B

Talk About It — Reporting problems

★   ★   ★   ★   ★

PRACTICE THE DIALOG

A Excuse me, Sonia. There's a problem with dryer number 18.

B What's wrong with it?

A The dryer won't start when customers put their quarters in the slot.

B Thanks for telling me. The repair person is coming here later today. Please make sure he fixes it.

PARTNER WORK

Work with a partner. Take turns reporting a problem with a machine you use at your workplace or school. Use the dialog above and the Useful Language.

ASAP PROJECT

Work with a team to create a notebook of information about different machines each person uses at work or school. Include the name of the machine and how it is used. Also list problems you often have with each machine and possible solutions for the problems. Complete this project as you work through the unit.

> **Useful Language**
>
> broken
>
> not working
>
> out of order

Unit 3

29

ASAP PROJECT

Have learners read the instructions. Discuss the project and its purpose with learners. Make sure that everyone understands. Help learners assign themselves to teams depending upon their skills, knowledge, interests, or other personal strengths. Have each team select a leader. Throughout the rest of the unit, allow time for learners to work on the project. Have the teams agree on a deadline when the project will be finished. For more information see "ASAP Project" on page vi.

Culture Note

Point out that machines that are not working properly can sometimes cause injuries. Employers greatly appreciate knowing about safety hazards in the workplace. Ask learners for examples of machines that can be dangerous when there is something wrong with them.

PREPARATION

1. Use picture cards to teach or review **clothes dryer, quarter,** and **repair person.** Display pictures or realia of broken machines to present the Useful Language.

2. Act out reporting a problem with a machine to a **repair person.**

PRESENTATION

1. Have learners read and discuss the Purpose Statement. For more information see "Purpose Statement" on page viii.

2. Focus attention on the illustration. Encourage learners to say as much as they can about it. Write learners' ideas on the board and/or restate them in acceptable English. Have them talk about what the people are doing and what machine they are discussing. Then present the dialog. See "Presenting a Dialog" on page ix.

3. Have partners read the Partner Work instructions. Focus attention on the Useful Language box. Help learners read the expressions. If necessary, model pronunciation. Then have learners complete the activity. Have learners switch partners and repeat the activity. Have one or two pairs present their dialogs to the class.

FOLLOW-UP

Problems with Machines: Have learners work in pairs. On slips of paper, write the names of ten machines learners use in the workplace. Have one partner in each pair draw a slip and describe a problem with the machine without naming the machine. The other partner should figure out the machine. Then have partners switch roles and repeat the activity. Ask each pair to tell the class what machines they named.

♦ Write the names of the ten machines on the board. Have the class brainstorm problems that each machine could have.

WORKBOOK

Unit 3, Exercise 3

Keep Talking — Creating solutions

PRACTICE THE DIALOG

A Hi, Jerry, how's your work going?

B Everything's fine. Earlier the cash register wouldn't scan items in plastic bags. But it's OK now.

A What did you do?

B Well, the scanner looked dirty, so I cleaned it.

A Good thinking, Jerry.

PARTNER WORK

Take turns telling your partner how you solved a problem with a machine. Use the dialog above and the Useful Language.

1. The telephone doesn't have a dial tone.

2. The TV in guest room 301 isn't working.

Useful Language

I'm having trouble . . .

Let's try . . .

Personal Dictionary ▸ Working with Machines

Write the words and phrases that you need to know.

_____

_____

30   Unit 3

Personal Dictionary

Have learners add the words in their Personal Dictionary to their *Workforce Writing Dictionary*. For more information see "Workforce Writing Dictionary" on page v.

PREPARATION

1. To teach or review **bar code, scanner,** and **scan,** display a product with a bar code. Role-play a grocery store clerk passing the package over the scanner repeatedly while expressing frustration that it won't scan.

2. Act out **creating a solution** to a simple mechanical problem, such as replacing batteries in a personal cassette player or cleaning the glass on an overhead projector. Have learners describe how you solved the problem.

PRESENTATION

1. Have learners read and discuss the Purpose Statement. For more information see "Purpose Statement" on page viii.

 2. Focus attention on the photograph. Encourage learners to say as much as they can about it. Have them speculate about what the people are doing and discussing. Write learners' ideas on the board and/or restate them in acceptable English. Then present the dialog. See "Presenting a Dialog" on page ix.

3. Have partners read the Partner Work instructions. Focus attention on the Useful Language box. Help learners read the expressions. If necessary, model pronunciation. Then have partners complete the activity. Have learners switch partners and repeat the activity. Have several pairs present each dialog to the class.

4. Have learners read the Personal Dictionary instructions. Then use the

Personal Dictionary procedures on page ix. Remind learners to add words to their dictionaries throughout the unit.

FOLLOW-UP

Problem/Solution: Have teams brainstorm solutions to mechanical problems with three machines team members commonly use at work. Have team reporters summarize their discussions for the class.

♦ Have teams make charts based on their discussions. The first column should list *Problems,* the second column, *Solutions.* Have teams exchange charts and add solutions to the second column. Post the charts in the classroom.

WORKBOOK

Unit 3, Exercise 4

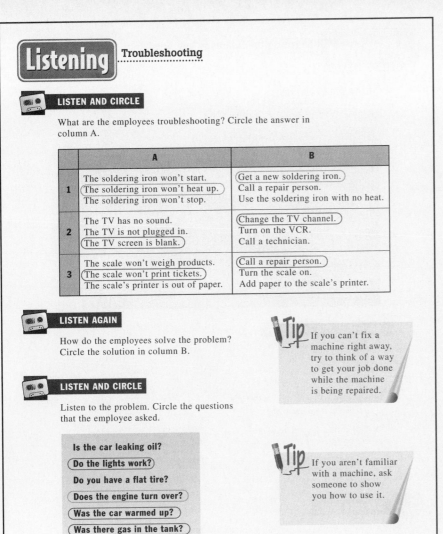

Listening · Troubleshooting

LISTEN AND CIRCLE

What are the employees troubleshooting? Circle the answer in column A.

	A	B
1	The soldering iron won't start. (The soldering iron won't heat up.) The soldering iron won't stop.	(Get a new soldering iron.) Call a repair person. Use the soldering iron with no heat.
2	The TV has no sound. The TV is not plugged in. (The TV screen is blank.)	(Change the TV channel.) Turn on the VCR. Call a technician.
3	The scale won't weigh products. (The scale won't print tickets.) The scale's printer is out of paper.	(Call a repair person.) Turn the scale on. Add paper to the scale's printer.

LISTEN AGAIN

How do the employees solve the problem? Circle the solution in column B.

LISTEN AND CIRCLE

Listen to the problem. Circle the questions that the employee asked.

- Is the car leaking oil?
- (Do the lights work?)
- Do you have a flat tire?
- (Does the engine turn over?)
- (Was the car warmed up?)
- (Was there gas in the tank?)

Tip If you can't fix a machine right away, try to think of a way to get your job done while the machine is being repaired.

Tip If you aren't familiar with a machine, ask someone to show you how to use it.

Unit 3

31

Language Note

*Tell learners that **troubleshooting** means "finding and eliminating the source of trouble in any kind of work," although the term is often applied specifically to mechanical breakdowns. Ask learners to describe ways they have heard people use the word.*

PREPARATION

1. Use a machine such as an electric pencil sharpener to model **troubleshooting.** Perform a few troubleshooting steps, such as making sure it is plugged in and emptying the shavings. As you work, ask questions such as "Is it plugged in? Is it jammed?" After each question, check to see if the troubleshooting solved the problem.

PRESENTATION

1. Have learners read and discuss the Purpose Statement. For more information see "Purpose Statement" on page viii. Focus attention on the chart. Discuss that the statements in the first column identify problems with machines. The statements in the second column identify solutions.

 2. Have learners read the Listen and Circle instructions. Then have them read the items. Make sure that everyone understands what to do. Then play the tape or read the Listening Transcript aloud two or more times as learners complete the activity. Have learners check their work. For more information see "Presenting a Listening Activity" on page ix.

 3. Have learners read the Listen Again instructions. Then follow the procedures in 2.

 4. Have learners read the Listen and Circle instructions and the questions in the box. Then follow the procedures in 2.

 Tip Have learners read the Tips. Have learners discuss how the advice will help them.

For more information, see "Presenting a Tip" on page ix.

FOLLOW-UP

What Could Go Wrong? Have learners work in teams. Give each team a picture card with a machine on it. Have the teams brainstorm a list of things that could go wrong with the machine and then write troubleshooting instructions for each problem.

♦ Have teams create a list of general questions individuals could use to troubleshoot a variety of mechanical problems in small business machines. (For example, "Is it plugged in?") Have team reporters share their list of questions.

WORKBOOK

Unit 3, Exercise 5

Report problems

Create solutions

★　　★　　★　　★　　★

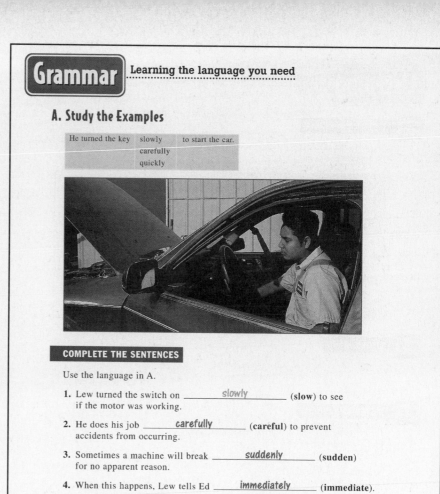

Grammar Learning the language you need

A. Study the Examples

He turned the key	slowly	to start the car.
	carefully	
	quickly	

COMPLETE THE SENTENCES

Use the language in A.

1. Lew turned the switch on _____ *slowly* _____ (**slow**) to see if the motor was working.

2. He does his job _____ *carefully* _____ (**careful**) to prevent accidents from occurring.

3. Sometimes a machine will break _____ *suddenly* _____ (**sudden**) for no apparent reason.

4. When this happens, Lew tells Ed _____ *immediately* _____ (**immediate**).

5. Then, he tries to find a solution _____ *quickly* _____ (**quick**).

PARTNER WORK

At your workplace or school, what do you do quickly? slowly? carefully? Why? Tell your partner. Share your partner's ideas with the class.

32

Unit 3

PREPARATION

Review the language in the grammar boxes with learners before they open their books, if necessary.

PRESENTATION

1. Have learners read and discuss the Purpose Statement. For more information see "Purpose Statement" on page viii.

2. Focus attention on the photograph. Encourage learners to say as much as they can about it. Write their ideas on the board and/or restate them in acceptable English.

3. Have learners read the grammar box in A. Have learners use the language in the box to say as many sentences as possible. Tell learners that they can use the grammar boxes throughout the unit to review or check sentence structures.

4. Have learners read the instructions for Complete the Sentences. If necessary, model the first item. Allow learners to complete the activity. Have learners check each other's work in pairs. Ask several learners to read their completed sentences aloud while the rest of the class checks their work.

5. Have learners read the Partner Work instructions. Make sure each pair knows what to do. Then have learners complete the activity. Have learners switch partners and repeat the activity. Ask several learners to present their partners' responses to the class.

B. Study the Examples

It's	going to	be fixed soon.
I'm		turn off the fax machine.
There's		be a reception in the hotel.

COMPLETE THE SENTENCES

Use the language in B.

1. There _'s going to be_____ (**be**) a training session tomorrow.
2. Mr. Williams and Mr. DiStefano ____are going to show____ (**show**) us how to use the new forklift.
3. I _'m going to attend_____ (**attend**) the training session.
4. We _'re going to learn_____ (**learn**) a new skill.
5. It _'s going to be_____ (**be**) a short training session.
6. The session _'s going to start_____ (**start**) at 1:30.
7. It _'s going to end_____ (**end**) at 2:00.

PARTNER WORK

Look at the pictures. What's going to happen? Tell your partner. Take turns completing the sentences.

The stock clerk ...   The car wash employee ...   The paramedics ...

TEAM WORK

What are you going to do at your workplace or school tomorrow? Tell the team.

---

6. Focus attention on the grammar box in B. Follow the procedures in 3.

7. Have learners read the instructions for Complete the Sentences. If necessary, model the first item. Allow learners to complete the activity. Have learners check each other's work in pairs. Ask several learners to read their sentences aloud while the rest of the class checks their work.

8. Focus attention on the illustrations. Encourage learners to say as much as they can about them. Write learners' ideas on the board and/or restate them in acceptable English. Then have partners read the Partner Work instructions. Make sure each pair knows what to do. If necessary, model the activity. Have learners switch partners and repeat the

activity. Ask several learners to present their completed sentences to the class.

9. Have learners read the Team Work instructions. Make sure everyone knows what to do. If necessary, model the activity. Then have teams complete the activity. Supply any language needed. Ask several teams to present one or two of their statements to the class.

FOLLOW-UP

I'm going to . . . Have the class create sentences that begin with "I'm going to. . . ." One learner starts by saying what he or she is going to do at work the next day. The next learner repeats the first learner's statement and says what he or she is going to do at work, and so on. Learners who can't repeat what everyone

is going to do drop out. Continue until only one person is left.

♦ Have learners work as partners to tell each other about machines they are going to troubleshoot. Ask them each to state at least three steps they are going to take. Have one or two learners present their partners' responses to the class.

WORKBOOK

Unit 3, Exercises 6A–6C

BLACKLINE MASTERS

Blackline Master: Unit 3

★   ★   ★   ★   ★

Reading and Writing — Using a suggestion box

READ THE SUGGESTION CARD

Some companies use suggestion boxes and cards to encourage employees to make suggestions for improvement.

Friendly Airlines — Suggestion Card

Name: *Ricardo Ramos*
Department: *baggage*
Phone number/extension: *555-2321 x311*
Date: *5/27/01*
Suggestion: *I think we ought to have the computer print passengers' names on their baggage tags. This will help us find the baggage if it is lost. It will help passengers find their baggage when they arrive at their destinations.*

Thank you! We appreciate your input!

ANSWER THE QUESTIONS

1. Who is making the suggestion? _____ *Ricardo Ramos*
2. What department is he in? _____ *baggage*
3. What is his phone number and extension? _____ *555-2321 x311*
4. What is his suggestion? *Have the computer print passengers' names on their baggage tags.*
5. How will his suggestion improve things? *It will help when baggage is lost. It will help passengers find their baggage when they arrive.*

ON YOUR JOB — DISCUSSION

How do you make suggestions for improvement at your workplace or school? Who do you talk to? Share your ideas with the class.

34   Unit 3

PREPARATION

1. Use realia or pictures to clarify **suggestion cards.** Ask learners if they have ever seen suggestion cards. Discuss other ways that people can make suggestions for improvement.

2. To present the language on this page, use realia or role-play putting a **baggage tag** on a piece of **baggage.**

PRESENTATION

1. Have learners read and discuss the Purpose Statement. For more information see "Purpose Statement" on page viii.

2. Have learners preview the suggestion card before they read. Encourage them to say everything they can about the card. Make sure they understand all the categories. Write their ideas on the board and/or restate them in acceptable English. Then have learners read the suggestion card independently.

3. Have learners read the Answer the Questions instructions. Make sure everyone knows what to do. Then have learners complete the activity. Ask several learners to share their answers with the class while the rest of the class checks their work.

4. Have learners read the Discussion questions. Make sure everyone knows what to do. Then have learners work in teams to discuss their ideas. Have team reporters share their ideas with the class.

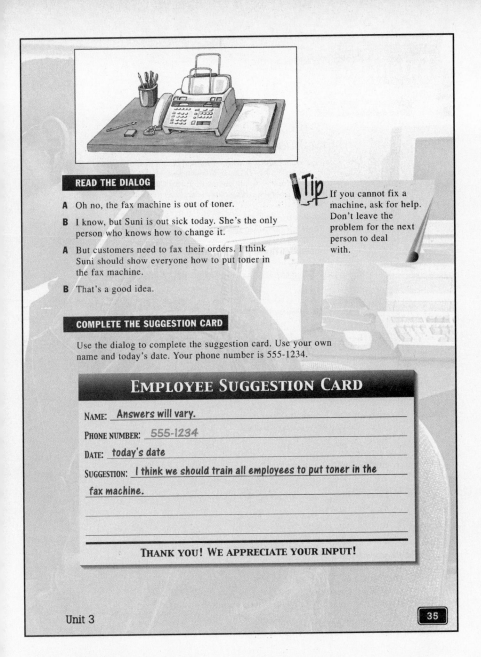

READ THE DIALOG

A Oh no, the fax machine is out of toner.

B I know, but Suni is out sick today. She's the only person who knows how to change it.

A But customers need to fax their orders. I think Suni should show everyone how to put toner in the fax machine.

B That's a good idea.

Tip If you cannot fix a machine, ask for help. Don't leave the problem for the next person to deal with.

COMPLETE THE SUGGESTION CARD

Use the dialog to complete the suggestion card. Use your own name and today's date. Your phone number is 555-1234.

EMPLOYEE SUGGESTION CARD

NAME: _Answers will vary._

PHONE NUMBER: _555-1234_

DATE: _today's date_

SUGGESTION: _I think we should train all employees to put toner in the fax machine._

THANK YOU! WE APPRECIATE YOUR INPUT!

Unit 3

35

---

6. Focus attention on the illustration. Encourage learners to say everything they can about the fax machine. Write their ideas on the board and/or restate them in acceptable English. Clarify vocabulary about parts of the fax machine. Present **toner** by explaining that toner is like ink in a copier and/or display a used toner cartridge. Then have learners read the dialog independently. Ask a few questions about it to make sure learners understand.

7. Have learners read the Complete the Suggestion Card instructions. Make sure everyone knows what to do. If necessary, model the first line of the activity. Then have learners complete the activity. Have learners discuss their completed suggestion cards with the class.

Tip Have learners read the Tip independently. Have learners discuss how the advice will help them. For more information, see "Presenting a Tip" on page ix.

FOLLOW-UP

Making Suggestions: Have learners work in teams to write a recommendation for an improvement at one team member's workplace or at a local business they use frequently. Ask one learner on each team to use a blank piece of paper to create the suggestion card. Have team reporters read the suggestion cards to the class.

♦ With the class, discuss positive ways to suggest improvements or make recommendations. Then have pairs create dialogs in which one partner suggests an improvement at his or her workplace or school and the other partner responds. Have several pairs present their dialogs to the class.

WORKBOOK

Unit 3, Exercises 7A–7D

★ ★ ★ ★ ★

Extension — Troubleshooting

READ THE ARTICLE

Troubleshooting

Do you have to troubleshoot at work? Troubleshooting means finding the source of problems. Think back on some problems with technology that you have had. Were you able to figure out the problem? Could you solve them by yourself? Here is a troubleshooting guide with some common problems and possible solutions.

Cars and Trucks
The engine does not start when you turn the key.
1. Check the battery.
2. Check the starter.

The brake pedal goes to the floor when you press it. The car doesn't stop.
1. Stop driving right away. Check the brakes and brake fluid.

Grocery Store
The scale does not print a label when you place food on it.
1. Be sure the scale's printer has paper in it.

Restaurant
A customer wants to pay with a debit card, but the machine won't read the card.
1. Be sure the machine is working properly.
2. Be sure the customer's card isn't damaged.

ANSWER THE QUESTIONS

These people are having problems. What do you recommend? Write the answers on a sheet of paper.

1. Dolores's car won't start.

2. Andrew just ran a stop sign. The brake pedal went to the floor when he pressed it, and the car didn't stop.

3. Glenn tried to weigh some meat, but the scale wouldn't print a label.

4. A restaurant customer tried to use her debit card to buy some hamburgers, but the machine wouldn't read the card.

 **Culture Notes**

Do you feel comfortable making suggestions? Why are you encouraged to make suggestions at your workplace or school?

36 Unit 3

SCANS Note

Remind learners that when troubleshooting it is a good idea to start by trying simple solutions and then moving on to more complicated solutions.

PREPARATION

1. If necessary, review **troubleshooting.** Follow the instructions in Preparation on page 31.

2. To present or review the machines in the article, display picture cards of a car engine, brake pedals, electronic scales, and a debit card reader. Display a debit card. Discuss learners' experiences with these items.

PRESENTATION

1. Have learners read and discuss the Purpose Statement. For more information see "Purpose Statement" on page viii. Have learners read the article independently.

2. Have learners preview the troubleshooting guide before they read. Encourage them to say everything they can about it. Make sure they understand all the categories. Write their ideas on the board and/or restate them in acceptable English. Then have learners read the troubleshooting guide independently.

3. Have learners read the instructions for Answer the Questions. Make sure everyone knows what to do. If necessary, model the first item. Then have learners complete the activity. Have learners review each other's work in pairs. Have several learners read their answers aloud while the rest of the class checks their work.

4. Have learners read Culture Notes and talk over their ideas in teams. Have team reporters share their ideas with the class. For more information see "Culture Notes" on page vii.

FOLLOW-UP

Troubleshooting: Have teams role-play a situation in which there is a problem with a machine. One learner should start by describing the problem; other team members should respond with troubleshooting questions. Have teams present their role-plays to the class.

♦ Have learners work in pairs. Have each pair choose either the grocery store or the restaurant problem in the article and create a dialog in which one learner is the customer and the other is the employee who solves the problem. Have several pairs present their dialogs to the class.

WORKBOOK

Unit 3, Exercise 8

 **How well can you use the skills in this unit?**
....

Complete the activities. Go over your work with a partner or your teacher.
Then complete the Performance Review on page 38.

SKILL 1   REPORT PROBLEMS

Think of a problem that occurs with a machine you use at
your workplace or school. Report the problem to a partner
or your teacher.

SKILL 2   CREATE SOLUTIONS

Your partner or your teacher needs help with the following
situations. Create a solution, and tell it to your partner or teacher.

The truck won't start.   The scanner isn't working.

SKILL 3   TROUBLESHOOT

The VCR in conference room 3 isn't working. Circle the things
you'll check before you call a repair person.

Is the tape in the VCR?	Is the TV turned to the right channel?
Is the conference room locked?	Are the TV and VCR plugged in?
Is the TV connected to the VCR?	Is the TV set to your favorite program?
Is the VCR a new model?	

Unit 3   37

PRESENTATION

Use any of the procedures in
"Evaluation," page x, with pages 37 and
38. Record individuals' results on the
Unit 3 Individual Competency Chart.
Record the class's results on the Class
Cumulative Competency Chart.

Use the dialog to complete the suggestion card. Use your own name and today's date.

A The fax machine is out of paper again. I'm expecting an important fax.

B I'm sorry. It seems like it's always out of paper.

A I agree. I think we should keep paper in the cabinet beside the fax machine. Then people wouldn't have to go to the supply room to get more paper. I'm going to fill out a suggestion card right now.

B That's a good idea. That would save all of us a lot of time.

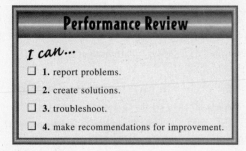

SUGGESTION CARD

NAME: Answers will vary.

DATE: today's date

SUGGESTION: I think we should keep the paper for the fax machine in the cabinet next to it. That would save people time.

THANK YOU! WE APPRECIATE YOUR INPUT!

Performance Review

I can...

☐ **1.** report problems.

☐ **2.** create solutions.

☐ **3.** troubleshoot.

☐ **4.** make recommendations for improvement.

Discussion

Work with a team. How will the skills help you? Make a list. Share the list with your class.

38   Unit 3

PRESENTATION

Follow the instructions on page 37.

INFORMAL WORKPLACE-SPECIFIC ASSESSMENT

Ask learners to describe a problem they've had with a machine at work and explain how they handled the problem.

WORKBOOK

Unit 3, Exercise 9

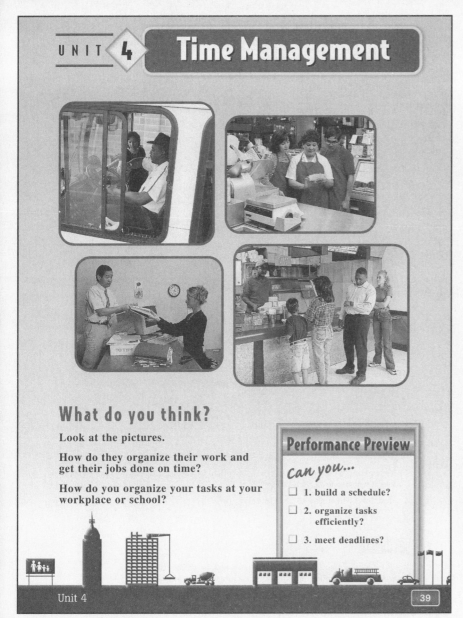

What do you think?

Look at the pictures.

How do they organize their work and get their jobs done on time?

How do you organize your tasks at your workplace or school?

Performance Preview

can you...

☐ 1. build a schedule?

☐ 2. organize tasks efficiently?

☐ 3. meet deadlines?

Unit 4 | 39

Unit 4 Overview
—SCANS Competencies—

★ Allocate time

★ Monitor performance

★ Organize and interpret information

Workforce Skills

● Build a schedule

● Organize tasks efficiently

● Meet deadlines

Materials

● Picture cards of people working under time pressure

● Samples of calendars, planners, and schedules; a clock

● Picture card of a car; pictures or realia of a copy machine, a computer, and a printer

● Copies of blank calendar pages

● Picture cards of walk-in refrigerator, grill, and tray

Unit Warm-Up

To stimulate discussion about the unit topic (organizing tasks to meet deadlines), show pictures of people working under time pressure, such as a cook. Discuss tasks the people have to do quickly. Ask how they can do them efficiently. Have learners name tasks they need to do efficiently at home or work.

★   ★   ★   ★   ★

WORKFORCE SKILLS (page 39)

Organize tasks efficiently

★   ★   ★   ★   ★

PREPARATION

Display samples of calendars, planners, and schedules. Help learners identify and name these materials. Encourage learners to tell which of these materials they use at home, school, or work. Ask what they use them for.

PRESENTATION

1. Focus attention on the photographs. Ask learners to speculate what the unit might be about. Write their ideas on the board and/or restate them in acceptable English.

2. Have learners talk about the pictures. Ask them to describe what is going on in each picture and what tasks the employees are trying to do efficiently. Ask what the employees have in common. Help learners identify the jobs depicted.

3. Help learners read the questions. Discuss the questions with the class.

4. You may want to use the Performance Preview to provide learners with an overview of the skills in the unit. Have learners read the list of skills and discuss what they will learn in the unit.

FOLLOW-UP

Daily Tasks: Have team members tell each other the tasks they have to do each day at work or at home. Have them answer these questions: *Which*

tasks take the longest? Which ones do you sometimes have trouble finishing on time? Have team reporters summarize their teams' discussions for the class.

♦ Have learners work in pairs. Each partner should choose a worker shown in one of the pictures on this page. Have the "workers" tell each other how they managed to get their jobs done on time that day. Ask several pairs to repeat their role-plays for the class.

WORKBOOK

Unit 4, Exercises 1A–1B

WORKFORCE SKILLS (page 40)

Organize tasks efficiently

★ ★ ★ ★ ★

Getting Started
Estimating time for tasks

TEAM WORK

Read the task list. Then look at the pictures. Match the pictures with the items on the list. Write the letters.

Tuesday Morning:

_a_ 1. Flush the radiator (45 minutes)

_c_ 2. Fix the flat tire (10 minutes)

_b_ 3. Change the oil (1/2 hour)

_d_ 4. Replace the tail light (10 minutes)

PARTNER WORK

Your partner is an auto mechanic who is fixing your car. Ask how long it will take to fix your car.

A How long will it take to change a flat tire?

B About ten minutes.

SURVEY

Work with a team. Each learner states a task he or she often does at work or school. Find out how long each task takes. Make a table.

40

Unit 4

Teaching Note

Use this page to introduce the new language in the unit. Whenever possible, encourage peer teaching. Supply any language learners need.

PREPARATION

1. Write a sample list of daily tasks on the board. Have learners discuss how they would organize the tasks efficiently.

2. Use a picture card of a car to present or review **radiator, flat tire, oil,** and **tail light.**

PRESENTATION

1. Read and discuss the Purpose Statement. For more information, see "Purpose Statement," page viii.

2. Focus attention on the task list and the illustrations. Encourage learners to say as much as they can about them. Write their ideas on the board and/or restate them in acceptable English.

3. Have teams read the Team Work instructions. Make sure each team knows what to do. Remind them they are responsible for making sure each member understands the new language. Have teams complete the activity. Ask team reporters to present the answers to the class.

4. Have partners read the Partner Work instructions. After partners complete the activity, have learners switch partners and repeat the activity. Have one or two pairs present their dialogs to the class.

 5. Have teams read the Survey instructions. Make sure everyone knows what to do. Then have teams complete the activity. Have teams compare tables. See "Survey" on page viii.

FOLLOW-UP

Bar Graph: Have teams use the information from the Survey tables to create bar graphs. The horizontal axis should show the tasks; the vertical axis should show the number of minutes each task takes. Post the graphs in the classroom.

◆ Have teams use the graphs to answer the following questions: What types of tasks take the most time to do? What types of tasks take the least time? Ask team reporters to summarize ideas for the class.

WORKBOOK

Unit 4, Exercises 2A–2B

Talk About It | Organizing tasks efficiently

 PRACTICE THE DIALOG

A When the lunch rush begins, we're very busy. So let's set up your work area and get started.

B OK, what do I do?

A Get the hamburger patties from the walk-in refrigerator. Then put them in the small refrigerator near the grill.

B What do I do next?

A At 11:30 take 12 hamburger patties and put them on the grill. Then close the top of the grill.

TEAM WORK

Look at the steps for cooking hamburgers. Put the steps in order.

__2__ **a.** Fill the refrigerator near the grill with hamburger patties.

__1__ **b.** Wash your hands.

__5__ **c.** Put the patties on a clean tray.

__4__ **d.** Open the grill and take out the cooked patties.

__3__ **e.** Put 12 patties on the grill, close the grill, and cook them.

 PARTNER WORK

Think of a task you do every day at your workplace or school. Tell your partner how you get ready for the task. Then say how you do the task. Use the dialog above.

ASAP
PROJECT

Work with a team. Think of a task for your team to organize, such as catering a dinner party, painting a house, or taking care of a customer's pet. Build a schedule. Complete this project as you work though the unit.

Unit 4

41

WORKFORCE SKILLS (page 41)

Organize tasks efficiently

★　　★　　★　　★　　★

ASAP
PROJECT

Have learners read the instructions. Discuss the project and its purpose with learners. Make sure that everyone understands. Help learners assign themselves to teams based upon their skills, knowledge, interests, or other personal strengths. Have each team select a leader. Throughout the rest of the unit, allow time for learners to work on the project. Have the teams agree on a deadline when the project will be finished. For more information see "ASAP Project" on page vi.

PREPARATION

Use picture cards and pantomime to present or review **walk-in refrigerator, grill,** and **tray.** Role-play a cook. Model the new language as you explain what you are doing.

PRESENTATION

1. Have learners read and discuss the Purpose Statement. For more information, see "Purpose Statement" on page viii.

 2. Focus attention on the illustration. Encourage learners to say as much as they can about it. Write learners' ideas on the board and/or restate them in acceptable English. Supply any language learners need. Then present the dialog. See "Presenting a Dialog" on page ix.

3. Have teams read the Team Work instructions. Make sure each team knows what to do. Then have teams complete the activity. Have team reporters share their answers with the class.

4. Have partners read the Partner Work instructions. Make sure each pair knows what to do. Then have learners complete the activity. Have learners switch partners and repeat the activity. Have one or two pairs present their dialogs to the class.

FOLLOW-UP

Task Masters: Divide the class into teams. On slips of paper, write different professions or jobs. Have each team draw a slip and brainstorm five tasks that a worker in that job might have to do in one day. Have them discuss how

the worker might do each task efficiently. Ask team reporters to summarize discussions for the class.

◆ Have teams put the tasks on their lists in order, with the task they would do first at the top. Have team reporters present the lists and explain the reasons for the order.

WORKBOOK

Unit 4, Exercises 3A–3B

★ ★ ★ ★ ★

Keep Talking
Organizing tasks efficiently

PRACTICE THE DIALOG

A We have a lot of work to do. Let's get organized.

B OK, I can start with the bedroom. First I'll put the sheets in the washing machine. While it's running, I'll make the bed. Then I'll do the vacuuming and dusting.

A Good idea. I'll start in the kitchen. I'll load the dishwasher. While it's running, I can wash the kitchen floor and counters.

PARTNER WORK

Tell your partner about two tasks that you can do at the same time. Use the dialog above and the Useful Language.

Useful Language

before   during   after

Tip Think of tasks that you can do while you are waiting for a machine to finish running.

Personal Dictionary Organizing Tasks

Write the words and phrases that you need to know.

_____

_____

_____

42

Unit 4

Personal Dictionary

Have learners add the words in their Personal Dictionary to their *Workforce Writing Dictionary*. For more information see "Workforce Writing Dictionary" on page v.

PREPARATION

1. To teach or review sequencing words, such as **while, before, during,** and **after,** pantomime a task with multiple steps, such as making soup and a sandwich. Use the language to describe and review the steps.

2. To present or review **washing machine, vacuuming,** and **dusting,** pantomime and identify the activities. Ask learners to pantomime and identify cleaning tasks they do.

PRESENTATION

1. Have learners read and discuss the Purpose Statement. See "Purpose Statement," page viii.

 2. Focus attention on the illustration. Encourage learners to say what the people are doing and discussing. Then present the dialog.

3. Have partners read the Partner Work instructions and the Useful Language. If necessary, model pronunciation. Have partners complete the activity, then switch partners and do it again. Ask a few pairs to present their dialogs.

4. Have learners read the Personal Dictionary instructions. Remind learners to add words to their dictionaries throughout the unit.

Tip Have learners read the Tip independently. Ask them to discuss how the advice will help them. See "Presenting a Tip" on page ix.

FOLLOW-UP

Home Maintenance: Have learners work in teams to brainstorm ten tasks they do when cleaning a workplace or a home. Ask teams to share their lists with the class. Generate a master list on the board.

♦ Have learners make individual three-column charts. The first column should list cleaning tasks they do at home or work. The second should show how many times a week they do each task. They should add a check-mark in the last column if the task can be done at the same time as other tasks. Have learners compare charts.

WORKBOOK

Unit 4, Exercises 4A–4B

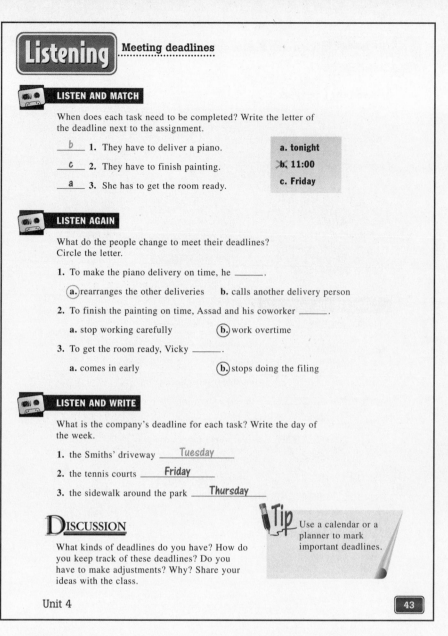

Listening — Meeting deadlines

LISTEN AND MATCH

When does each task need to be completed? Write the letter of the deadline next to the assignment.

_b_ 1. They have to deliver a piano.

_c_ 2. They have to finish painting.

_a_ 3. She has to get the room ready.

a. tonight
b. 11:00
c. Friday

LISTEN AGAIN

What do the people change to meet their deadlines? Circle the letter.

1. To make the piano delivery on time, he _____.

   (a.) rearranges the other deliveries   b. calls another delivery person

2. To finish the painting on time, Assad and his coworker _____.

   a. stop working carefully   (b.) work overtime

3. To get the room ready, Vicky _____.

   a. comes in early   (b.) stops doing the filing

LISTEN AND WRITE

What is the company's deadline for each task? Write the day of the week.

1. the Smiths' driveway _Tuesday_

2. the tennis courts _Friday_

3. the sidewalk around the park _Thursday_

DISCUSSION

What kinds of deadlines do you have? How do you keep track of these deadlines? Do you have to make adjustments? Why? Share your ideas with the class.

 Tip Use a calendar or a planner to mark important deadlines.

Unit 4

43

WORKFORCE SKILLS (page 43)

Meet deadlines

★　　★　　★　　★　　★

Language Note

Point out or review that there are different ways to write the time of day in English: for example, 5:00, five o'clock, 5 A.M., 5 P.M., 12:00, noon, and midnight.

PREPARATION

1. Explain that a **deadline** is the date and time when a task must be completed. Discuss deadlines learners need to meet at work.

2. Use the clock to review time. Display various times and have learners say and write them. Similarly, use a large calendar to review days of the week and months. Use a daily planner to review **today, tonight,** and **tomorrow.**

PRESENTATION

1. Have learners read and discuss the Purpose Statement. See "Purpose Statement," page viii.

 2. Have learners read the Listen and Match instructions and the items. Then play the

tape or read the Listening Transcript aloud two or more times as learners complete the activity. Have learners check their work.

 3. Have learners read the Listen Again instructions. Then follow the procedures in 2.

4. Have learners read the Listen and Write instructions. Then follow the procedures in 2.

5. Have learners read the Discussion questions. Then have them discuss their responses in teams. Have teams share their ideas with the class.

 Tip Have learners read the Tip. Ask how the advice will help them.

FOLLOW-UP

Meeting Deadlines: Have individual learners write lists of tasks they have to do that have deadlines in the next few weeks. Learners should write the deadline date next to each task. Have partners compare lists. Then ask a few learners to present their lists to the class.

♦ Distribute blank calendar pages. Have individuals transfer the information from their lists to the calendars, writing the tasks on the appropriate deadline dates. Display the completed calendar pages.

WORKBOOK

Unit 4, Exercise 5

SCANS Note

Point out to learners that accurately noting the length of time they spend on a work project will improve their ability to organize their time in the future. Discuss why the timely completion of tasks is important for success in the workplace.

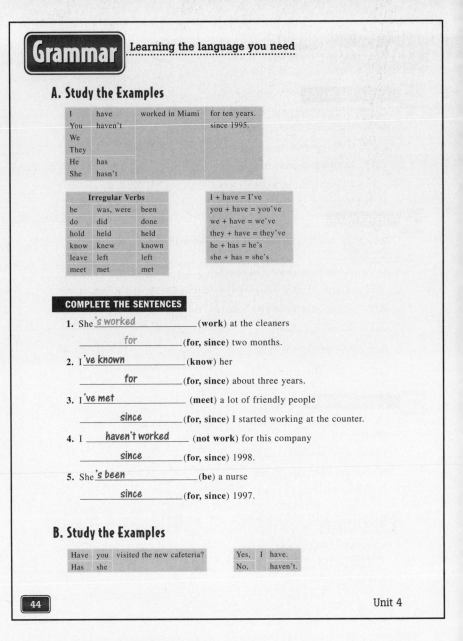

Grammar — Learning the language you need

A. Study the Examples

I	have	worked in Miami	for ten years.
You	haven't		since 1995.
We			
They			
He	has		
She	hasn't		

Irregular Verbs		
be	was, were	been
do	did	done
hold	held	held
know	knew	known
leave	left	left
meet	met	met

I + have = I've
you + have = you've
we + have = we've
they + have = they've
he + has = he's
she + has = she's

COMPLETE THE SENTENCES

1. She *'s worked* ___(**work**) at the cleaners
   for ___(**for, since**) two months.

2. I *'ve known* ___(**know**) her
   for ___(**for, since**) about three years.

3. I *'ve met* ___(**meet**) a lot of friendly people
   since ___(**for, since**) I started working at the counter.

4. I *haven't worked* ___(**not work**) for this company
   since ___(**for, since**) 1998.

5. She *'s been* ___(**be**) a nurse
   since ___(**for, since**) 1997.

B. Study the Examples

| Have | you | visited the new cafeteria? | | Yes, | I | have. |
| Has | she | | | No, | | haven't. |

44 · Unit 4

PREPARATION

Review the language in the grammar boxes with learners before they open their books, if necessary. Use pantomime and realia to present or review **hold.** With the help of a learner, act out **meet** and **leave.**

PRESENTATION

1. Have learners read and discuss the Purpose Statement. For more information, see "Purpose Statement" on page viii.

2. Have learners read the grammar boxes in A. Have learners use the language in the boxes to say as many sentences as possible. Tell learners that they can use the grammar boxes throughout the unit to review or check sentence structures.

3. Focus attention on Complete the Sentences. If necessary, model the first item. Allow learners to complete the activity. Have learners check each other's work in pairs. Ask several learners to read their completed sentences aloud while the rest of the class checks their work.

4. Focus attention on the grammar boxes in B. Follow the procedures in 2.

Complete the sentences to answer the questions. Use the language in B.

1. Have you talked to the site managers?

   Yes, _____ I have _____ .

2. Have they done anything about the parking problem?

   No, _____ they haven't _____ .

3. Have you written to them?

   No, _____ I haven't _____ .

4. Have they held a meeting?

   No, _____ they haven't _____ .

5. Has Mrs. West talked to you about it?

   Yes, _____ she has _____ .

C. Study the Examples

"This job is interesting."	Tim thinks (that) this job is interesting.
"I need a job."	Frances says (that) she needs a job.
"Factories provide jobs."	Eva agrees (that) factories provide jobs.

Read the dialog. Then summarize it using the language in C.

1. **A** This city is expensive, Jan.

   B I agree. This city is expensive.

   _____ Jan agrees (that) this city is expensive. _____

2. **A** You could get a job at the factory, Alberto.

   B Yes, I'll get a job at the factory.

   _____ Alberto says (that) he'll get a job at the factory. _____

3. **A** What do you think about the factory, Bethany?

   B The factory is noisy.

   _____ Bethany thinks (that) the factory is noisy. _____

Unit 4

45

---

5. Have learners read the instructions for Answer the Questions. If necessary, model the first item. Allow learners to complete the activity. Have a different individual read each question and answer aloud while the rest of the class checks their work.

6. Focus attention on the grammar box in C. Follow the procedures in 2.

7. Have learners read the instructions for Write the Summary. If necessary, model the first item by writing the summary on the board. Allow learners to complete the activity. Have learners check each other's work in pairs. Ask several learners to read their summaries aloud while the rest of the class checks their work.

FOLLOW-UP

Have or Haven't: Ask learners to work in pairs. Have one partner ask five questions using "have," for example: "Have you done your homework yet?" or "Have you had lunch?" The other partner should answer the questions. Ask several pairs to present their questions and answers to the class.

♦ Have pairs write their dialogs. Then have them rewrite the questions and answers using "he" or "she" as the subject. Check each pair's work.

WORKBOOK

Unit 4, Exercises 6A–6C

BLACKLINE MASTERS

Blackline Master: Unit 4

★　　★　　★　　★　　★

Culture Note

Discuss differences in the typical workday among different cultures. Point out that in the United States a typical full-time employee works eight hours a day with a break for lunch. Ask learners to talk about their schedules in the United States and in other countries.

Reading and Writing   Scheduling

READ THE SCHEDULE

Malika works at Downtown Copy Shop. She's in charge of opening the store every day. Read her schedule for opening the store.

DOWNTOWN COPY SHOP
110 West End Avenue • 555-3280 • Open 7:00 to 10:00 for all your copying needs

Opening the Store

6:30 Arrive at work, enter the store, turn off the alarm, turn on the lights, and lock the door. Clock in.

6:35 Turn on the copy machines and computers. Let them warm up for 15 minutes. Fill the copy machines with paper.

6:45 Turn on the cash register and count the change in the drawer.

6:50 Check the copy machines to make sure they are all working.

7:00 Unlock the front door. Turn on the OPEN sign.

CHECK THE SCHEDULE

Malika is on vacation this week, and Don is in charge of opening the store. Malika gave Don the schedule. Did Don follow the schedule? Write *yes* or *no*.

yes **1.** Don turned on the copy machines and computers at 6:35.

yes **2.** Don unlocked the door at 7:00.

_no_   **3.** Don turned on the OPEN sign at 6:30.

_no_   **4.** Don checked the copy machines at 7:50.

yes **5.** Don put paper in the copy machines at 6:35.

ON YOUR JOB   DISCUSSION

Don is supposed to turn on the copiers and computers at 6:35 because they need 15 minutes to warm up. What will go wrong if Don turns them on at 6:55? What will go wrong at your workplace or school if employees don't follow the schedule?

46   Unit 4

PREPARATION

1. Present or review what a schedule is by writing your typical morning schedule on the board. Include tasks you do and the times you do them. Ask one or two volunteers to write their morning schedules on the board.

2. Use pictures or realia to present or review **copier, copy machine, computer,** and **computer printer.**

PRESENTATION

1. Have learners read and discuss the Purpose Statement. For more information see "Purpose Statement" on page viii.

2. Have learners preview the schedule before they read. See "Prereading" on page x. Encourage learners to say everything they can about the schedule.

Write their ideas on the board and/or restate them in acceptable English. Then have learners read the schedule independently.

3. Have learners read the instructions for Check the Schedule. Make sure everyone knows what to do. Then have learners complete the activity. Ask several learners to share their answers with the class while the rest of the class checks their work.

ON YOUR JOB **4.** Have learners read the Discussion questions and work in teams to discuss them. Have teams compare ideas.

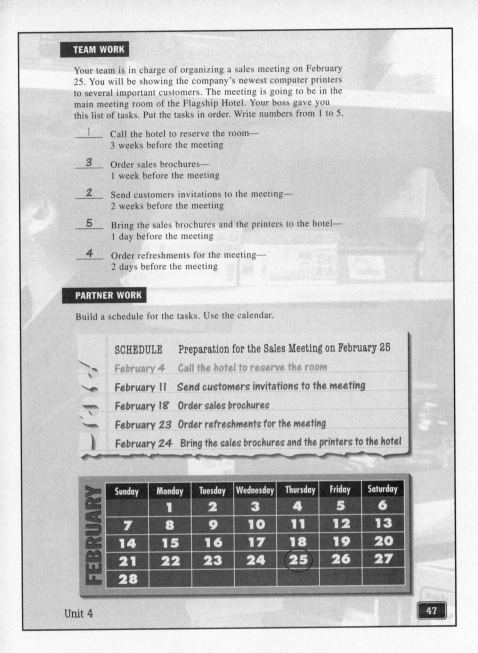

TEAM WORK

Your team is in charge of organizing a sales meeting on February 25. You will be showing the company's newest computer printers to several important customers. The meeting is going to be in the main meeting room of the Flagship Hotel. Your boss gave you this list of tasks. Put the tasks in order. Write numbers from 1 to 5.

_1_ Call the hotel to reserve the room—
3 weeks before the meeting

_3_ Order sales brochures—
1 week before the meeting

_2_ Send customers invitations to the meeting—
2 weeks before the meeting

_5_ Bring the sales brochures and the printers to the hotel—
1 day before the meeting

_4_ Order refreshments for the meeting—
2 days before the meeting

PARTNER WORK

Build a schedule for the tasks. Use the calendar.

SCHEDULE   Preparation for the Sales Meeting on February 25

February 4   Call the hotel to reserve the room

February 11   Send customers invitations to the meeting

February 18   Order sales brochures

February 23   Order refreshments for the meeting

February 24   Bring the sales brochures and the printers to the hotel

FEBRUARY	Sunday	Monday	Tuesday	Wednesday	Thursday	Friday	Saturday
		1	2	3	4	5	6
	7	8	9	10	11	12	13
	14	15	16	17	18	19	20
	21	22	23	24	(25)	26	27
	28						

Unit 4   47

---

5. Have learners read the Team Work instructions. Make sure everyone knows what to do. Then have teams complete the activity. Have team reporters share their teams' answers with the class.

6. Have learners reread the tasks in Team Work and look at the calendar in Partner Work. Help them find the meeting date on the calendar. Ask why "February 4" is the first date on the schedule. Make sure everyone knows what to do. Then have partners complete the Partner Work activity. Have several pairs present their schedules to the class, while the rest of the class checks their work.

FOLLOW-UP

Build a Schedule: Have teams think of a class project they might like to plan, such as cleaning their company's outdoor picnic area or painting their classroom. Then have them build schedules for completing the project. Suggest that they: (1) Write a list of tasks that need to be done. (2) Decide and note how far in advance each task should be done. (3) Put the tasks in order by numbering them. Ask team reporters to identify the project and read the ordered task lists to the class.

♦ Give each team a blank calendar page. Have them decide on and circle an end date for the project, then write the tasks on the appropriate dates. Post the calendars in the classroom.

WORKBOOK

Unit 4, Exercises 7A–7B

WORKFORCE SKILLS (page 48)

Build a schedule

Organize tasks efficiently

Meet deadlines

★　　★　　★　　★　　★

Teaching Note

Explain to learners that there is no single best method for organizing tasks to meet deadlines. Some people rely on portable planners, while others use task lists or desk calendars. Encourage learners to experiment until they find the method that works best for them.

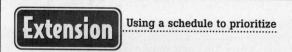 **Using a schedule to prioritize**

READ THE DELIVERY SCHEDULE

Alan delivers groceries to customers' homes. Read his schedule.

Customer	Notes
Mr. Santos	He wants his groceries after 4:00.
Mrs. Robinson	She lives near Mr. Schultz.
Mrs. Cho	Deliver her groceries between 10:30 and 11:00.
Mr. Anderson	He needs his groceries any time today, and he lives far away.
Mr. Schultz	**He needs his groceries as soon as possible. **URGENT

ANSWER THE QUESTIONS

Help Alan organize his deliveries.

1. Alan will probably not deliver Mr. Anderson's groceries first. Why?

　　Mr. Anderson needs his groceries any time today, and he lives far away.

2. Whose groceries should Alan deliver first? Why?

　　Mr. Schultz's, because he needs them as soon as possible.

3. Whose order can Alan combine with Mr. Schultz's? Why?

　　Mrs. Robinson's, because she lives near Mr. Schultz.

4. Which two customers' groceries will Alan probably deliver last?

　　Mr. Santos's and Mr. Anderson's

 **Culture Notes**

Good customer service is a priority. How does good scheduling help with customer service at your workplace? What happens if employees don't follow the schedule?

48　　　　　　　　　　　　　　　　　　　　　　　　　　　Unit 4

PREPARATION

Ask learners to identify useful language for prioritizing tasks, for example, **first, second, third, before, during,** and **after.** Write the words on the board.

PRESENTATION

1. Have learners read and discuss the Purpose Statement. See "Purpose Statement," page viii.

2. Have learners preview the schedule and say everything they can about it. Write their ideas on the board and/or restate them in acceptable English. Then have learners read the schedule.

3. Have learners read the instructions for Answer the Questions. Make sure everyone knows what to do. If necessary, model the first item. Allow learners to complete the activity. Have learners

review each other's work in pairs. Have several learners read their answers aloud while the rest of the class checks their work.

 4. Have learners read Culture Notes and talk over their responses in teams. Have team reporters share their ideas with the class. Ask the teams to compare ideas. See "Culture Notes," page vii.

FOLLOW-UP

Priorities: Have teams discuss how learners decide which work tasks to do first. Are learners' priorities determined by deadlines, customer service, employer requests, or something else? As team reporters list the factors team members mention, write a master list on the board.

◆ Help the class create a table that shows how many learners use each item on the board to prioritize tasks. Then have the class create a bar graph that shows the information. The horizontal axis should show the factors, the vertical axis should show the number of learners that use them. Display the graph in the classroom.

WORKBOOK

Unit 4, Exercise 8

48　　　　　　　　　　　　　　　　　　　　　　　　　　English ASAP

Performance Check

How well can you use the skills in this unit?

Complete the activities. Go over your work with a partner or your teacher. Then complete the Performance Review on page 50.

SKILL 1   BUILD A SCHEDULE

Mike is in charge of making 200 sandwiches for a lunch meeting on Monday, April 24. Put the tasks in order. Number them from 1 (first) to 5 (last).

__2__   Schedule employees to make the sandwiches—
4 days before April 24

__1__   Order bread, meat, and cheese—
5 days before April 24

__4__   Deliver the sandwiches—
10:00 on April 24

__3__   Pick up the bread from the bakery—
1 day before April 24

Use the information and the calendar to build a schedule.

Schedule
Preparations for the lunch meeting at City Hall on Monday, April 24

April 19   Order bread, meat, and cheese

April 20   Schedule employees to make the sandwiches

April 23   Pick up the bread from the bakery

April 24   Deliver the sandwiches by 10:00

APRIL

Sunday	Monday	Tuesday	Wednesday	Thursday	Friday	Saturday
						1
2	3	4	5	6	7	8
9	10	11	12	13	14	15
16	17	18	19	20	21	22
23	(24)	25	26	27	28	29
30						

Unit 4

49

PRESENTATION

Use any of the procedures in "Evaluation," page x, with pages 49 and 50. Record individuals' results on the Unit 4 Individual Competency Chart. Record the class's results on the Class Cumulative Competency Chart.

SKILL 2   ORGANIZE TASKS EFFICIENTLY

Think of a task you do every day at your workplace or school.
Tell your partner or teacher how you get ready for the task. Then
say how you do the task. Tell how you can organize the work to
save time.

SKILL 3   MEET DEADLINES

Listen to the dialog. What's the deadline for each task? Write the
letter of the deadline next to the assignment.

_b_ **1.** flower delivery   **a. Saturday 4:00 p.m.**

_c_ **2.** tile job   **b. Thursday 8:30 a.m.**

_a_ **3.** wedding cake   **c. Tuesday 3:00 p.m.**

Performance Review

I can...

☐ **1.** build a schedule.

☐ **2.** organize tasks efficiently.

☐ **3.** meet deadlines.

DISCUSSION

Work with a team. How will the skills help you? Make a list.
Share the list with your class.

PRESENTATION

Follow the instructions on page 49.

INFORMAL WORKPLACE-
SPECIFIC ASSESSMENT

Ask learners to discuss their workplace
schedule with you and to say which tasks
are most important.

WORKBOOK

Unit 4, Exercise 9

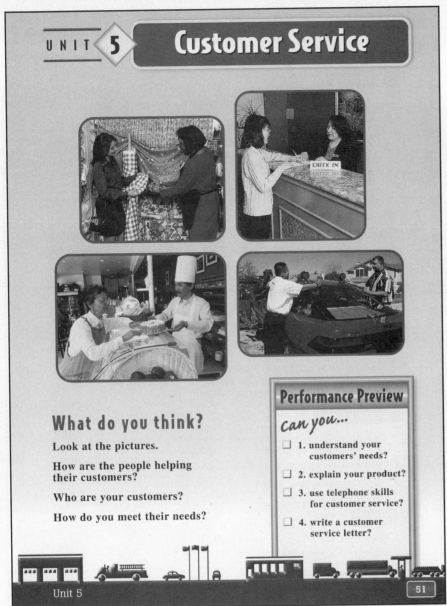

UNIT 5 — Customer Service

What do you think?

Look at the pictures.

How are the people helping their customers?

Who are your customers?

How do you meet their needs?

Performance Preview

can you...

☐ 1. understand your customers' needs?

☐ 2. explain your product?

☐ 3. use telephone skills for customer service?

☐ 4. write a customer service letter?

Unit 5

51

Unit 5 Overview
—SCANS Competencies—

★ Serve customers
★ Solve problems
★ Communicate information
★ Understand social systems

Workforce Skills

● Understand your customers' needs
● Explain your product
● Use telephone skills for customer service
● Write a customer service letter

Materials

● Picture cards of workers interacting with customers
● Pictures cards of economy and luxury cars
● A running shoe, a telephone
● Product catalogs
● Samples of customer service letters

Unit Warm-Up

To stimulate discussion about the unit topic (developing customer service skills), show pictures of people helping customers. Discuss what is happening in each picture. Ask learners to describe the kind of service they appreciate when they are customers.

★   ★   ★   ★   ★

WORKFORCE SKILLS (page 51)

Understand your customers' needs

Explain your product

★   ★   ★   ★   ★

PREPARATION

1. Explain that customer service means "helping customers." Help learners name times they provide customer service and times they receive it. Encourage learners to use peer teaching to clarify new vocabulary.

2. Have learners discuss the needs of new "customers" at your school. What are some questions new learners might ask?

PRESENTATION

1. Focus attention on the photographs. Ask learners to say what the unit might

be about. Write their ideas on the board and/or restate them in acceptable English.

2. Have learners talk about the photos. Ask learners to identify the employee and the customer in each picture. Have learners describe how the employees are meeting their customers' needs.

3. Help learners read the questions. Discuss the questions with the class.

4. You may want to use the Performance Preview to provide learners with an overview of the skills in the unit. Have learners read the list of skills and discuss what they will learn in the unit.

FOLLOW-UP

Role-Play: Have partners role-play situations in which an employee explains a product or a service to a customer. Encourage learners to explain products

or services their own workplaces offer. Encourage "customers" to ask questions. Have one or two pairs present their role-plays to the class.

♦ Ask partners to write the dialog they used in their role-play. Have them team up with another pair of learners, switch dialogs, and perform them for the pair that wrote them.

WORKBOOK

Unit 5, Exercises 1A–1B

WORKFORCE SKILLS (page 52)

Understand your customers' needs

Explain your product

★　　★　　★　　★　　★

Teaching Note

Use this page to introduce the new language in the unit. Whenever possible, encourage peer teaching. Supply any language the learners need.

Getting Started   Helping customers

TEAM WORK

What is each person saying to the customer? Write the letter. Can you think of anything else each person might say?

a. We don't have any economy cars available, so I'm giving you a free upgrade to a bigger car.

b. I think you'll like this phone. It has more features than the cheaper model.

c. The clinic is open from 7:00 in the morning to 6:00 at night Monday to Friday. Would you like to make an appointment?

PARTNER WORK

Look at the pictures again. What other questions do you think the customers might ask? Student A is the customer. Student B responds.

A Can I make an appointment to see Dr. Lear?

B Sure, what's your name?

ON YOUR JOB SURVEY

Work with a team. What questions do customers and other workers ask? Make a list. Share your list with the class.

52   Unit 5

PREPARATION

1. Display pictures of products and ask learners what employees might say to customers about them.

2. Use picture cards or realia to present or review **economy, upgrade,** and **model.** For example, show two cars and ask: *Which one is the economy car?*

PRESENTATION

1. Have learners read and discuss the Purpose Statement. For more information see "Purpose Statement" on page viii.

2. Focus attention on the illustrations. Encourage learners to say as much as they can about them. Write their ideas on the board and/or restate them in acceptable English.

3. Have teams read the Team Work instructions. Make sure each team

knows what to do. Remind teams that they are responsible for making sure that each member understands the new language. Then have teams complete the activity. Have team reporters share their answers with the class.

4. Have partners read the Partner Work instructions. Make sure each pair knows what to do. If necessary, model the activity. Then have partners complete the activity. Have learners switch partners and repeat the activity. Supply any language needed. Have one or two pairs present their dialogs to the class.

 5. Have teams read the Survey instructions. Make sure everyone knows what to do. Then have teams complete the activity. Have team reporters share their teams' lists with the class. For more information, see "Survey" on page viii.

FOLLOW-UP

Chart: Have teams use the information from the Survey to make a chart. In the first column, have them list questions customers frequently ask. In the second column, have them write possible responses to the questions. Display the charts in the classroom.

♦ Ask individual learners to choose from the chart one question a customer at their workplace might ask. Have them write the question, then write the answer they would provide. Ask several learners to share their questions and answers with the class.

WORKBOOK

Unit 5, Exercises 2A–2B

---

52   English ASAP

Talk About It — Understanding your customers' needs

 PRACTICE THE DIALOG

A May I help you find something?

B Yes, I'm looking for a pair of running shoes.

A We have lots of shoes for runners. What size do you need?

B I wear a size eight, but it has to have a narrow heel.

A No problem. I'll bring out a few pairs with a narrow heel. You can see which pair feels the most comfortable. I'll be right back.

ON YOUR JOB — PARTNER WORK

Your partner is your customer in a department store. Ask questions to find out your customer's needs. Use the dialog above and the Useful Language.

ASAP **PROJECT**

Work with a team. Develop a list of guidelines that are important in good customer service, such as greeting customers politely. Think about examples from your workplace or other workplaces. Use your list to create a "Good Customer Service" poster or booklet. Complete this project as you work through the unit.

Useful Language

How can I help you?

Are you looking for anything special?

What style do you want?

What color would you like?

Unit 5   53

ASAP **PROJECT**

Have learners read the instructions. Discuss the project and its purpose with learners. Make sure that everyone understands. Help learners assign themselves to teams depending upon their skills, knowledge, interests, or other personal strengths. Have each team select a leader. Throughout the rest of the unit, allow time for learners to work on the project. Have the teams agree on a deadline when the project will be finished. For more information see "ASAP Project" on page vi.

PREPARATION

To present or review new language, display a running shoe and identify the **size, heel, style,** and **color.** Have learners suggest other products these words could describe. For example, **size** could describe a pizza.

PRESENTATION

1. Have learners read and discuss the Purpose Statement. For more information see "Purpose Statement" on page viii.

 2. Focus attention on the photograph. Encourage learners to say as much as they can about it. Have them identify the type of store and suggest what the people might be saying. Write learners' ideas on the board and/or restate them in acceptable English. Then present the dialog. See "Presenting a Dialog" on page ix.

 3. Have partners read the Partner Work instructions. Focus attention on the Useful Language box. Help learners read the expressions. If necessary, model pronunciation. Make sure each pair knows what to do. Then have learners complete the activity. Have learners switch partners and repeat the activity. Have one or two pairs present their dialogs to the class.

FOLLOW-UP

Quality Service: Have learners work in pairs. On slips of paper, write the names of various products, such as "book," "computer," "lettuce," and "floor wax." Have pairs draw slips. One partner should role-play a customer who asks questions about the product; the other, a store employee who tries to meet the customer's needs. Have several pairs present their role-plays to the class.

♦ Have pairs write a list of questions customers at their workplaces might ask about products or services. Have them share their lists with the class.

WORKBOOK

Unit 5, Exercises 3A–3B

WORKFORCE SKILLS (page 54)

Explain your product

★ ★ ★ ★ ★

Keep Talking Explaining your product

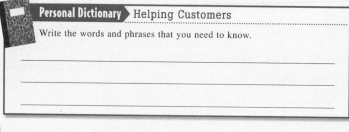

PRACTICE THE DIALOG

A Welcome to Maria's Pizza. How can I help you?

B I'd like a pizza large enough for three people. What size should I get?

A Well, the large pizza is enough for two or three people. But our special is a small pizza for half price when you order a medium pizza. That's more pizza for less money.

B Then I'll take the special. By the way, what's home-style crust?

A It's an extra thick crust.

B I see. I'd rather have the thin crust.

PARTNER WORK

Your partner is the customer. Explain one of these products to your customer. Answer any questions your customer may ask.

1. a color TV   **2.** a telephone   **3.** a clock radio

Personal Dictionary ▸ Helping Customers

Write the words and phrases that you need to know.

_____

_____

_____

54   Unit 5

Personal Dictionary

Have learners add the words in their Personal Dictionary to their *Workforce Writing Dictionary*. For more information see "Workforce Writing Dictionary" on page v.

PREPARATION

Explain that the word "special" is often used to indicate an item or combination of items a business offers at a reduced price. Provide examples of specials that restaurants, deli counters, and other businesses might offer. Encourage learners whose workplaces offer "specials" to describe them to the class.

PRESENTATION

1. Have learners read and discuss the Purpose Statement. For more information see "Purpose Statement" on page viii.

 2. Focus attention on the illustration. Encourage learners to say as much as they can about it. Help them identify the type of business shown. Discuss what they think the people are doing and

saying. Then present the dialog. See "Presenting a Dialog" on page ix.

 3. Have partners read the Partner Work instructions. Make sure each pair knows what to do. If necessary, model the activity. Then have partners complete the activity. Have learners change partners and repeat the activity. Have several pairs present their dialogs to the class.

4. Have learners read the Personal Dictionary instructions. Then use the Personal Dictionary procedures on page ix. Remind learners to continue to add words to their dictionaries throughout the unit.

FOLLOW-UP

Familiar Products: Ask learners to take turns explaining a product or

service at work. Have the rest of the class ask for additional information about the product.

♦ Divide the class into teams. Write the names of different products on slips of paper. Have learners draw slips and explain the product without saying its name. Other team members figure out the product. Continue until each learner has had a turn explaining a product.

WORKBOOK

Unit 5, Exercise 4

---

54   English ASAP

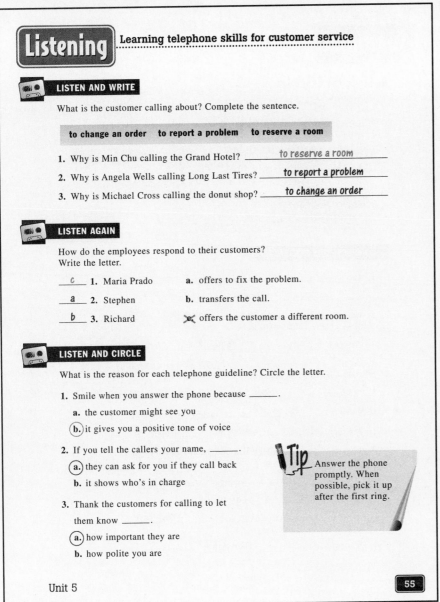

Listening — Learning telephone skills for customer service

LISTEN AND WRITE

What is the customer calling about? Complete the sentence.

| to change an order | to report a problem | to reserve a room |

1. Why is Min Chu calling the Grand Hotel? ___to reserve a room___

2. Why is Angela Wells calling Long Last Tires? ___to report a problem___

3. Why is Michael Cross calling the donut shop? ___to change an order___

LISTEN AGAIN

How do the employees respond to their customers?
Write the letter.

__c__ 1. Maria Prado   **a.** offers to fix the problem.

__a__ 2. Stephen   **b.** transfers the call.

__b__ 3. Richard   ~~**c.** offers the customer a different room.~~

LISTEN AND CIRCLE

What is the reason for each telephone guideline? Circle the letter.

1. Smile when you answer the phone because _____.

   a. the customer might see you

   (**b.**) it gives you a positive tone of voice

2. If you tell the callers your name, _____.

   (**a.**) they can ask for you if they call back

   b. it shows who's in charge

3. Thank the customers for calling to let them know _____.

   (**a.**) how important they are

   b. how polite you are

Tip Answer the phone promptly. When possible, pick it up after the first ring.

Unit 5   **55**

SCANS Note

Explain that being equally polite and helpful to people of all cultures and backgrounds is an aspect of good customer service. Ask learners to talk about times they've seen people receive unsatisfactory service because of their age, sex, or cultural background.

PREPARATION

1. Review telephone skills by modeling the language you use to answer the phone politely, put someone on hold, and transfer a call. Have a few learners who use phones at work model how they greet customers on the phone.

2. Show learners a catalog and explain how people use it to order products by phone.

PRESENTATION

1. Have learners read and discuss the Purpose Statement. For more information see "Purpose Statement" on page viii.

 2. Have learners read the Listen and Write instructions. Then have them read the items. Make sure that everyone understands the instructions. If necessary, model the first item. Then play the tape or read the Listening Transcript aloud two or more times as learners complete the activity. Check learners' work. For more information see "Presenting a Listening Activity" on page ix.

 3. Have learners read the Listen Again instructions. Then follow the procedures in 2.

 4. Have learners read the Listen and Circle instructions. Then follow the procedures in 2.

Tip Have learners read the Tip and discuss how the advice will help them. For more information, see "Presenting a Tip" on page ix.

FOLLOW-UP

Phone Orders: Give each pair of learners a catalog or a few pages of a catalog. Have them create a dialog in which one person orders something from the catalog and the other takes the order over the phone. The customer should ask several questions about the product before ordering it. Have several pairs present their dialogs to the class.

♦ Have partners role-play situations in which a customer has a problem with a product and an employee responds. Ask partners to switch roles and repeat the activity. Have several pairs present their role-plays to the class.

WORKBOOK

Unit 5, Exercise 5

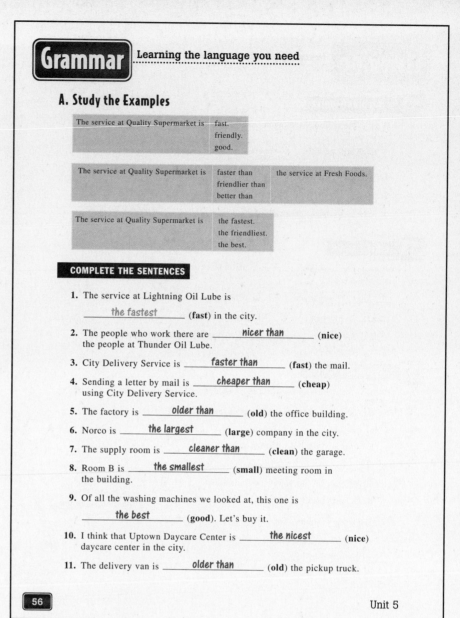

Grammar Learning the language you need

A. Study the Examples

The service at Quality Supermarket is	fast. friendly. good.	
The service at Quality Supermarket is	faster than friendlier than better than	the service at Fresh Foods.
The service at Quality Supermarket is	the fastest. the friendliest. the best.	

COMPLETE THE SENTENCES

1. The service at Lightning Oil Lube is
   _____the fastest_____ (**fast**) in the city.

2. The people who work there are _____nicer than_____ (**nice**) the people at Thunder Oil Lube.

3. City Delivery Service is _____faster than_____ (**fast**) the mail.

4. Sending a letter by mail is _____cheaper than_____ (**cheap**) using City Delivery Service.

5. The factory is _____older than_____ (**old**) the office building.

6. Norco is _____the largest_____ (**large**) company in the city.

7. The supply room is _____cleaner than_____ (**clean**) the garage.

8. Room B is _____the smallest_____ (**small**) meeting room in the building.

9. Of all the washing machines we looked at, this one is
   _____the best_____ (**good**). Let's buy it.

10. I think that Uptown Daycare Center is _____the nicest_____ (**nice**) daycare center in the city.

11. The delivery van is _____older than_____ (**old**) the pickup truck.

56

Unit 5

Language Note

Explain or review the pattern for adding **-er** *or* **-est** *to adjectives that end in* **-y**, *for example* **friendly, friendlier, friendliest**. *Discuss comparative and superlative forms of other adjectives that end in* **-y**, *such as* **happy, busy, funny,** *and* **easy.**

PREPARATION

Review the language in the grammar boxes with learners before they open their books, if necessary.

PRESENTATION

1. Have learners read and discuss the Purpose Statement. For more information see "Purpose Statement" on page viii.

2. Have learners read the grammar boxes in A. Have learners use the language in the boxes to say as many sentences as possible. Tell learners that they can use the grammar boxes throughout the unit to review or check sentence structures.

3. Focus attention on Complete the Sentences. Make sure learners know what to do. If necessary, model the first item. Allow learners to complete the activity.

Have learners check each other's work in pairs. Ask several learners to read their completed sentences aloud while the rest of the class checks their work.

B. Study the Examples

The waiters at Market Grill are	efficient.
	helpful.
	courteous.

The waiters at Super Pasta are	more efficient than	the staff at Market Grill.
	more helpful than	
	more courteous than	

The waiters at Circle Cafe are	the most efficient.
	the most helpful.
	the most courteous.

COMPLETE THE SENTENCES

Use the language in B.

1. The Green River Cafe is ____more expensive than____ (**expensive**)
   The Central Grill.

2. The waiters at The Oven are ____more helpful than____ (**helpful**)
   the waiters at The Central Grill.

3. The Green River Cafe has ____the most helpful____ (**helpful**)
   waiters in town.

4. The Green River Cafe is ____the most expensive____ (**expensive**)
   restaurant in town.

5. The Green River Cafe is also ____the most famous____ (**famous**)
   restaurant in town.

6. Working at the counter is ____more interesting than____ (**interesting**)
   taking orders over the phone.

7. This is ____the most delicious____ (**delicious**) food I've ever eaten!

TEAM WORK

Work with your team. Talk about stores and restaurants where you live. Which ones are the nicest, cleanest, cheapest, most expensive, most convenient, best, and worst? Use the language in A and B.

Tip Some adjectives are irregular.
good   better   best
bad   worse   worst

Unit 5

57

---

4. Focus attention on the grammar boxes in B. Follow the procedures in 2.

5. Have learners read the instructions for Complete the Sentences. Make sure that everyone knows what to do. If necessary, model the first item. Allow learners to complete the activity. Have learners check each other's work in pairs. Ask several learners to read their answers aloud while the rest of the class checks their work.

6. Have teams read the Team Work instructions. Make sure everyone knows what to do. If necessary, model the activity. Then have teams complete the activity. Ask several teams to present their conversations to the class.

 Tip Have learners read the Tip independently and discuss how the advice will help them.

For more information, see "Presenting a Tip" on page ix.

FOLLOW-UP

What I Like Most: Have the class make a list of local bests, such as the best employer, the best working conditions, and the store with the best customer service. Then have partners take turns telling each other about the places on the list, using the word "most." For example, a learner might say, "I like Better Books because their selection is the most complete." Have several pairs present their dialogs to the class.

♦ Ask learners to write two sentences that might appear in an advertisement for the product or service offered by their workplace. Encourage them to use the language in A and B. Have several learners read their sentences to the class.

WORKBOOK

Unit 5, Exercise 6

BLACKLINE MASTERS

Blackline Master: Unit 5

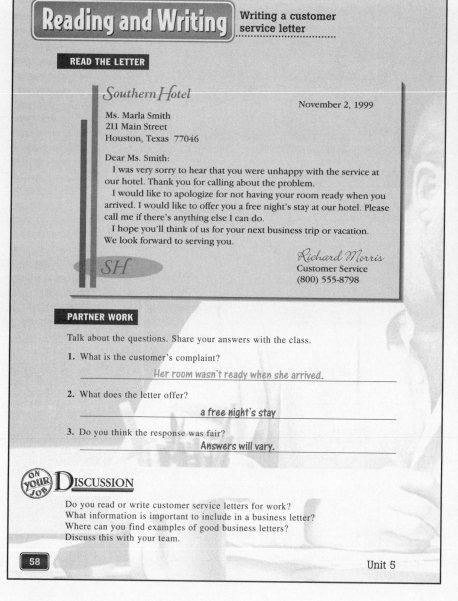

Reading and Writing — Writing a customer service letter

READ THE LETTER

Southern Hotel

November 2, 1999

Ms. Marla Smith
211 Main Street
Houston, Texas 77046

Dear Ms. Smith:

  I was very sorry to hear that you were unhappy with the service at our hotel. Thank you for calling about the problem.

  I would like to apologize for not having your room ready when you arrived. I would like to offer you a free night's stay at our hotel. Please call me if there's anything else I can do.

  I hope you'll think of us for your next business trip or vacation. We look forward to serving you.

Richard Morris
Customer Service
(800) 555-8798

SH

PARTNER WORK

Talk about the questions. Share your answers with the class.

1. What is the customer's complaint?

    Her room wasn't ready when she arrived.

2. What does the letter offer?

    a free night's stay

3. Do you think the response was fair?

    Answers will vary.

DISCUSSION (ON YOUR JOB)

Do you read or write customer service letters for work? What information is important to include in a business letter? Where can you find examples of good business letters? Discuss this with your team.

58

Unit 5

Culture Note

Discuss differences in customer service policies at different businesses. For example, in some stores, it is the policy for employees to offer help to customers. In other stores, it is the policy for the employee to wait for customers to approach them. Ask learners what the policy is at their workplace and how comfortable they are with it.

PREPARATION

1. To explain or review what a customer service letter is, show learners sample customer service letters. Review the structure of the letter by pointing out the heading, the date, the inside address, the salutation, the body of the letter, and the signature.

2. Preteach or review **apologize** by role-playing an employee who apologizes to a customer. Then ask volunteers to role-play apologies.

PRESENTATION

1. Have learners read and discuss the Purpose Statement. For more information see "Purpose Statement" on page viii.

2. Have learners preview the letter before they read. Encourage learners to say everything they can about the letter.

Write their ideas on the board and/or restate them in acceptable English. Then have learners read the letter independently.

3. Have partners read the instructions for Partner Work. Make sure each pair knows what to do. If necessary, model the first item. Then have learners complete the activity. Ask several pairs to share their answers with the class while the rest of the class checks their work.

4. Have learners read the Discussion questions. Then have learners work in teams to discuss their ideas. Have team reporters share their teams' ideas with the class.

Unit 5

WRITE A CUSTOMER SERVICE LETTER

Write a customer service letter in response to one of these complaints.

- You work for a restaurant. You are writing to a customer who wrote a letter saying that her food was cold and that the cooks wouldn't heat it up for her.

- You work for City Water Company. You are writing to correct a bill on which the customer was charged for one month's service twice.

- You work for a supermarket. You are writing to a customer who sent a letter that said her ice cream tasted terrible.

Answers will vary.

TEAM WORK

Make a list of different reasons you might send customer service letters at your workplace or school. Share your list with the class.

Unit 5

59

Teaching Note

You may choose to have learners work in pairs to complete the Write a Customer Service Letter activity.

6. Have learners read the Write a Customer Service Letter instructions. Make sure everyone knows what to do. Ensure students understand that they will write in response to only one of the situations. (In advanced classes, you might assign one of the other scenarios as homework and/or allow learners to write about situations from their workplaces.) Then have learners complete the activity. Check learners' work.

7. Have teams read the Team Work instructions and complete the activity. Have team reporters present the lists to the class.

FOLLOW-UP

You're the Customer: Ask teams to discuss the different ways businesses try to sell them products or services, for example, through letters, telephone calls, and face-to-face interaction. Which way do learners prefer? Why? Have team reporters share the teams' ideas with the class.

◆ Give each team a card with a customer complaint on it. Have teams discuss the appropriate response to the complaint and write a letter in response to the customer. Have team reporters read the letters to the class.

WORKBOOK

Unit 5, Exercises 7A–7C

Use telephone skills for customer service

★ ★ ★ ★ ★

SCANS Note

Do learners always know the appropriate person to transfer a customer's call to? Discuss how understanding the organization of the company they work for and knowing the responsibilities of the other employees can help them provide good customer service.

 Extension Using telephone skills for customer service

READ THE GUIDELINES

Home Catalog Company

Customer Service Telephone Guidelines

Our goal is to provide excellent customer service. We want our customers to know that we offer the best service in the business.

1. Always answer the phone promptly. Answer on the first ring, if possible.
2. Always tell the customer your name. Answer with this greeting:
   Hello, this is _____ . You've reached the Home Catalog Company. Thank you for calling.
3. Remember to smile. It makes you feel good, and it makes you sound friendly.
4. When you take an order, make sure you get all the information you need to fill out the form.
5. When handling a customer complaint, always apologize. Explain the policy to the customer. Try to find a way to solve the problem.
6. If necessary, allow the customer to speak to your supervisor.
7. Always thank the customer for calling!

ANSWER THE QUESTIONS

Write the answers on your own paper.

1. When should you answer the phone?
2. Should you tell the customer your name?
3. Should you allow the customer to talk to a supervisor?
4. Should you end each phone call by thanking the customer for calling?

PARTNER WORK

Your partner is the customer. Use the guidelines to respond to your customer's telephone call.

 Culture Notes

A customer just complained to you about some bad customer service she received from another employee. What do you do? What if you think the customer isn't telling the truth?

60 Unit 5

PREPARATION

If necessary, review language related to using the telephone politely. Follow the instructions on page 55.

PRESENTATION

1. Have learners read and discuss the Purpose Statement. For more information see "Purpose Statement" on page viii.

2. Have learners preview the Customer Service Telephone Guidelines. Encourage them to say everything they can about them. Write their ideas on the board and/or restate them in acceptable English. Then have learners read the Guidelines independently.

3. Have learners read the instructions for Answer the Questions. Make sure everyone knows what to do. If necessary, model the first item. Then have learners

complete the activity. Have learners review each other's work in pairs. Have several learners read their answers aloud while the rest of the class checks their work.

4. Have partners read the Partner Work instructions. Make sure everyone knows what to do. Then have pairs complete the activity. Have one or two pairs present their dialogs to the class.

5. Have learners read Culture Notes and talk over their ideas in teams. Have team reporters share their ideas with the class. Ask teams to compare ideas. For more information see "Culture Notes" on page vii.

FOLLOW-UP

Ideal Service: Have teams discuss the kinds of customer service they would

like to receive when they have a complaint about a product or a service. Then assign each team a customer service problem, such as a broken toy or a hotel room in which the air conditioner doesn't work. Ask the team to come up with an appropriate solution. Have teams share their problems and solutions with the class.

♦ Have teams discuss the worst customer service problems team members have experienced as employees. How did they handle the situations? Ask teams to discuss the best ways to handle difficult situations with customers. Have team reporters summarize their teams' discussions for the class.

WORKBOOK

Unit 5, Exercise 8

Performance Check

How well can you use the skills in this unit?
....

Complete the activities. Go over your work with a partner or your teacher.
Then complete the Performance Review on page 62.

SKILL 1 — UNDERSTAND YOUR CUSTOMERS' NEEDS

You are a salesperson at Discount Department Store. A customer comes into the store and wants to buy clothes, shoes, or another product. Your partner or your teacher is the customer. Ask questions to find out what your customer needs.

SKILL 2 — EXPLAIN YOUR PRODUCT

Explain one of the products. Answer any questions your customer may ask. Your partner or teacher is the customer.

1. an automatic dishwasher
2. hiking boots
3. a color TV
4. a telephone

SKILL 3 — USE TELEPHONE SKILLS FOR CUSTOMER SERVICE

Read the customer service guidelines. Work with a partner or your teacher to answer a customer service phone call.

Customer Service Telephone Guidelines

1. Always answer the phone promptly. Answer on the first ring, if possible.
2. Always tell the customer your name. Answer with this greeting: *Hello, this is _____ . You've reached the Country Kitchen Catalog Company. Thank you for calling.*
3. Remember to smile. It makes you feel good, and it makes you sound friendly.
4. When you take an order, make sure you get all the information you need to fill out the form.
5. Always thank the customer for calling!

Unit 5

61

PRESENTATION

Use any of the procedures in "Evaluation," page x, with pages 61 and 62. Record individuals' results on the Unit 5 Individual Competency Chart. Record the class's results on the Class Cumulative Competency Chart.

Use the situation below to write a customer service letter.

You work for Music CDs by Mail. You are writing in response to a customer who ordered a CD but did not receive it.

Answers will vary.

Music CDs by Mail

Today's date

Ms. Jill Easton

2304 South Market Street

Springfield, Missouri 65806

Dear Ms. Easton:

I'm sorry that you haven't received your CD. I'm mailing your CD, along with a coupon for a free CD, to you today. Please let me know if I can help you in any other way. Thanks for your business.

Abena Morrison

Music CDs by Mail

Performance Review

I can...

❑ 1. understand my customers' needs.

❑ 2. explain my product.

❑ 3. use telephone skills for customer service.

❑ 4. write a customer service letter.

Discussion

Work with a team. How will the skills help you? Make a list. Share the list with your class.

62

Unit 5

PRESENTATION

Follow the instructions on page 61.

INFORMAL WORKPLACE-SPECIFIC ASSESSMENT

Ask learners to describe two ways they provide good customer service in the workplace.

WORKBOOK

Unit 5, Exercise 9

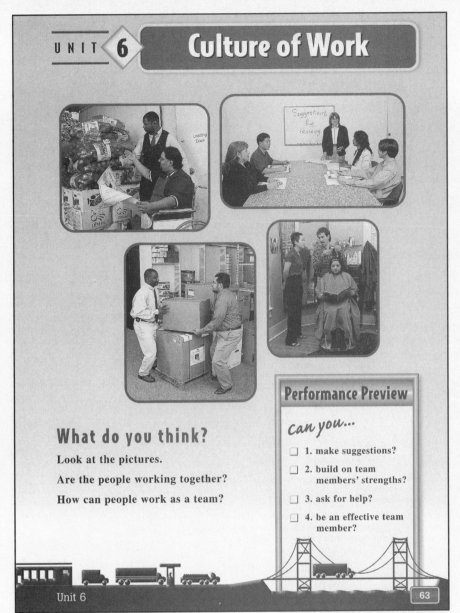

UNIT 6 — Culture of Work

What do you think?
Look at the pictures.

Are the people working together?

How can people work as a team?

Performance Preview

Can you...

☐ 1. make suggestions?

☐ 2. build on team members' strengths?

☐ 3. ask for help?

☐ 4. be an effective team member?

Unit 6

63

Unit 6 Overview
—SCANS Competencies—

★ Communicate information

★ Work on teams

★ Understand social systems

★ Understand organizational systems

Workforce Skills

● Make suggestions

● Build on team members' strengths

● Ask for help

● Be an effective team member

Materials

● Picture cards or realia of a supermarket display, a break room, a broom, some trash

● Pictures or realia of posters, fliers, and booths

● Realia of a schedule and an agenda

● Sample evaluation forms, such as those guests fill out at restaurants or hotels

Unit Warm-Up

To stimulate discussion about the unit topic (working effectively as part of a team), ask a few volunteers to help you move a table or a desk. Discuss how the volunteers' help made the work easier. Ask how learners felt about helping you.

★   ★   ★   ★   ★

WORKFORCE SKILLS (page 63)

Make suggestions

Ask for help

Be an effective team member

★   ★   ★   ★   ★

PREPARATION

1. To present or review what it means to make a **suggestion,** ask learners how you could make the classroom more colorful. Write their ideas on the board and identify them as "suggestions." Ask learners to talk about times they have made suggestions at their workplaces.

2. Explain that being an effective team member involves working well with others. Ask learners to talk about times they have worked with others.

PRESENTATION

1. Focus attention on the photographs. Ask learners what they think the unit might be about. Write their ideas on the board and/or restate them in acceptable English.

2. Have learners talk about the photos. Ask them to describe how the people in each photograph are working together. Encourage learners to use peer teaching to clarify any unfamiliar vocabulary.

3. Help learners read the questions. Discuss the questions with the class.

4. You may want to use the Performance Preview to provide learners with an overview of the skills in the unit. Have learners read the list of skills and discuss what they will learn in this unit.

FOLLOW-UP

Working Together: Have partners create dialogs in which one learner asks for help with a task at work or school and the other agrees to help. Ask several pairs to present their dialogs to the class.

◆ Ask partners to recreate their dialogs. This time, however, the second learner is not able to help and politely explains why. Have several pairs present their dialogs to the class.

WORKBOOK

Unit 6, Exercises 1A–1B

Make suggestions

★　　★　　★　　★　　★

Teaching Note

Use this page to introduce the new language in the unit. Whenever possible, encourage peer teaching. Supply any language learners need.

Getting Started — Making suggestions

TEAM WORK

Match the suggestion with the situation. Can you think of other suggestions?

a. **Let's straighten up this display.**

b. **Why don't you let me help you with that?**

c. **Maybe someone else has an idea.**

PARTNER WORK

Student A makes a suggestion. Student B responds.

A Let's clean up the trash in the break room.

B OK, I'll get a broom.

 SURVEY

Think of a situation at your workplace or school that could be improved. Ask three classmates to make a suggestion that might help. Share their suggestions with the class.

64   Unit 6

PREPARATION

1. Present or review what it means to make a suggestion. Follow the procedure in Preparation on page 63.

2. Use picture cards or realia to teach or review **display, trash, break room,** and **broom.** Ask learners to describe displays they have seen in supermarkets or other stores.

PRESENTATION

1. Have learners read and discuss the Purpose Statement. See "Purpose Statement," page viii.

2. Focus attention on the pictures. Encourage learners to say as much as they can about them. Write their ideas on the board and/or restate them in acceptable English.

3. Have teams read the Team Work instructions. Make sure each team knows what to do. Then have teams complete the activity. Have team reporters share their teams' answers with the class.

4. Have partners read the Partner Work instructions. If necessary, model the activity. Then have partners complete the activity. Have learners switch partners and repeat the activity. Supply any language needed. Have a few pairs present their conversations. See "Partner Work and Team Work" on page viii.

 5. Have learners read the Survey instructions. Make sure everyone knows what to do. Then give learners time to complete the activity. Have several learners share their classmates' suggestions with the class. For more information, see "Survey" on page viii.

FOLLOW-UP

Helpful Suggestions: Ask individuals to write the three suggestions they received in the survey. Next to each, ask them to note if the suggestion is "very helpful," "possibly helpful," or "probably not helpful." Have several learners share "very helpful" suggestions with the class.

◆ Help the class create a pie chart to show the percent of suggestions in each category. (For more information on pie charts, see "Survey," page viii.) Display the pie chart and discuss the results with the class.

WORKBOOK

Unit 6, Exercises 2A–2B

Talk About It — Building on team members' strengths

 PRACTICE THE DIALOG

A We need to find a few more people to help with the Health Fair. Who can make posters?

B Maybe Ali can do that. He's good at drawing.

A That's a good idea. We also need someone to plan the activities.

B Marla seems very organized. Let's ask her.

C I'd like to help. I can set up the booths.

A Great. Thanks for offering.

Useful Language

We need someone to set up the chairs.

I need help making a flier.

Why don't we ask her to rent some tables?

 PARTNER WORK

You're planning a safety campaign at your workplace or school. First make a list of things that need to be done. Then think of people in your class who can do each of the tasks well. Use the dialog and Useful Language above.

ASAP PROJECT

Make a list of your own strengths. Get into teams and share your strengths with your team. Then think of several jobs that each team member might do well. Write down the jobs that your team suggested for you. Complete this project as you work through the unit.

Unit 6

`65`

ASAP PROJECT

Have learners read the instructions. Discuss the project and its purpose with learners. Make sure that everyone understands. Help learners assign themselves to teams depending upon their skills, knowledge, interests, or other personal strengths. Have each team select a leader. Throughout the rest of the unit, allow time for learners to work on the project. Have the teams agree on a deadline when the project will be finished. For more information see "ASAP Project" on page vi.

PREPARATION

1. Explain that a person's **strengths** are the things that person does well. Give examples of your strengths as a teacher. Then have learners give examples of their strengths on the job.

2. To present or review new language, display realia or show pictures of **posters, fliers,** and **booths.** Ask learners where they have seen these items. Explain that a **safety campaign** is an organized effort to teach people at a workplace to work safely. A safety campaign might use posters, fliers, and announcements. Discuss why campaigns use posters and fliers. If possible, show safety posters from the learners' workplaces.

PRESENTATION

1. Have learners read and discuss the Purpose Statement. For more information see "Purpose Statement" on page viii.

2. Focus attention on the illustration. Encourage learners to say as much as they can about it. Help them identify the people's occupation and ask them to describe what the people are doing. Then present the dialog. See "Presenting a Dialog" on page ix.

 3. Have partners read the Partner Work instructions. Help learners read the sentences in the Useful Language box. If necessary, model pronunciation and clarify the language. Make sure each pair knows what to do. Then have learners complete the activity. Have one or two pairs present their lists and assignments to the class.

FOLLOW-UP

Ideal Team: Ask teams to imagine that their task is to build a house. Have them decide who will do various tasks, such as design the house, pour the foundation, put up walls, put in electricity and plumbing, paint, decorate, and landscape. Have team reporters tell the class who is doing what and why.

♦ Help the class create a master list of class members' strengths. Post the list in the classroom.

WORKBOOK

Unit 6, Exercises 3A–3B

★   ★   ★   ★   ★

Personal Dictionary

Have learners add the words in their Personal Dictionary to their *Workforce Writing Dictionary.* For more information see "Workforce Writing Dictionary" on page v.

Keep Talking   Asking for help

 PRACTICE THE DIALOG

A   Beatrice, it's getting late, and I have a lot to do. Do you have time to help me?

B   Sure, Bruce. Just let me put this away.

A   Thanks. I have to wash the windows in the reception area. If I don't get help, I won't finish on time.

B   No problem. If we work together, we'll finish soon.

 PARTNER WORK

Think of a task you might need help with at work such as completing a large project. Then take turns asking your partner for help. Use the dialog and Useful Language above.

Useful Language

I don't think I can finish this by myself.

Are you busy right now?

Can you help me out?

Personal Dictionary ▸ Working in Teams

Write the words and phrases that you need to know.

_____

_____

_____

66   Unit 6

PREPARATION

To teach or review polite ways to ask for help, ask learners to help you with small classroom tasks, such as erasing the blackboard or adjusting window shades. Have learners identify the polite phrases you use. Write them on the board.

PRESENTATION

1. Have learners read and discuss the Purpose Statement. For more information see "Purpose Statement" on page viii.

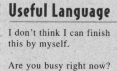 **2.** Focus attention on the photograph. Encourage learners to say as much as they can about it. Have them speculate about what the people are doing and saying. Then present the dialog. See "Presenting a Dialog" on page ix.

3. Have partners read the Partner Work instructions. Make sure everyone knows what to do. Focus attention on the Useful Language box. If necessary, model pronunciation. Then have partners complete the activity. Have learners switch partners and repeat the activity. Have one or two pairs present their dialogs to the class.

4. Have learners read the Personal Dictionary instructions. Then use the Personal Dictionary procedures on page ix. Remind learners to continue to add words to their dictionaries throughout the unit.

FOLLOW-UP

Just Ask: Have partners draw a slip of paper with a task on it, such as "Hang a

picture," or "Rake the leaves." One partner should ask for help with the task, the other should respond. Have a few pairs present their dialogs to the class.

◆ Have learners work in teams. Ask team members to discuss instances when they asked for help at work. Who did they ask for help? Did they find it difficult to ask for help? Why? Have team reporters share their teams' ideas with the class.

WORKBOOK

Unit 6, Exercises 4A–4B

Listening
Working cooperatively

LISTEN AND CIRCLE

What are the people talking about? Circle the problem in column A.

	A	B
1	(The plants might get damaged.) The greenhouse has a leak. It's cloudy.	Listen to the weather report. (Work together.) Water the plants.
2	The memo's unclear. The boss won't listen. (Meetings last too long.)	Have more meetings. Work longer hours. (Send out an agenda.)
3	The beds are too old. (The rooms aren't always clean.) The guests are messy.	(Make a checklist.) Hire more housekeepers. Buy new tables.

LISTEN AGAIN

How do the people want to solve the problems? Circle the suggestion in column B.

LISTEN AND ANSWER

Circle the letter of the answer.

1. What do the people need to do?
   a. They need to agree on a work schedule.
   b. They need to get ready for an inspection.

2. Why does someone have to be at the office at 8:30?
   a. Someone has to turn on the machines.
   b. Someone has to answer the phones.

DISCUSSION

Did the people solve the problem? Who will work from 8:30 to 4:30? If necessary, listen to the conversation again. What can people do if they do not agree on a solution?

Unit 6

67

Make suggestions

Be an effective team member

Ask for help

★   ★   ★   ★   ★

SCANS Note

Tell learners that knowing the specific responsibilities of the employees at their workplace can help them decide who to ask for help with a particular task or problem. Discuss ways learners can find out the job responsibilities of each employee at their workplace.

PREPARATION

1. Display and identify a **schedule.** Then write a schedule on the board that represents **flex-time.** Help learners understand how a flex-time schedule is different. Ask learners what their schedules at work are like.

2. Pantomime an **inspection.** Ask learners if inspections occur at their workplaces and what they are for.

3. Display and identify an **agenda.**

PRESENTATION

1. Have learners read and discuss the Purpose Statement. For more information see "Purpose Statement" on page viii.

 2. Have learners read the Listen and Circle instructions. Then have them read column A in the chart independently. Use peer-

teaching to clarify any unfamiliar vocabulary. Make sure everyone knows what to do. If necessary, model the first item. Then play the tape or read the Listening Transcript aloud two or more times as learners complete the activity. Check learners' work. For more information see "Presenting a Listening Activity" on page ix.

 3. Have learners read the Listen Again instructions. Then have them read column B in the chart. Then follow the procedures in 2.

 4. Have learners read the Listen and Answer instructions. Then follow the procedures in 2.

5. Have learners read the Discussion questions. Then have them work in teams to answer the questions. Have team

reporters share their teams' ideas with the class.

FOLLOW-UP

How Many People Does It Take? Have learners work in teams. Ask teams to create three-column charts with these headings: "Alone," "With a Partner," and "With a Group." Then have them decide on appropriate tasks to write in each column. Display the completed charts around the room.

♦ Ask partners to discuss what they like and what they dislike about working alone. Have several pairs present their ideas to the class.

WORKBOOK

Unit 6, Exercises 5A–5B

Ask for help

Be an effective team member

★   ★   ★   ★   ★

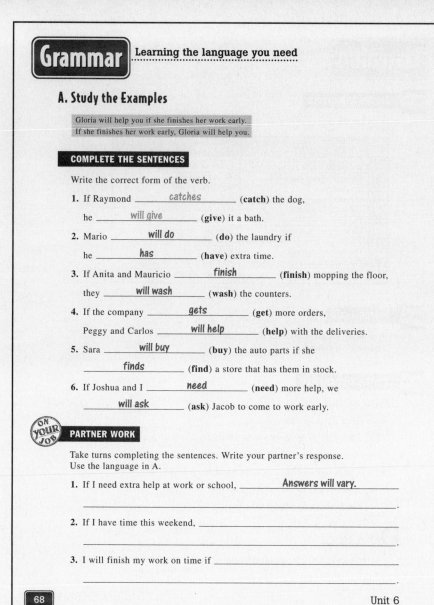

Grammar ·· Learning the language you need ··········

A. Study the Examples

> Gloria will help you if she finishes her work early.
> If she finishes her work early, Gloria will help you.

COMPLETE THE SENTENCES

Write the correct form of the verb.

1. If Raymond _____catches_____ (**catch**) the dog,
   he _____will give_____ (**give**) it a bath.

2. Mario _____will do_____ (**do**) the laundry if
   he _____has_____ (**have**) extra time.

3. If Anita and Mauricio _____finish_____ (**finish**) mopping the floor,
   they _____will wash_____ (**wash**) the counters.

4. If the company _____gets_____ (**get**) more orders,
   Peggy and Carlos _____will help_____ (**help**) with the deliveries.

5. Sara _____will buy_____ (**buy**) the auto parts if she
   _____finds_____ (**find**) a store that has them in stock.

6. If Joshua and I _____need_____ (**need**) more help, we
   _____will ask_____ (**ask**) Jacob to come to work early.

 PARTNER WORK

Take turns completing the sentences. Write your partner's response.
Use the language in A.

1. If I need extra help at work or school, _____Answers will vary._____
   _____.

2. If I have time this weekend, _____
   _____.

3. I will finish my work on time if _____
   _____.

68   Unit 6

PREPARATION

Review the language in the grammar
box with learners before they open their
books, if necessary. Teach or review
early by drawing two clocks on the
board, each with a time early or late in
your class session. Identify one time as
"early," the other as "late."

PRESENTATION

1. Have learners read and discuss the
Purpose Statement. For more information
see "Purpose Statement" on page viii.

2. Have learners read the grammar box
in A. Have learners use the language in
the box to say as many sentences as
possible. Tell learners that they can use
the grammar box throughout the unit to
review or check sentence structures.

3. Have learners read the instructions
for Complete the Sentences. Make sure
learners know what to do. If necessary,
model the first item. Allow learners to
complete the activity. Have learners
check each other's work in pairs. Ask
several learners to read their completed
sentences aloud while the rest of the
class checks their work.

4. Have pairs read the Partner
Work instructions. Make sure
everyone knows what to do.
If necessary, model the first item. Then
have pairs complete the activity. Ask
several pairs to present their answers to
the class.

B. Study the Examples

> If Ignacio doesn't need help, I'll leave early.
> If Ignacio asks for help, I won't leave early.

COMPLETE THE SENTENCES

Write the correct form of the verb. Use the language in B.

1. If Cheng ___doesn't talk___ (**not talk**) to her boss today,

   she ___'ll try___ (**try**) again tomorrow.

2. If Miguel ___explains___ (**explain**) the situation clearly,

   he ___won't need___ (**not need**) to repeat his directions.

3. If I ___don't go___ (**not go**) to the auto parts store this morning,

   I ___'ll go___ (**go**) this afternoon.

4. If you ___leave___ (**leave**) home early,

   you ___won't be___ (**not be**) late to work.

C. Study the Examples

Raymond	seems	worried.
	looks	
Bill and Pat	feel	

WRITE

Look at the picture. The employee wants to catch the dog to give it a bath. How do you think the dog feels? The employee? Write sentences on a sheet of paper. Read your sentences to the class. Use the language in C.

Unit 6

69

---

5. Focus attention on the grammar box in B. Follow the procedures in 2.

6. Have learners read the instructions for Complete the Sentences. Follow the procedures in 3.

7. Focus attention on the grammar box in C. Follow the procedures in 2.

8. Focus attention on the illustration. Encourage learners to say as much as they can about it. Then have learners read the Write instructions. Make sure everyone knows what to do. If necessary, model the activity. Then have learners complete the activity. Ask several learners to read their sentences aloud to the class.

FOLLOW-UP

Seem, Feel, Help: Have learners work in groups of three. Write these dialog prompts on the board:

A: "You seem _____."

B: "I feel _____."

C: "Maybe it will help if _____."

Have learners complete the sentences as they say the dialog. Ask them to repeat the activity three times so each learner can be A, B, and C. Have a few groups say their dialogs to the class.

◆ Have learners write their dialogs. Check their work.

WORKBOOK

Unit 6, Exercises 6A–6C

BLACKLINE MASTERS

Blackline Master: Unit 6

Build on team members' strengths

Be an effective team member

★   ★   ★   ★   ★

Language Note

*Review the way an apostrophe is used to mark the place in a contraction where one or more letters are omitted. Ask which letter(s) the apostrophe replaces in each of these contractions: **does not = doesn't, is not = isn't, can not = can't,** and **will not = won't.** Have learners form other contractions, for example, of: **has not, it will,** and **he is.***

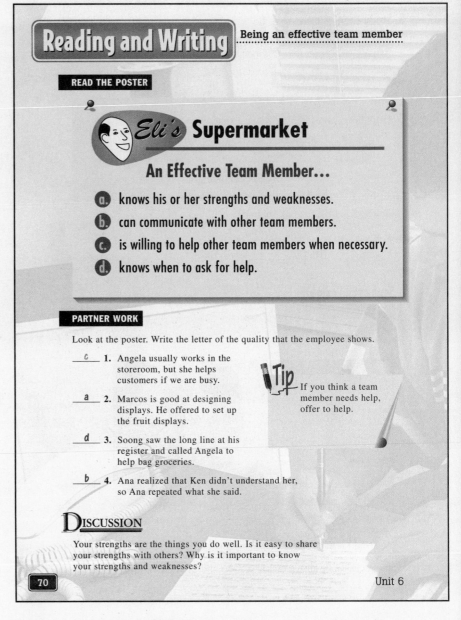

Reading and Writing   Being an effective team member

READ THE POSTER

Eli's Supermarket

An Effective Team Member...

a. knows his or her strengths and weaknesses.

b. can communicate with other team members.

c. is willing to help other team members when necessary.

d. knows when to ask for help.

PARTNER WORK

Look at the poster. Write the letter of the quality that the employee shows.

_c_   **1.** Angela usually works in the storeroom, but she helps customers if we are busy.

_a_   **2.** Marcos is good at designing displays. He offered to set up the fruit displays.

_d_   **3.** Soong saw the long line at his register and called Angela to help bag groceries.

_b_   **4.** Ana realized that Ken didn't understand her, so Ana repeated what she said.

Tip If you think a team member needs help, offer to help.

Discussion

Your strengths are the things you do well. Is it easy to share your strengths with others? Why is it important to know your strengths and weaknesses?

70   Unit 6

PREPARATION

Display and identify a **poster.** Have learners describe posters they've seen. Ask what purpose they served.

PRESENTATION

1. Have learners read and discuss the Purpose Statement. For more information see "Purpose Statement" on page viii.

2. Have learners preview the poster before they read. For more information, see "Prereading" on page x. Encourage learners to say everything they can about the poster. Write their ideas on the board and/or restate them in acceptable English. Then, have learners read the poster independently.

3. Have partners read the instructions for Partner Work. Make sure each pair knows what to do. If necessary, model

the first item. Then have learners complete the activity. Ask several pairs to share their answers with the class while the rest of the class checks their work.

4. Have learners read the Discussion questions. Then have learners work in teams to discuss their ideas. Have team reporters share their teams' ideas with the class. Have teams compare ideas.

Tip Have learners read the Tip independently and discuss how the advice will help them. For more information, see "Presenting a Tip" on page ix.

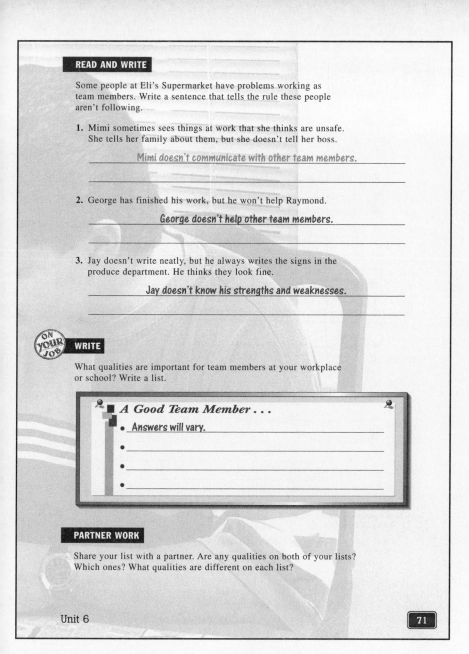

READ AND WRITE

Some people at Eli's Supermarket have problems working as team members. Write a sentence that tells the rule these people aren't following.

1. Mimi sometimes sees things at work that she thinks are unsafe. She tells her family about them, but she doesn't tell her boss.

    Mimi doesn't communicate with other team members.

2. George has finished his work, but he won't help Raymond.

    George doesn't help other team members.

3. Jay doesn't write neatly, but he always writes the signs in the produce department. He thinks they look fine.

    Jay doesn't know his strengths and weaknesses.

WRITE

What qualities are important for team members at your workplace or school? Write a list.

> ■ *A Good Team Member . . .*
> - Answers will vary.
> - _____
> - _____
> - _____

PARTNER WORK

Share your list with a partner. Are any qualities on both of your lists? Which ones? What qualities are different on each list?

Unit 6   71

---

5. Have learners read the Read and Write instructions. Make sure everyone knows what to do. If necessary, model the first item. Then have learners complete the activity. Pair learners to compare sentences. Have several learners present their work to the class.

 6. Have learners read the Write instructions. If necessary, model the activity by suggesting some qualities that the staff and faculty at your school exhibit when they work together as a team. Then have learners complete the activity. Have several learners read their lists aloud.

7. Have partners read the Partner Work instructions and complete the Partner Work activity. Have several pairs present their answers to the class.

FOLLOW-UP

Better and Better: Have teams discuss how people can become more effective team members at work or at school. Have learners take turns identifying something they would like to improve about the way they work in teams. Other team members can suggest ways to improve in that area. Have teams compare ideas.

♦ Have teams discuss what they find most challenging about working with other people. Have teams write lists of qualities or behaviors that make people difficult to work with. Have team reporters present their teams' ideas to the class.

WORKBOOK

Unit 6, Exercises 7A–7B

WORKFORCE SKILLS (page 72)

Build on team members' strengths

Be an effective team member

★　　★　　★　　★　　★

Culture Note

Tell learners that different workplaces expect different levels of cooperation among coworkers. Some employers expect employees to work independently; others expect teamwork. Ask learners what level of teamwork their employers expect. How did their employers let them know what they expected?

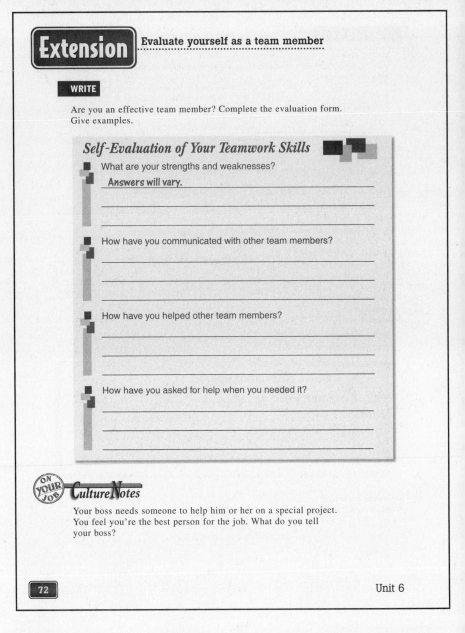

Extension ········ Evaluate yourself as a team member

WRITE

Are you an effective team member? Complete the evaluation form. Give examples.

Self-Evaluation of Your Teamwork Skills

■ What are your strengths and weaknesses?

  Answers will vary.

  _____

  _____

■ How have you communicated with other team members?

  _____

  _____

  _____

■ How have you helped other team members?

  _____

  _____

  _____

■ How have you asked for help when you needed it?

  _____

  _____

  _____

Culture Notes

Your boss needs someone to help him or her on a special project. You feel you're the best person for the job. What do you tell your boss?

72   Unit 6

PREPARATION

1. If necessary, review what it means to be an effective team member. See Preparation on page 63.

2. Display sample **evaluation** forms. Discuss their purpose. Ask learners where they've seen and/or used these kinds of forms.

PRESENTATION

1. Have learners read and discuss the Purpose Statement. For more information see "Purpose Statement" on page viii.

2. Have learners preview the evaluation form. Encourage them to say everything they can about it. Write their ideas on the board and/or restate them in acceptable English. Then, have learners read the form independently.

3. Have learners read the instructions for Write. Make sure everyone knows what to do. If necessary, model the first item. Then have learners complete the activity. Have learners review each other's work in pairs. Ask several learners to read their answers aloud.

 4. Have learners read Culture Notes and talk over their ideas in teams. Have team reporters share their teams' ideas with the class. For more information see "Culture Notes" on page vii.

FOLLOW-UP

Interview: Have learners work in pairs. Have one learner interview the other for a job and ask about teamwork skills. The other learner should describe his or her strengths as a team member.

Have partners switch roles and repeat. Have several pairs present their interviews to the class.

♦ Have teams discuss ways to boost and support team spirit. How does a team leader keep team members motivated to achieve a goal? Have teams compare ideas.

WORKBOOK

Unit 6, Exercise 8

Performance Check
How well can you use the skills in this unit?

Complete the activities. Go over your work with a partner or your teacher. Then complete the Performance Review on page 74.

SKILL 1   MAKE SUGGESTIONS

Match the suggestion to the situation.

> a. Let's work together to clean this up.
> b. Maybe someone else has an idea.
> c. Why don't I help you with that?

SKILL 2   BUILD ON TEAM MEMBERS' STRENGTHS

Your partner or teacher asks you who can help with a job. You think that another person can do the job well. Suggest to your partner or teacher that the other person should do the job. Then talk about a job that you can do well.

SKILL 3   ASK FOR HELP

Ask your partner or teacher for help with one of the following things.

1. lift a box
2. clean up the waiting room
3. pass out fliers

Unit 6   73

PRESENTATION

Use any of the procedures in "Evaluation," page x, with pages 73 and 74. Record individuals' results on the Unit 6 Individual Competency Chart. Record the class's results on the Class Cumulative Competency Chart.

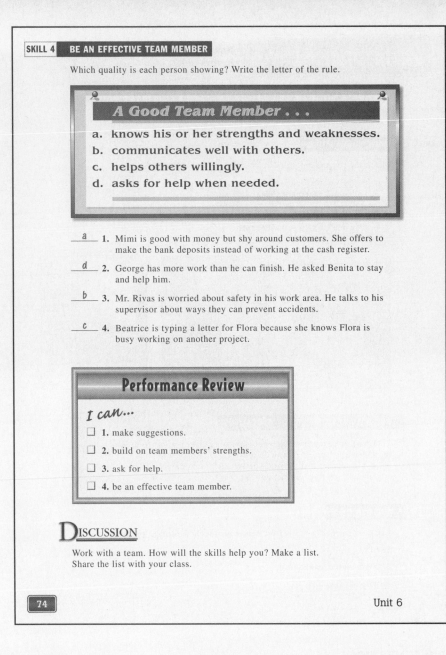

Which quality is each person showing? Write the letter of the rule.

A Good Team Member . . .

a. knows his or her strengths and weaknesses.

b. communicates well with others.

c. helps others willingly.

d. asks for help when needed.

__a__ **1.** Mimi is good with money but shy around customers. She offers to make the bank deposits instead of working at the cash register.

__d__ **2.** George has more work than he can finish. He asked Benita to stay and help him.

__b__ **3.** Mr. Rivas is worried about safety in his work area. He talks to his supervisor about ways they can prevent accidents.

__c__ **4.** Beatrice is typing a letter for Flora because she knows Flora is busy working on another project.

Performance Review

I can...

☐ **1.** make suggestions.

☐ **2.** build on team members' strengths.

☐ **3.** ask for help.

☐ **4.** be an effective team member.

DISCUSSION

Work with a team. How will the skills help you? Make a list. Share the list with your class.

74   Unit 6

PRESENTATION

Follow the instructions on page 73.

INFORMAL WORKPLACE-SPECIFIC ASSESSMENT

Ask learners to discuss times they work as team members. Have them explain their special strengths as team members.

WORKBOOK

Unit 6, Exercise 9

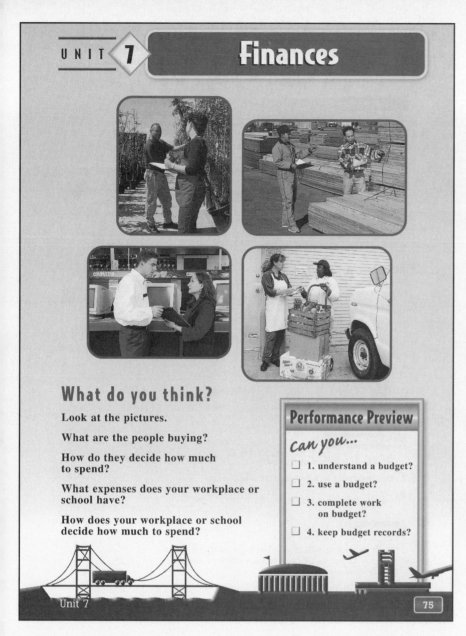

Unit 7

75

Unit 7 Overview
—SCANS Competencies—

★ Allocate resources
★ Acquire and evaluate data
★ Interpret information
★ Monitor and correct performance

Workforce Skills

• Understand a budget
• Use a budget
• Complete work on budget
• Keep budget records

Materials

• From a newspaper: ads showing different prices for the same kind of item, sale circulars from supermarkets
• Copies of a restaurant menu
• Picture cards or realia of cleaning supplies, a moving truck, a uniform, a seamstress, a bouquet of flowers, paint, crayons, paper, pencils, and glue
• A sample budget showing income and expenses

Unit Warm-Up

To get learners thinking about the unit topic (working with budgets), display ads showing different prices for the same kind of item, such as ladders or brooms. Ask learners to talk about which to buy.

★　　★　　★　　★　　★

WORKFORCE SKILLS (page 75)

Understand a budget

★　　★　　★　　★　　★

PREPARATION

1. Display and identify a sample budget. Point to the appropriate sections of the budget as you present or review **income** and **expenses.** Discuss the purpose of a budget.

2. Ask learners when they have used a budget. Ask why they used it and what it helped them do.

PRESENTATION

1. Focus attention on the photographs. Ask learners to say what the unit might be about. Write their ideas on the board and/or restate them in acceptable English.

2. Have learners talk about the photos. Ask them to describe what the employees are doing. Ask how each person might use a budget.

3. Help learners read the questions. Discuss the questions with the class.

4. You may want to use the Performance Preview to provide learners with an overview of the skills in the unit. Have learners read the list of skills and discuss what they will learn in this unit.

FOLLOW-UP

Budget Talk: Have learners work in pairs. Have each pair choose one of the photographs on this page and create a dialog that might take place between the people in the picture. Have several pairs present their dialogs to the class.

♦ Have teams talk about why companies use budgets. Encourage them to use examples from their own workplaces. Ask team reporters to share their teams' ideas with the class.

WORKBOOK

Unit 7, Exercises 1A–1B

★　　★　　★　　★　　★

Getting Started — Understanding a budget

TEAM WORK

Jack Brown made this budget for a job at The Fence Company. Compare how much money Jack budgeted to how much was actually spent. Write whether the builder is under budget, over budget, or on budget for each item.

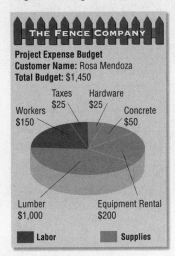

THE FENCE COMPANY

Project Expense Budget
Customer Name: Rosa Mendoza
Total Budget: $1,450

Taxes $25　Hardware $25
Workers $150　Concrete $50
Lumber $1,000　Equipment Rental $200

■ Labor　■ Supplies

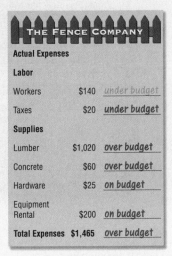

THE FENCE COMPANY

Actual Expenses

Labor		
Workers	$140	*under budget*
Taxes	$20	*under budget*
Supplies		
Lumber	$1,020	*over budget*
Concrete	$60	*over budget*
Hardware	$25	*on budget*
Equipment Rental	$200	*on budget*
Total Expenses	**$1,465**	*over budget*

PARTNER WORK

Take turns talking about the budget.

A How much did Jack budget to pay the workers?

B $150.

SURVEY

Work with a team. Make a budget for the expenses of an average worker for one day. Include expenses such as transportation and lunch.

76

Unit 7

Teaching Note

Use this page to introduce the new language in the unit. Whenever possible, encourage peer teaching. Supply any language learners need.

PREPARATION

1. To present or review **budget,** see Preparation on page 75.

2. To present or review **over budget, under budget,** and **on budget** write a dollar amount on the board. Then write or say other amounts and identify them as "over," "under," or "on" budget. Finally, ask learners to tell if amounts you name are over, under, or on budget.

PRESENTATION

1. Have learners read and discuss the Purpose Statement. See "Purpose Statement" on page viii.

2. Focus attention on the budget. Encourage learners to say as much as they can about it. Write their ideas on the board and/or restate them in acceptable English.

3. Have teams read the Team Work instructions. Make sure each team knows what to do. If necessary, model the first item. Have teams complete the activity. Ask team reporters to share their teams' answers with the class.

4. Have partners read the Partner Work instructions. If necessary, model the activity. Then have partners complete the activity. Have learners switch partners and repeat the activity. Have one or two pairs present their conversations to the class. For more information, see "Partner Work and Team Work" on page viii.

5. Have teams read the Survey instructions and complete the activity. Have team reporters share their budgets with the class. For more information, see "Survey" on page viii.

FOLLOW-UP

Over Budget? Have pairs discuss how a typical worker who is spending too much money can decrease work expenses such as lunch, transportation, and work clothing. Ask several pairs to present their ideas to the class.

◆ Have learners survey themselves to find out how many learners keep a written record of their daily expenses and how many do not. Help them create a pie chart to show the percent in each category.

WORKBOOK

Unit 7, Exercises 2A–2B

Talk About It — Using a budget

 PRACTICE THE DIALOG

A I'd like you to plan and buy the snacks for the center this week.

B How about cheese and crackers? The kids really like that.

A Cheese might be too expensive for our budget.

B What if I get cheese and crackers for two days and bananas, raisins, and pretzels for the other days?

A Sounds good. Why don't you check the costs and see if it fits our budget?

PARTNER WORK

You and your partner are buying refreshments for a meeting. You have a budget of $50 to serve twenty people. Talk about what you can buy to stay on budget. Use the dialog above and the price list.

Midtown Market
Refreshments Menu

Item	Price
24 cans of soda	$6.00
Coffee and tea for 20	$8.00
Fruit juice for 20	$12.00
Fresh fruit tray for 20	$25.00
Cookies & brownies for 20	$30.00
Sandwiches for 20	$45.00

ASAP
PROJECT

Work with a team. Why do people go over budget? How can they stay on budget? Make a list of tips. Write tips for home, work, and school. Share your list with the class. Complete this project as you work through the unit.

Unit 7

77

ASAP
PROJECT

Have learners read the instructions. Discuss the project and its purpose with learners. Make sure that everyone understands. Help learners assign themselves to teams depending upon their skills, knowledge, interests, or other personal strengths. Have each team select a leader. Throughout the rest of the unit, allow time for learners to work on the project. Have the teams agree on a deadline when the project will be finished. For more information see "ASAP Project" on page vi.

PREPARATION

1. To teach or review **refreshments** and the specific foods on the price list, use realia or a sales circular from a supermarket.

2. If necessary, review **on budget, over budget,** and **under budget.** Follow the instructions in Preparation on page 76.

PRESENTATION

1. Have learners read and discuss the Purpose Statement. For more information see "Purpose Statement" on page viii.

2. Focus attention on the photo. Encourage learners to say as much as they can about it. Have them identify the workplace shown and say what they think the people are talking about. Then present

the dialog. See "Presenting a Dialog" on page ix.

3. Have partners read the Partner Work instructions. Help learners read the price list. Make sure each pair knows what to do. Then have learners complete the activity. Have learners switch partners and repeat the activity. Supply any language needed. Have one or two pairs present their dialogs to the class.

FOLLOW-UP

Staying on Budget: Have learners work in teams. Give each team a copy of a menu from the same restaurant. Tell learners that they need to plan a lunch for ten people at the restaurant. They can spend a total of two hundred and fifty dollars. Have each team use the menus to decide what to serve and

figure the total cost. Post the budgets in the classroom.

♦ Have teams compare and discuss the budgets. Did every team choose the same meal? Are different options available even when following a budget? Have teams identify other options that would also fit the budget. Ask team reporters to summarize their discussions for the class.

WORKBOOK

Unit 7, Exercises 3A–3B

★　　★　　★　　★　　★

Personal Dictionary

Have learners add the words in their Personal Dictionary to their *Workforce Writing Dictionary.* For more information see "Workforce Writing Dictionary" on page v.

Keep Talking — Completing work on budget

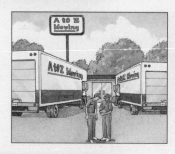 

 PRACTICE THE DIALOG

A This moving job is bigger than we thought. If we use the small truck, we'll have to make two trips.

B That'll take too long. We only budgeted for one trip.

A Let's see if one of the bigger trucks is available.

B That's a good idea. Then we can do it in one trip.

TEAM WORK

Read the situations. Agree on a solution for each problem.

1. Your team needs to complete a project this week, but there aren't enough workers. The company can't afford to pay you overtime.

2. You need to buy cleaning supplies, but your regular supplier has gone out of business. Some items from the new supplier are more expensive.

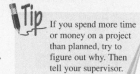 If you spend more time or money on a project than planned, try to figure out why. Then tell your supervisor.

Personal Dictionary — Using a budget

Write the words and phrases that you need to know.

_____

_____

78   Unit 7

PREPARATION

Use realia or pictures to present or review **moving truck** and **cleaning supplies.** To explain **overtime,** tell learners that hourly employees who work more than a certain number of hours (usually 8 hours in a day or 40 hours a week) are paid additional bonus pay. Ask learners to explain their companies' rules for overtime.

PRESENTATION

1. Have learners read and discuss the Purpose Statement. For more information see "Purpose Statement" on page viii.

2. Focus attention on the illustrations. Encourage learners to say as much as they can about them and identify the people's occupation. Ask what they

think the people are discussing. Then present the dialog. See "Presenting a Dialog" on page ix.

3. Have teams read the Team Work instructions. Make sure everyone knows what to do. If necessary, model the activity. Then have teams complete the activity. Have several teams present their conversations to the class.

4. Have learners read the Personal Dictionary instructions. Then use the Personal Dictionary procedures on page ix. Remind learners to add words to their dictionaries throughout the unit.

Have learners read the Tip independently. Have learners discuss how the advice will help them. For more information, see "Presenting a Tip" on page ix.

FOLLOW-UP

Problem/Solution: Write these businesses on separate slips of paper: **Lawn Maintenance, Restaurant, Gas Station,** and **Child Care Center.** Have each team choose a slip. Ask teams to think of three budgeting problems the business could have. Then ask learners to provide solutions for each problem. Ask team reporters to share their teams' ideas with the class.

♦ Have partners role-play situations in which an employee explains to a supervisor why a project has gone over budget. Have several pairs present their role-plays to the class.

WORKBOOK

Unit 7, Exercise 4

 **Adjusting spending to stay on budget**

 LISTEN AND CIRCLE

What is causing the budget problem? Circle the letter.

1. Tranh needs to change the menu because _____.
   a. the client added people to the guest list
   b. he spent too much money on the meat

2. Malika needed to save money on the costumes because _____.
   a. last year she was over budget
   b. the price of some of the materials went up

3. Ramona has to find another supplier because _____.
   a. the prices on some of the flowers went up
   b. her regular supplier is in Hawaii

 LISTEN AGAIN

How will the employees adjust their spending? Match the people with their solutions. Write the letter.

___c___ 1. Tranh   a. use less of an expensive material

___a___ 2. Malika   b. get a better price from another supplier

___b___ 3. Ramona   ✖ use a different, cheaper product

LISTEN AND CIRCLE

How can the people stay on budget? Circle the letters.

a. use another supplier   b. plan ahead
c. substitute a different product   d. start over if you have a problem
e. budget more money than you need   f. complain to your friends

DISCUSSION

Why do people go over budget? What are ways people can stay on budget? Make a list. Share your list with the class.

Unit 7   79

SCANS Note

Encourage learners to keep records of items related to their home and work budgets. Have volunteers explain the systems they use to keep track of income and expenses.

PREPARATION

1. Use realia, pictures, and pantomime to present or review **uniform, seamstress,** and **bouquet.**

2. Present or review **cheap** and **expensive** by talking about items in the supermarket sales circular. Give an example of how to make an **adjustment** to a budget by **substituting** a less expensive item.

PRESENTATION

1. Have learners read and discuss the Purpose Statement. For more information see "Purpose Statement" on page viii.

 2. Have learners read the Listen and Circle instructions. Then have them read the items. Make sure that everyone understands the

instructions. If necessary, model the first item. Then play the tape or read the Listening Transcript aloud two or more times as learners complete the activity. Check learners' work. For more information see "Presenting a Listening Activity" on page ix.

 3. Have learners read the Listen Again instructions. Then follow the procedures in 2.

4. Have learners read the Listen and Circle instructions. Then follow the procedures in 2.

5. Have learners read the Discussion questions. Then have them work in teams to discuss their ideas. Have team reporters share their lists with the class.

FOLLOW-UP

Budgeting Tips: Have partners role-play situations in which one employee describes a budget problem and the other offers advice on how to solve it. Have several pairs present their role-plays to the class.

♦ Have partners write the advice in the form of a list of tips. Display the tips in the classroom.

WORKBOOK

Unit 7, Exercises 5A–5B

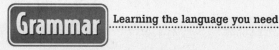

A. Study the Examples

| I finished the roof | fifteen minutes ago. |
| | two weeks ago. |

Schedule	Ali Hashimi
8:00 A.M.	start work
9:00 A.M.	add up the expenses
10:00 A.M.	write the new budget
11:30 A.M.	eat lunch

ANSWER THE QUESTIONS

It's 12:00 noon now. Use the schedule and the language in A.

1. When did Ali Hashimi write the new budget? *He wrote it two hours ago.*

2. When did he start work? *He started work four hours ago.*

3. When did he eat lunch? *He ate lunch half an hour ago.*

4. When did he add up the expenses? *He did it three hours ago.*

 **PARTNER WORK**

Talk about what you did earlier today at your workplace or school. Use the language in A.

80

Unit 7

PREPARATION

Review the language in the grammar boxes with learners before they open their books, if necessary. To teach or review **ago,** tell learners what you did an hour ago, such as, "I arrived at school an hour ago." Repeat for **already** and **yet,** modeling with sentences such as, "I have already arrived" and "I haven't left yet."

PRESENTATION

1. Have learners read and discuss the Purpose Statement. For more information see "Purpose Statement" on page viii.

2. Have learners read the grammar box in A. Have learners use the language in the box to say as many sentences as possible. Tell learners that they can use the grammar box throughout the unit to review or check sentence structures.

3. Focus attention on the photo and the schedule. Encourage learners to say as much as they can about them. Ask what the man at the desk is doing and what the schedule shows.

4. Have learners read the instructions for Answer the Questions. Make sure learners know what to do. If necessary, model the first item. Allow learners to complete the activity. Have learners check each other's work in pairs. Ask several learners to read their answers aloud while the rest of the class checks their work.

5. Have pairs read the Partner Work instructions. Make sure everyone knows what to do. If necessary, model the activity. Then have

partners complete the activity. Have several pairs present their dialogs to the class.

B. Study the Examples

> Have you finished the roof yet?

> I've already finished the roof.
> I haven't finished the roof yet.

COMPLETE THE DIALOG

Write the correct form of the word, and circle *already* or *yet*. Use the language in B.

A Allison, _____have_____ you _____written_____

(**write**) the holiday schedule (**already** / (**yet**))?

B Yes, I've ((**already**) / **yet**) _____finished_____ (**finish**) it.

A _____Has_____ Mr. Patterson _____seen_____

(**see**) it (**already** / (**yet**))?

B No, I _____haven't shown_____ (**show**) it to him.

A _____Have_____ you _____worked_____ (**work**)

on hiring an extra housekeeper (**already** / (**yet**))?

B Yes, I 've_____ ((**already**) / **yet**)

_____hired_____ (**hire**) someone to help out over the

holidays.

A _____Has_____ the new housekeeper

_____started_____ (**start**) working (**already** / (**yet**))?

B Yes, she 's_____ ((**already**) / **yet**)

_____completed_____ (**complete**) the training session. She's

working on the third floor.

PARTNER WORK

What have you done today? What haven't you done yet? Write a list. Share your list with the class. Ask about other learners' lists.

---

6. Focus attention on the grammar boxes in B. Follow the procedures in 2.

7. Have learners read the instructions for Complete the Dialog. If necessary, model the first item. Then have learners complete the activity independently. Have learners check each other's work in pairs. Have a different learner read each sentence aloud as the rest of the class checks their answers.

8. Have partners read the Partner Work instructions. Make sure everyone knows what to do. If necessary, model the activity. Then have partners complete the activity. Ask pairs to share their lists with the class.

FOLLOW-UP

Already, Yet, Ago: Have one learner ask the next learner a question using **already** or **yet**, as in "Have you done your homework yet?" The learner who responds should use the word **already, yet,** or **ago,** as in, "I've already finished my homework," and then ask the next learner a question using **already** or **yet.** Continue until everyone has asked and answered a question.

◆ Repeat the activity, but have learners work in teams and ask them to write down their questions and answers. The first learner should write a question using **already** or **yet** and pass the paper to the next learner. This learner writes an answer using **already** or **ago** and writes another question. When everyone has asked and answered a question, check learners' work.

WORKBOOK

Unit 7, Exercises 6A–6B

BLACKLINE MASTERS

Blackline Master: Unit 7

WORKFORCE SKILLS
(pages 82–83)

Keep budget records

★　　★　　★　　★　　★

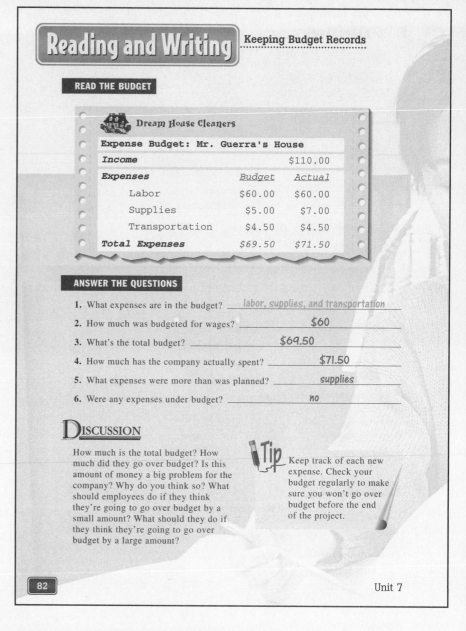

Reading and Writing
Keeping Budget Records

READ THE BUDGET

Dream House Cleaners

Expense Budget: Mr. Guerra's House

Income		$110.00
Expenses	*Budget*	*Actual*
Labor	$60.00	$60.00
Supplies	$5.00	$7.00
Transportation	$4.50	$4.50
Total Expenses	*$69.50*	*$71.50*

ANSWER THE QUESTIONS

1. What expenses are in the budget? _labor, supplies, and transportation_
2. How much was budgeted for wages? **$60**
3. What's the total budget? **$69.50**
4. How much has the company actually spent? **$71.50**
5. What expenses were more than was planned? **supplies**
6. Were any expenses under budget? **no**

DISCUSSION

How much is the total budget? How much did they go over budget? Is this amount of money a big problem for the company? Why do you think so? What should employees do if they think they're going to go over budget by a small amount? What should they do if they think they're going to go over budget by a large amount?

Tip Keep track of each new expense. Check your budget regularly to make sure you won't go over budget before the end of the project.

82

Unit 7

PREPARATION

To clarify the difference between **budgeted** and **actual expenses**, use peer teaching or review **over, under,** and **on budget** following the procedures on page 76.

PRESENTATION

1. Have learners read and discuss the Purpose Statement. For more information see "Purpose Statement" on page viii.

2. Have learners preview the budget before they read. Encourage learners to say everything they can about the budget. Write their ideas on the board and/or restate them in acceptable English. Then have learners read the budget independently.

3. Have learners read the instructions for Answer the Questions. Make sure everyone knows what to do. If necessary, model the first item. Then have learners complete the activity. Ask several learners to share their answers with the class while the rest of the class checks their work.

4. Have learners read the Discussion questions. Make sure everyone knows what to do. Then have learners work in teams to discuss their ideas. Have team reporters share their teams' answers with the class.

Tip Have learners read the Tip independently. Provide any clarification needed. For more information, see "Presenting a Tip" on page ix.

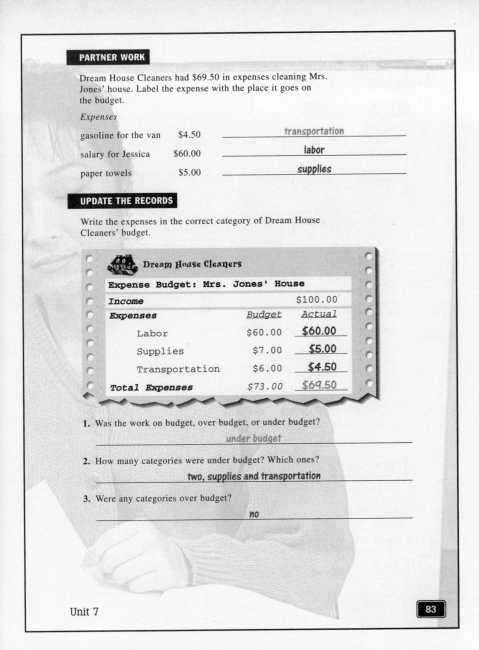

Dream House Cleaners had $69.50 in expenses cleaning Mrs. Jones' house. Label the expense with the place it goes on the budget.

Expenses

gasoline for the van	$4.50	*transportation*
salary for Jessica	$60.00	*labor*
paper towels	$5.00	*supplies*

UPDATE THE RECORDS

Write the expenses in the correct category of Dream House Cleaners' budget.

Dream House Cleaners

Expense Budget: Mrs. Jones' House

	Budget	*Actual*
Income	$100.00	
Expenses		
Labor	$60.00	**$60.00**
Supplies	$7.00	**$5.00**
Transportation	$6.00	**$4.50**
Total Expenses	$73.00	$69.50

1. Was the work on budget, over budget, or under budget?

under budget

2. How many categories were under budget? Which ones?

two, supplies and transportation

3. Were any categories over budget?

no

Unit 7

83

---

5. Have partners read the Partner Work instructions. Make sure everyone knows what to do. Then have pairs complete the activity. Check learners' work.

6. Have learners read the instructions for Update the Records. Make sure everyone knows what to do. Then have learners complete the activity. Check learners' budgets. Then have several students say their answers aloud while the rest of the class checks their work.

FOLLOW-UP

Record-Keeping: Have teams create budgets. Give each team a slip of paper with a project description and a total project budget, such as: "Company picnic for 15 people: $200." Have teams create budgets for the project. Post the budgets in the classroom.

♦ Have teams discuss how to estimate expenses for a budget. What kind of information do they need? How could they find it? Have teams compare ideas.

WORKBOOK

Unit 7, Exercises 7A–7B

WORKFORCE SKILLS (page 84)

Use a budget

Complete work on budget

★   ★   ★   ★   ★

Language Note

*Discuss that the verb **cost** is the same in both present and past tense. Have learners use the verb in sample sentences in both tenses, such as "Today, the books cost $12," and "Yesterday the books cost $11."*

 **Prioritizing purchases**

READ THE PRICE LIST

Mr. Abernathy wants his classroom aide to order the supplies on the list. Read Mr. Abernathy's list and the price list. Then answer the questions.

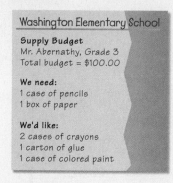

Washington Elementary School

Supply Budget
Mr. Abernathy, Grade 3
Total budget = $100.00

We need:
1 case of pencils
1 box of paper

We'd like:
2 cases of crayons
1 carton of glue
1 case of colored paint

Lings School Supplies
44 River Street
Mankato, MN 44625
(324) 555-2214

Price List

Item	Price
Case of colored paint	$30.00
Case of crayons	$20.00
Box of paper	$20.00
Carton of glue	$10.00
Case of pencils	$10.00

1. What supplies does he need most?

   <u>I case of pencils and I box of paper</u>

2. How much do these things cost together?

   $30

3. How much does everything on the list cost? ____ $110

Discussion

Mr. Abernathy's total budget is $100. Is this enough money for everything he wants? What can the classroom aide do to stay on budget? Why?

 **Culture Notes**

You think you know a way your company can save money on supplies. What do you do? Why?

Unit 7

PREPARATION

1. To present or review the school supply vocabulary on the page, display and identify pencils, paint, crayons, paper, and glue. Explain that all these items are **school supplies.** Identify, or have learners identify, each item.

2. Explain that **prioritizing** means deciding what is most important. Have learners rank the school supplies in your display in order of importance for a student in high school. Ask if they would rank, or **prioritize,** the items differently for preschool children. Discuss that different people have different **priorities,** or things that are important to them.

PRESENTATION

1. Have learners read and discuss the

Purpose Statement. See "Purpose Statement" on page viii.

2. Have learners preview the lists. Encourage them to say everything they can about them. Then have learners read the lists independently.

3. Have learners read the Read the Price List instructions. Make sure everyone knows what to do. Then have learners complete the activity. Have several learners read their answers aloud while the rest of the class checks their work.

4. Have learners read the Discussion questions. Then have learners work in teams to discuss their ideas. Have team reporters share their teams' ideas with the class.

 5. Have learners read Culture Notes and talk over their ideas in teams. Have team reporters

share the ideas with the class. See "Culture Notes," page vii.

FOLLOW-UP

Calculations: Prepare copies of a sample budget for a project relevant to learners' workplaces. Include line items and prices for several items, but not totals. Ask learners to calculate the expenses for each item and the total expense of the event. Have teams compare calculations.

♦ Tell learners the overall budget has changed and they now have a hundred dollars less to spend. Have teams discuss what they would do. Have team leaders share the revised budgets with the class.

WORKBOOK

Unit 7, Exercise 8

Performance Check) How well can you use the skills
in this unit?
....

Complete the activities. Go over your work with a partner or your teacher.
Then complete the Performance Review on page 86.

SKILL 1   UNDERSTAND A BUDGET

Write *under budget*, *over budget*, or *on budget* for each item.

Sunshine Day Care   **Monthly Classroom Budget**

Expenses		Budget	Actual	
Supplies	Paper	$25	$20	under budget
	Crayons	$20	$15	under budget
Snacks	Food	$100	$105	over budget
	Drinks	$35	$35	on budget
Total Expenses		$180	$175	under budget

SKILL 2   USE A BUDGET

You are buying snacks for a staff
meeting. You have a budget of $25.
You need to buy snacks for 10 people.
Talk with a partner or your teacher
about what you can buy to stay on
budget. Use the price list.

SWEET HILL CATERING

Snack Menu
Item	Price
12 cans of soda	$4.00
Coffee and tea for 10	$6.00
Fresh fruit tray for 10	$14.00
Cookies and brownies for 10	$15.00

SKILL 3   COMPLETE WORK ON BUDGET

Study the scenarios and think of solutions for each problem.
Tell your ideas to a partner or your teacher.

1. You are a carpenter with orders for a cabinet and some
   bookshelves. You discover that you have ordered too much
   wood for the cabinet you are working on.

2. You have to deliver thirty potted plants to an office building.
   The price of the ceramic pots you usually use has gone up.

Unit 7   85

PRESENTATION

Use any of the procedures in
"Evaluation," page x, with pages 85
and 86. Record individuals' results on
the Unit 7 Individual Competency
Chart. Record the class's results on the
Class Cumulative Competency Chart.

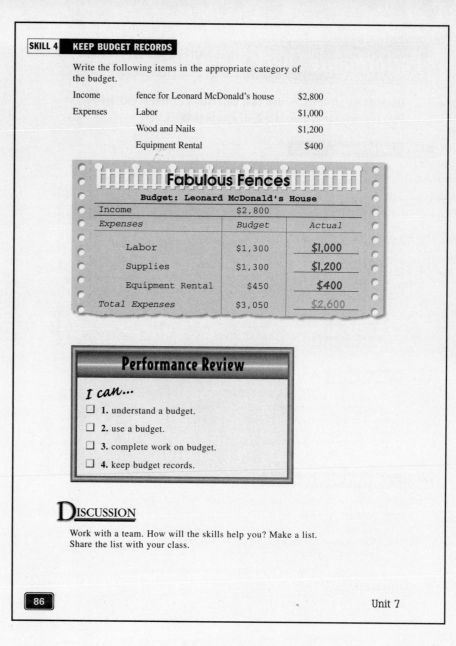

Write the following items in the appropriate category of the budget.

Income	fence for Leonard McDonald's house	$2,800
Expenses	Labor	$1,000
	Wood and Nails	$1,200
	Equipment Rental	$400

Fabulous Fences

Budget: Leonard McDonald's House

Income		$2,800	
Expenses		*Budget*	*Actual*
Labor		$1,300	$1,000
Supplies		$1,300	$1,200
Equipment Rental		$450	$400
Total Expenses		$3,050	$2,600

Performance Review

I can...

☐ **1.** understand a budget.

☐ **2.** use a budget.

☐ **3.** complete work on budget.

☐ **4.** keep budget records.

Discussion

Work with a team. How will the skills help you? Make a list. Share the list with your class.

PRESENTATION

Follow the instructions on page 85.

INFORMAL WORKPLACE-SPECIFIC ASSESSMENT

Ask learners to discuss how budgets affect them and what they do to stay on budget at work.

WORKBOOK

Unit 7, Exercise 9

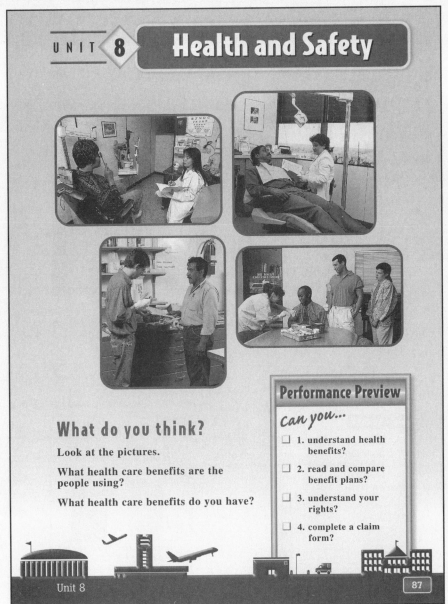

What do you think?

Look at the pictures.

What health care benefits are the people using?

What health care benefits do you have?

Performance Preview

can you...

☐ 1. understand health benefits?

☐ 2. read and compare benefit plans?

☐ 3. understand your rights?

☐ 4. complete a claim form?

Unit 8

87

Unit 8 Overview
—SCANS Competencies—

★ Evaluate and interpret information

★ Understand organizational systems

★ Communicate information

Workforce Skills

● Understand health benefits

● Read and compare benefit plans

● Understand your rights

● Complete a claim form

Materials

● Samples of an insurance claim form, brochures describing health plans, and paycheck stubs showing salary deductions for health benefits

● Realia or picture cards of a knife, a burn, a cut, gloves, boots, cotton, fire-proof clothes, and a car

Unit Warm-Up

To stimulate discussion about the unit topic (employee benefits), act out injuring yourself on the job. Ask what learners think you should do. Discuss times learners have hurt themselves at work.

★   ★   ★   ★   ★

WORKFORCE SKILLS (page 87)

Understand health benefits

★   ★   ★   ★   ★

PREPARATION

1. Explain that **health care benefits** are plans that some employers provide to help workers pay for health care. Ask learners to name the different kinds of health care people need, such as dental care, allergy shots, and eye exams.

2. Display and identify a **claim form.** Discuss when an employee might need to use such a form.

PRESENTATION

1. Focus attention on the photographs. Ask learners what they think the unit might be about. Write their ideas on the

board and/or restate them in acceptable English.

2. Have learners talk about the photographs. Ask them to describe how the employees in each photo are using health benefits.

3. Help learners read the questions. Discuss the questions with the class.

4. You may want to use the Performance Preview to provide learners with an overview of the skills in the unit. Have learners read the list of skills and discuss what they will learn in this unit.

FOLLOW-UP

Role-Play: Have partners create pantomimes in which an employee receives health care, such as X rays, dental care, or vision service. Then have two pairs work together. Have them

take turns performing their pantomimes and identifying the type of health care.

◆ Help the class create a list of all the different kinds of health care that learners pantomimed. Post the list in the classroom.

WORKBOOK

Unit 8, Exercises 1A–1B

Teaching Note

Use this page to introduce the new language in the unit. Whenever possible, encourage peer teaching. Supply any language learners need.

Getting Started — Using employee benefits

TEAM WORK

What are the people doing? What employee benefit are they using? Use the Useful Language. What other benefits can you name?

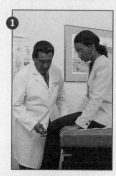 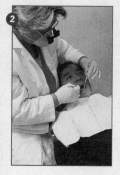 

PARTNER WORK

Take turns asking questions about the health care benefits.

A What does dental insurance cover?

B It pays for visits to the dentist.

Useful Language

dental insurance

family leave

health care plan

 SURVEY

Make a list of all the different types of health care benefits your employers offer. Find out how many students have each benefit. Use the information to make a bar graph.

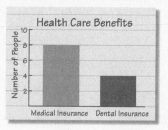

Health Care Benefits (bar graph: Number of People / Medical Insurance, Dental Insurance)

88

Unit 8

PREPARATION

To teach or review **health benefits,** see Preparation on page 87. Explain that health benefits are one type of **employee benefits.** Another is **family leave,** which enables employees to take a longer time off, for example, to care for a newborn baby.

PRESENTATION

1. Have learners read and discuss the Purpose Statement. See "Purpose Statement," page viii.

2. Focus attention on the illustrations. Encourage learners to say as much as they can about them. Write their ideas on the board and/or restate them in acceptable English.

3. Have teams read the Team Work instructions. Make sure each team knows what to do. Then have teams complete the activity. Have team reporters summarize the discussions for the class.

4. Have partners read the Partner Work instructions. Focus attention on the Useful Language box. If necessary, model pronunciation. Have each learner complete the activity with two different partners. Have one or two pairs present their dialogs to the class. See "Partner Work and Team Work," page viii.

 5. Have teams read the Survey instructions and complete the activity. Ask them to share their bar graphs with the class. See "Survey," page viii.

FOLLOW-UP

Employee Benefits: Have teams discuss the information from the Survey activity. Which benefits do team members receive? Which ones do they use most often? Ask team reporters to share responses with the class.

◆ Have teams rank the benefits in the graphs according to importance. Which benefits do they value the most? Why? Which ones would they like to have? Have team reporters share their teams' rankings with the class.

WORKBOOK

Unit 8, Exercises 2A–2B

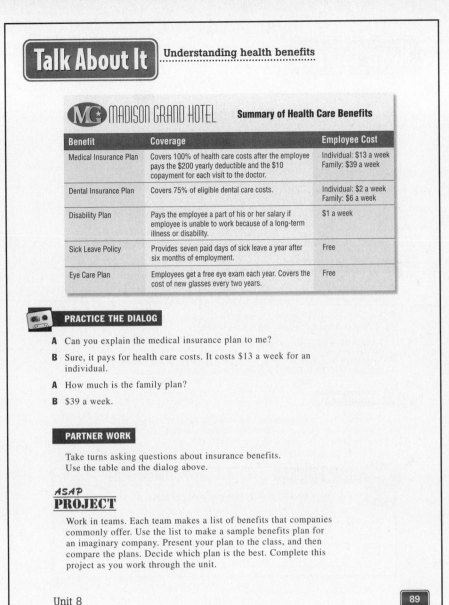

Talk About It   Understanding health benefits

MADISON GRAND HOTEL — Summary of Health Care Benefits

Benefit	Coverage	Employee Cost
Medical Insurance Plan	Covers 100% of health care costs after the employee pays the $200 yearly deductible and the $10 copayment for each visit to the doctor.	Individual: $13 a week Family: $39 a week
Dental Insurance Plan	Covers 75% of eligible dental care costs.	Individual: $2 a week Family: $6 a week
Disability Plan	Pays the employee a part of his or her salary if employee is unable to work because of a long-term illness or disability.	$1 a week
Sick Leave Policy	Provides seven paid days of sick leave a year after six months of employment.	Free
Eye Care Plan	Employees get a free eye exam each year. Covers the cost of new glasses every two years.	Free

PRACTICE THE DIALOG

A Can you explain the medical insurance plan to me?

B Sure, it pays for health care costs. It costs $13 a week for an individual.

A How much is the family plan?

B $39 a week.

PARTNER WORK

Take turns asking questions about insurance benefits. Use the table and the dialog above.

ASAP PROJECT

Work in teams. Each team makes a list of benefits that companies commonly offer. Use the list to make a sample benefits plan for an imaginary company. Present your plan to the class, and then compare the plans. Decide which plan is the best. Complete this project as you work through the unit.

Unit 8   89

PREPARATION

Find and display a page in a health care manual that summarizes health care benefits. Help learners understand the terms. Explain that a **sick leave policy** allows employees to take paid days off from work when they are ill. Explain that a **disability plan** enables employees to receive part of their income if they have to miss work for a long time as a result of illness or injury.

PRESENTATION

1. Have learners read and discuss the Purpose Statement. For more information see "Purpose Statement" on page viii.

 2. Focus attention on the chart. Encourage learners to say as much as they can about it. Have them identify the types of

benefits shown. Then present the dialog. See "Presenting a Dialog" on page ix.

3. Have partners read the Partner Work instructions. Make sure each pair knows what to do. Then have learners complete the activity. Have learners switch partners and repeat the activity. Have one or two pairs present their dialogs to the class.

FOLLOW-UP

Who Should You Call? Have teams brainstorm a list of resources for information about health insurance benefits. Who can they ask for information? How can they contact benefits experts who are not at their workplace? Have team reporters share the ideas with the class.

♦ Have learners work in pairs to create a dialog in which an employee contacts

one of the resources on the list and asks questions about health insurance benefits. Have learners switch roles and repeat the exercise. Ask one or two pairs to present their dialogs to the class.

WORKBOOK

Unit 8, Exercise 3

ASAP PROJECT

Have learners read the instructions. Discuss the project and its purpose with learners. Make sure that everyone understands. Help learners assign themselves to teams depending upon their skills, knowledge, interests, or other personal strengths. Have each team select a leader. Throughout the rest of the unit, allow time for learners to work on the project. Have the teams agree on a deadline when the project will be finished. For more information see "ASAP Project" on page vi.

WORKFORCE SKILLS (page 90)

Read and compare benefit plans

★   ★   ★   ★   ★

Personal Dictionary

Have learners add the words in their Personal Dictionary to their *Workforce Writing Dictionary*. For more information see "Workforce Writing Dictionary" on page v.

Keep Talking Comparing benefits

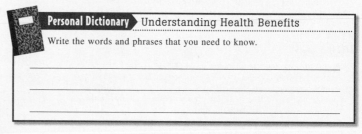

	ABC Health Plan	First Health Plan
Salary Deduction	$5 per week	$6.50 per week
Doctor's Visit Copayment	$5	$15
Doctors	Any participating doctor	Any doctor
Hospital Care Copayment	10%	None
Preventive Care	Free annual physical exams	Free annual physical exams and free immunizations

PRACTICE THE DIALOG

A I just became eligible for employee benefits. I need to decide which health insurance plan to choose. Can you tell me about them?

B With ABC Health Plan the copayment for a doctor's visit is only $5. With First Health Plan the copayment is $15.

A I see. ABC sounds like a better deal.

B It depends how you look at it. With ABC you have to use certain doctors. With First Health you can go to any doctor you want.

PARTNER WORK

Continue comparing the health care plans. Take turns asking questions. Use the dialog above. Which plan sounds better to you? Why? Tell the class.

Personal Dictionary Understanding Health Benefits

Write the words and phrases that you need to know.

_____

_____

_____

90   Unit 8

PREPARATION

1. Use sample paycheck stubs to identify and clarify **salary deductions.**

2. Present or review **copayment** by putting up a "Doctor's Office" sign, then acting out paying a receptionist five or ten dollars. Explain that insurance covers the rest of the cost of the doctor's visit.

3. Explain that **preventive care** keeps people from getting sick. Use role-play and a calendar to identify examples, such as an **annual physical exam** and **immunizations.**

4. Display and identify lists of **participating doctors** in a Health Insurance Brochure.

PRESENTATION

1. Have learners read and discuss the Purpose Statement. See "Purpose Statement," page viii.

2. Focus attention on the table. Help learners identify the categories in the table. Then present the dialog. See "Presenting a Dialog," page ix.

3. Have partners read the Partner Work instructions. Then have partners complete the activity. Have learners switch partners and repeat. Have learners say which plan they want and explain why.

4. Have learners read the Personal Dictionary instructions. Remind learners to add words to their dictionaries throughout the unit. See the Personal Dictionary procedures, page ix.

FOLLOW-UP

What's Your Plan? Have partners choose one of the health plans in the table on this page and role-play a patient and a cashier at a doctor's office. The patient tells the cashier the reason for the visit, and the cashier uses information about the health plan to tell the patient what to pay. Ask a few pairs to present their role-plays to the class.

♦ Have the class discuss who pays for health benefits. Ask questions, such as *Who pays the doctor when an employee has a free physical exam?* Write learners' ideas on the board and/or restate them in acceptable English.

WORKBOOK

Unit 8, Exercises 4A–4C

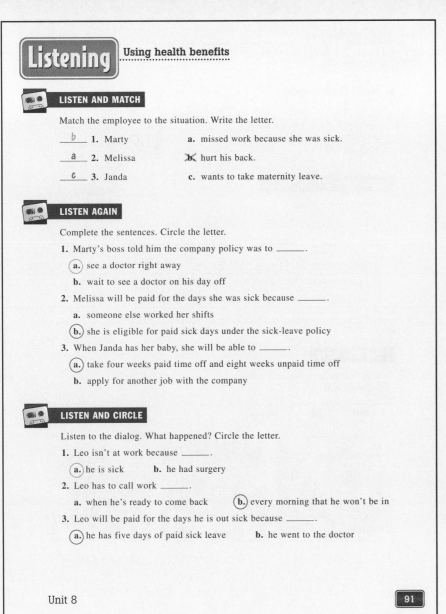

Listening — Using health benefits

LISTEN AND MATCH

Match the employee to the situation. Write the letter.

_b_ **1.** Marty   **a.** missed work because she was sick.

_a_ **2.** Melissa   **b.** hurt his back.

_c_ **3.** Janda   **c.** wants to take maternity leave.

LISTEN AGAIN

Complete the sentences. Circle the letter.

1. Marty's boss told him the company policy was to _____.

    (a.) see a doctor right away

    b. wait to see a doctor on his day off

2. Melissa will be paid for the days she was sick because _____.

    a. someone else worked her shifts

    (b.) she is eligible for paid sick days under the sick-leave policy

3. When Janda has her baby, she will be able to _____.

    (a.) take four weeks paid time off and eight weeks unpaid time off

    b. apply for another job with the company

LISTEN AND CIRCLE

Listen to the dialog. What happened? Circle the letter.

1. Leo isn't at work because _____.

    (a.) he is sick   **b.** he had surgery

2. Leo has to call work _____.

    a. when he's ready to come back   **(b.)** every morning that he won't be in

3. Leo will be paid for the days he is out sick because _____.

    (a.) he has five days of paid sick leave   **b.** he went to the doctor

Unit 8   **91**

SCANS Note

Tell learners that it is useful to know who to contact with questions about benefits issues. Many companies have Human Resources Departments to handle employees' health care questions. Ask learners whether their companies have Human Resources Departments. Have volunteers discuss their experiences with Human Resources Departments.

PREPARATION

1. To present or review **family leave** and **sick leave,** refer to Preparation on pages 88 and 89. Use **company policy** in several sample sentences to help learners figure out what the phrase means.

2. Have learners brainstorm valid and invalid reasons employees might miss work.

PRESENTATION

1. Have learners read and discuss the Purpose Statement. For more information see "Purpose Statement" on page viii.

 2. Have learners read the Listen and Match instructions. Then have them read the items. Use peer-teaching to clarify any unfamiliar vocabulary. Make sure that everyone understands the instructions. If necessary, model the first item. Then play the tape or read the Listening Transcript aloud two or more times as learners complete the activity. Check learners' work. For more information see "Presenting a Listening Activity" on page ix.

 3. Have learners read the Listen Again instructions. Then follow the procedures in 2.

 4. Have learners read the Listen and Circle instructions. Then follow the procedures in 2.

FOLLOW-UP

Name That Benefit: Give partners a slip of paper that tells a reason for missing work, such as "bad headache," "surgery," or "new baby." Have pairs discuss what the employees can expect in the way of benefits. Will they be paid? For how long? If so, which benefit applies? Ask pairs to summarize their discussions for the class.

♦ Have partners ask each other questions about times they missed work and the benefits they used. Ask them to write their dialogs. Check pairs' work.

WORKBOOK

Unit 8, Exercise 5

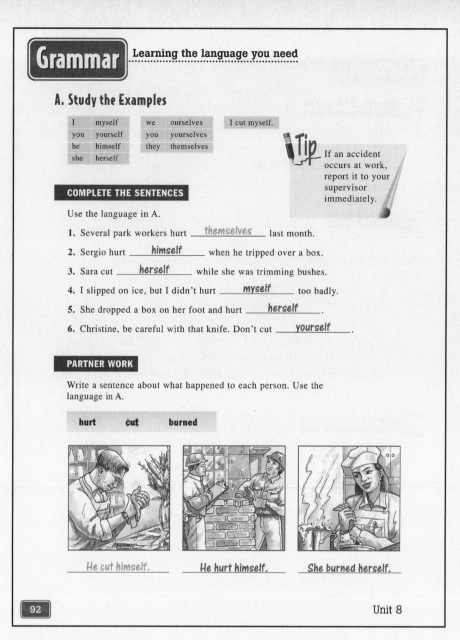

Grammar Learning the language you need

A. Study the Examples

I	myself	we	ourselves		I cut myself.
you	yourself	you	yourselves		
he	himself	they	themselves		
she	herself				

Tip If an accident occurs at work, report it to your supervisor immediately.

COMPLETE THE SENTENCES

Use the language in A.

1. Several park workers hurt _____themselves_____ last month.

2. Sergio hurt _____himself_____ when he tripped over a box.

3. Sara cut _____herself_____ while she was trimming bushes.

4. I slipped on ice, but I didn't hurt _____myself_____ too badly.

5. She dropped a box on her foot and hurt _____herself_____ .

6. Christine, be careful with that knife. Don't cut _____yourself_____ .

PARTNER WORK

Write a sentence about what happened to each person. Use the language in A.

hurt	cut	burned

He cut himself.   _He hurt himself._   _She burned herself._

92   Unit 8

Language Note

*Have learners brainstorm words and phrases related to injuries. You may want to start the list on the board with words used on these pages: **hurt, tripped, cut,** and **accident.***

PREPARATION

1. Review the language in the grammar boxes with learners before they open their books, if necessary.

2. Use picture cards, realia, or pantomime to present or review **knife, burn, cut, tripped, slipped, gloves, boots, cotton,** and **fire-proof clothes.**

PRESENTATION

1. Have learners read and discuss the Purpose Statement. For more information see "Purpose Statement" on page viii.

2. Have learners read the grammar boxes in A. Have learners use the language in the boxes to say as many sentences as possible. Tell learners that they can use the grammar boxes throughout the unit to review or check sentence structures.

3. Have learners read the instructions for Complete the Sentences. Make sure learners know what to do. If necessary, model the first item. Allow learners to complete the activity. Have learners check each other's work in pairs. Ask several learners to read their completed sentences aloud while the rest of the class checks their work.

4. Focus attention on the illustrations. Have learners say as much as they can about them. Then have pairs read the Partner Work instructions. Make sure everyone knows what to do. If necessary, model the first item. Then have pairs complete the activity. Ask several pairs to present their answers to the class.

Tip Have learners read the Tip independently. Have them discuss how the advice will help them. See "Presenting a Tip," page ix.

B. Study the Examples

| My workplace provides | care for my children. |
| | child care. |

Tip Before you take a job, find out about the benefits you'll get.

COMPLETE THE DIALOG

Use the language in B.

A Does this **company** have a **policy** for sick leave?

B Yes, the _____ company policy _____ provides ten paid sick days a year.

A Does your company provide **benefits** for **employees**?

B Yes, we have great _____ employee benefits _____ .

A Does the company provide **training** on **safety**?

B Yes, the _____ safety training _____ program helps make sure we don't have any accidents at work.

C. Study the Example

| Hong wore thick heavy fire-proof clothes. |

ANSWER THE QUESTIONS

Read the sentences. Answer the questions. Use the language in C.

1. Dawn wears gloves at work. They're white. They're made of cotton. Dawn uses them for gardening. What does Dawn wear?

   _____ Dawn wears white cotton gardening gloves. _____

2. Gerald bought some boots. The boots are black. They're made of leather. He wears them at work. What did Gerald buy for work?

   _____ Gerald bought some black leather work boots. _____

3. Linda has a hat. It's yellow. It's made of cotton. She wears it in the sun. What does Linda have?

   _____ Linda has a yellow cotton sun hat. _____

---

5. Focus attention on the grammar box in B. Follow the procedures in 2.

6. Have learners read the instructions for Complete the Dialog. Make sure everyone knows what to do. If necessary, model the first item. Allow learners to complete the activity. Have learners check each other's work in pairs. Ask several learners to read their answers aloud while the rest of the class checks their work.

7. Focus attention on the grammar box in C. Follow the procedures in 2.

8. Have learners read the Answer the Questions instructions. Make sure everyone knows what to do. If necessary, model the first item. Then have learners complete the activity. Ask several learners to read their sentences to the class.

Tip Have learners read the Tip independently. Have learners discuss how the advice will help them. For more information, see "Presenting a Tip" on page ix.

FOLLOW-UP

Adding Adjectives: Have learners take turns describing an object in the classroom. Ask one learner to start by saying a sentence such as, "Hong has a green notebook." The next learner should add an adjective to the sentence, such as, "Hong has a dark green notebook." Continue until there are three or four adjectives in the sentence. Then have the next learner describe another object. Continue until everyone has contributed.

♦ Have learners work in pairs. Ask each learner to say three sentences, each of which uses multiple adjectives to describe his or her partner's clothes or possessions. Ask several pairs to present their sentences to the class.

WORKBOOK

Unit 8, Exercises 6A–6C

BLACKLINE MASTERS

Blackline Master: Unit 8

Understand health benefits

Complete a claim form

★   ★   ★   ★   ★

READ THE BENEFIT PLAN

National Auto Painting
Summary of Employee Health Benefits

Benefit	Description	Eligible Employees Full-Time	Part-Time
Sick Leave	One paid sick day for every 30 days of employment, available after the first 90 days of work.	X	X
Health Insurance Plan	The company pays half the cost of the employee's health coverage plan. The plan is available after 60 days of employment.	X	
Disability Plan	This plan is optional. The employee pays all premiums.	X	
Workers' Compensation	The plan pays the employee's medical costs due to injury on the job. The employer pays the premiums.	X	X
Extended Leave for accident, illness, or birth, adoption, or foster care of a child	Up to 12 weeks unpaid, job-protected leave guaranteed by the Family and Medical Leave Act. Some part-time employees are eligible.	X	

ANSWER THE QUESTIONS

1. Who's eligible for sick leave? _____ *all employees*

2. How long do new full-time employees have to wait to get health insurance?
   _____ *60 days*

3. Who is eligible for Workers' Compensation? _____ *all employees*

4. How many paid sick days do workers get?
   _____ *1 for every 30 days of employment*

5. How much time can a full-time employee take off for extended leave?
   _____ *up to 12 weeks*

 DISCUSSION

Do full-time and part-time employees receive the same benefits at your workplace? Discuss the differences in benefits that come with different jobs.

94

Unit 8

Culture Note

Tell learners that health insurance may not cover all treatments or medications, such as experimental drugs, "alternative treatments," or mental health treatments. If learners do not know exactly what their health insurance covers, ask them to suggest ways they can find out.

PREPARATION

1. Explain that **Worker's Compensation** is a government plan that pays medical expenses for employees who are injured on the job. Display and identify a **claim form.** Discuss its use.

2. Present or review **optional** as something a person can choose to take or not take. Display a picture of a car and, as you indicate various features, ask learners which are "optional."

3. To review or present **Family and Medical Leave Act, sick leave,** and **disability plan,** see Preparation on pages 88 and 89. Explain that **premiums** are payments for insurance.

PRESENTATION

1. Have learners read and discuss the Purpose Statement. For more information see "Purpose Statement" on page viii.

2. Have learners preview the benefit plan before they read. For more information, see "Prereading" on page x. Encourage learners to say everything they can about it. Write their ideas on the board and/or restate them in acceptable English. Then have learners read the plan independently.

3. Focus learners' attention on Answer the Questions. Make sure everyone knows what to do. If necessary, model the first item. Then have learners complete the activity. Ask several learners to share their answers with the class while the rest of the class checks their work.

ON YOUR JOB **4.** Have learners read the Discussion questions. Then have learners work in teams to discuss their ideas. Have team reporters share their teams' ideas with the class.

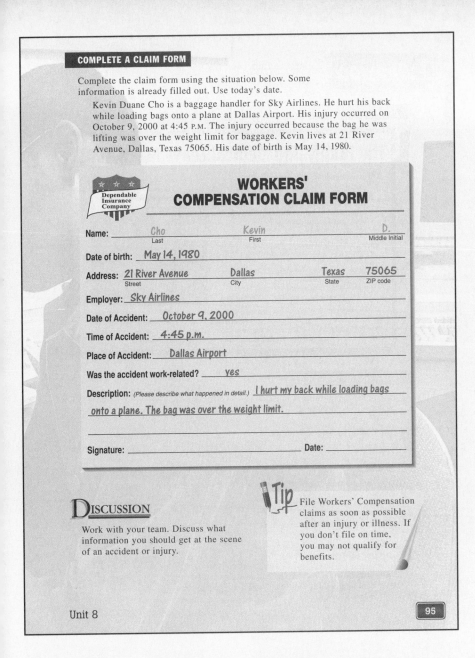

Complete the claim form using the situation below. Some information is already filled out. Use today's date.

Kevin Duane Cho is a baggage handler for Sky Airlines. He hurt his back while loading bags onto a plane at Dallas Airport. His injury occurred on October 9, 2000 at 4:45 P.M. The injury occurred because the bag he was lifting was over the weight limit for baggage. Kevin lives at 21 River Avenue, Dallas, Texas 75065. His date of birth is May 14, 1980.

Dependable Insurance Company

WORKERS' COMPENSATION CLAIM FORM

Name: _____Cho_____ _____Kevin_____ _____D._____
　　　　　Last　　　　　　First　　　　　Middle Initial

Date of birth: May 14, 1980

Address: 21 River Avenue　　Dallas　　Texas　75065
　　　　　Street　　　　　　City　　　State　ZIP code

Employer: Sky Airlines

Date of Accident: October 9, 2000

Time of Accident: 4:45 p.m.

Place of Accident: Dallas Airport

Was the accident work-related? yes

Description: (Please describe what happened in detail.) I hurt my back while loading bags onto a plane. The bag was over the weight limit.

Signature: _____　　Date: _____

DISCUSSION

Work with your team. Discuss what information you should get at the scene of an accident or injury.

Tip File Workers' Compensation claims as soon as possible after an injury or illness. If you don't file on time, you may not qualify for benefits.

Unit 8

95

---

5. Have learners preview the claim form. Encourage learners to say everything they can about it. Use peer teaching to clarify unfamiliar terms. Then have learners read the situation and the claim form independently.

6. Have learners read the Complete a Claim Form instructions. Make sure everyone knows what to do. If necessary, model the first item. Then have learners complete the activity. Check learners' work.

7. Have learners read the Discussion instructions. Then have learners work in teams to discuss their ideas. Have team reporters share the teams' ideas with the class.

 Have learners read the Tip independently. Have learners discuss how the advice will

help them. For more information, see "Presenting a Tip" on page ix.

FOLLOW-UP

Workers' Compensation: Have teams write a description of an injury at a workplace. Ask them to include all the details they think are important. Then distribute blank Workers' Compensation claim forms. Ask teams to complete them for the injury they described. Have team reporters read the claim forms to the class.

♦ Have partners role-play an employee at National Auto Painting and a benefits specialist at the same company. The employee should ask questions about the plan and the specialist should respond. Then have learners switch roles. Ask several pairs to present their dialogs to the class.

WORKBOOK

Unit 8, Exercises 7A–7B

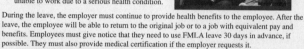

READ THE ARTICLE

The Family and Medical Leave Act of 1993

The Family and Medical Leave Act, or FMLA, allows employees to take up to 12 weeks of unpaid leave during the year. Employees are eligible to take unpaid leave if they:

- work for a covered employer that employs more than 50 workers.
- have worked for the employer for 12 months.
- have worked at least 1,250 hours over the previous 12 months.

Unpaid leave may be taken for the following reasons:

- to have a baby, or to care for a newborn baby or adopted or foster child.
- to take care of a spouse, child, or parent with a serious health condition.
- to take medical leave when the employee is unable to work due to a serious health condition.

During the leave, the employer must continue to provide health benefits to the employee. After the leave, the employee will be able to return to the original job or to a job with equivalent pay and benefits. Employees must give notice that they need to use FMLA leave 30 days in advance, if possible. They must also provide medical certification if the employer requests it.

ANSWER THE QUESTIONS

1. You have worked for a large company for three years. Will you lose your job if you need to take off 12 weeks to care for a new baby?

   _____ no _____

2. How long can you miss work under the FMLA?

   _____ 12 weeks _____

3. When should you tell your employer that you need to take time off?

   _____ 30 days before _____

4. While you are on leave, will your health benefits continue? _____ yes

 **Culture Notes**

Talk about how health benefits help employees. Do they help employers? What can people do if their employers don't offer benefits?

96   Unit 8

Teaching Note

Encourage learners to use the library and the Internet as sources of information about health care and government plans that protect employees.

Language Note

Ask learners to name other benefits-related abbreviations they see or hear, such as HMO, PPO, IRA, 401K, and so on. Clarify as needed.

PREPARATION

If necessary, review **family leave.** Follow instructions on page 88. Tell learners that the name of the law that created family leave is the Family and Medical Leave Act, or FMLA.

PRESENTATION

1. Have learners read and discuss the Purpose Statement. See "Purpose Statement," page viii.

2. Have learners preview the article. See "Prereading" on page x. Use peer teaching to clarify unfamiliar words. Then have learners read the article independently.

3. Have learners read the instructions for Answer the Questions. Then have them complete the activity. Have several learners read their answers aloud as the rest of the class checks their work.

 4. Have learners read Culture Notes and talk over their ideas in teams. Have team reporters tell the teams' ideas to the class. See "Culture Notes," page vii.

FOLLOW-UP

Eligibility: Write descriptions of individual worker's situations on slips of paper, for example, "Matt works for Uptown Movers, a company with 15 employees, and his wife just had a baby." Have each team pick a slip and explain why the employee is or is not eligible for benefits under the Family and Medical Leave Act. Have teams share the decisions with the class.

♦ Have teams figure out how many eight-hour days in twelve months an employee would have to work to be eligible for unpaid leave. How many four-hour days? Have teams compare answers. If answers aren't identical, help learners recalculate.

WORKBOOK

Unit 8, Exercise 8

Performance Check
How well can you use the skills in this unit?
....

Complete the activities. Go over your work with a partner or your teacher. Then complete the Performance Review on page 98.

SKILL 1   UNDERSTAND HEALTH BENEFITS

You work for Miguel's Body Shop. You have the following employee benefits: health insurance, dental insurance, disability insurance, and a sick leave policy that includes three paid sick days per year. Explain each benefit to your partner or your teacher.

SKILL 2   READ AND COMPARE BENEFIT PLANS

Read the health insurance plans. Then tell your partner or teacher which plan is better in the following categories: doctor's visits, hospital deductible, and doctor/hospital choices.

	National Health Care	State Health Plan
Doctor's Visit Copayment	$5	$15
Doctors/Hospitals	Any participating doctor or hospital	Any doctor or hospital
Hospital and emergency medical care	$300 deductible, pays 80% of expenses after deductible is paid	$500 deductible, pays 80% of expenses after deductible is paid

SKILL 3   UNDERSTAND YOUR RIGHTS

Read the article. Which sentences are correct? Circle the numbers.

Family and Medical Leave Act (FMLA)

Under the FMLA, eligible employees can take up to 12 weeks unpaid time off work to care for a new baby or a sick family member. Employees who have a serious illness can also take time off. During the leave, the employer is required to continue the employee's health benefits. After the leave, the employee can return to the old job or to a job with the same pay and benefits.

(1.) Under the FMLA, eligible employees can take time off if they have a serious illness.

2. If you take unpaid leave under the FMLA, you can lose your job or your health benefits.

Unit 8

97

PRESENTATION

Use any of the procedures in "Evaluation," page x, with pages 97 and 98. Record individuals' results on the Unit 8 Individual Competency Chart. Record the class's results on the Class Cumulative Competency Chart.

Complete the claim form using the situation below. Some information is already filled out. Use today's date.

Marty L. Rumman is a baggage handler for Blue Bird Bus Lines. He hurt his shoulder while lifting bags on October 12, 1999 at 5:45 P.M. The injury occurred at City Bus Station. The bag he was lifting was too heavy. Marty's address is 45 Willow Avenue, Los Angeles, California, 90040. His date of birth is March 14, 1979.

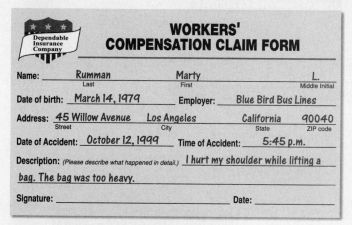

WORKERS' COMPENSATION CLAIM FORM

Dependable Insurance Company

Name: ___Rumman___   ___Marty___   ___L.___
            Last   First   Middle Initial

Date of birth: ___March 14, 1979___   Employer: ___Blue Bird Bus Lines___

Address: ___45 Willow Avenue___   ___Los Angeles___   ___California___   ___90040___
          Street   City   State   ZIP code

Date of Accident: ___October 12, 1999___   Time of Accident: ___5:45 p.m.___

Description: *(Please describe what happened in detail.)* ___I hurt my shoulder while lifting a___ ___bag. The bag was too heavy.___

Signature: _____   Date: _____

Performance Review

I can...

☐ 1. understand health benefits.

☐ 2. read and compare benefit plans.

☐ 3. understand my rights.

☐ 4. complete a claim form.

DISCUSSION

Work with a team. How will the skills help you? Make a list. Share the list with your class.

PRESENTATION

Follow the instructions on page 97.

INFORMAL WORKPLACE-SPECIFIC ASSESSMENT

Ask learners to describe health benefits they receive and the employee rights they are entitled to.

WORKBOOK

Unit 8, Exercise 9

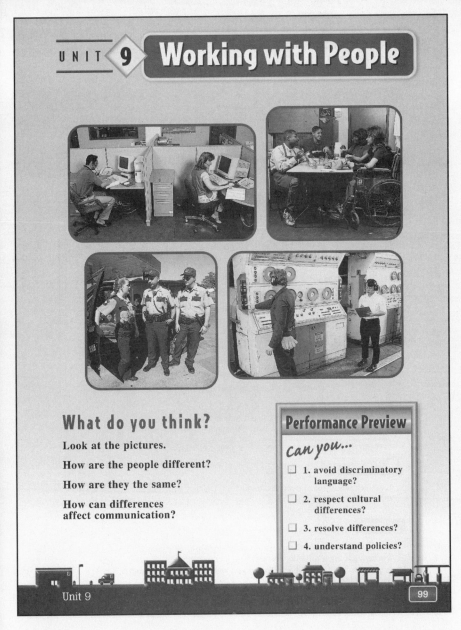

UNIT 9 — Working with People

What do you think?

Look at the pictures.

How are the people different?

How are they the same?

How can differences affect communication?

Performance Preview

Can you...

☐ 1. avoid discriminatory language?

☐ 2. respect cultural differences?

☐ 3. resolve differences?

☐ 4. understand policies?

Unit 9

Unit 9 Overview
—SCANS Competencies—

- Work well with people from culturally diverse backgrounds
- Understand social systems
- Negotiate
- Interpret information

Workforce Skills

- Avoid discriminatory language
- Respect cultural differences
- Resolve differences
- Understand policies

Materials

- Picture cards of culturally diverse people working together
- Picture cards of employees in appropriate and inappropriate dress
- Samples of a work schedule
- A picture card of a wedding and a wheelchair ramp

Unit Warm-Up

To get learners thinking about the unit topic (workers' rights), show photos of culturally diverse people working together. Discuss cultural diversity at learners' jobs.

★   ★   ★   ★   ★

WORKFORCE SKILLS (page 99)

Respect cultural differences

★   ★   ★   ★   ★

PREPARATION

Discuss with learners reasons people don't get along at work. Ask learners to name ways workers can get along better.

PRESENTATION

1. Focus attention on the photographs. Ask learners what the unit might be about. Write their ideas on the board and/or restate them in acceptable English.

2. Have learners talk about the pictures. Ask what's going on in each. Discuss how the employees in each photo are interacting.

3. Help learners read the questions. Discuss the questions with the class.

4. You may want to use the Performance Preview to provide learners with an overview of the skills in the unit. Have learners read the list of skills and discuss what they will learn in this unit.

FOLLOW-UP

Discussing Differences: Have teams create two-column charts with the columns labeled "challenging" and "rewarding." In the first column, teams should write things they find challenging about working with people from different backgrounds; in the second column, things they find rewarding. Post the charts. Discuss them with the class.

◆ Have teams create tables showing team members' cultural backgrounds.

Have teams share the tables and discuss the variety of cultures represented in the class.

WORKBOOK

Unit 9, Exercises 1A–1B

★　　★　　★　　★　　★

Getting Started ······ Avoiding discriminatory language

TEAM WORK

What do you know about avoiding discriminatory language?
Complete the survey.

Discrimination in the Workplace

Complete the following survey to find out how well you know how to avoid
discriminatory language. Write *yes* if the statement is appropriate. Write *no* if
the statement should be avoided.

___yes___ 1. We hired Ms. Grimes as the new office assistant because she scored the
highest on the typing test.

___no___ 2. Women are never allowed to work in the mail room. There's too much
heavy lifting.

___yes___ 3. This job involves taking orders from customers in Mexico, so the employee
needs to know Spanish.

___no___ 4. You were laid off instead of John because you're 63 years old. You'd
probably retire soon anyway.

___yes___ 5. There's a wheelchair ramp at the side door for employees with handicaps.

___yes___ 6. We have a new project coming up. The first three people who sign up can
start working on it.

___yes___ 7. We gave the big office to Tondra because she needs privacy for meetings
and interviews.

___no___ 8. Mauricio wasn't promoted because the job requires a lot of travel, and he
has young children. A parent shouldn't be away from home a lot.

DISCUSSION

Look at each of the statements marked *no*. Discuss what makes
the statements inappropriate.

SURVEY

Look at the results of the questions in Team Work. How many
learners got eight answers correct? seven correct? Make a bar
graph. Discuss the results. What do you want to learn in this unit
about avoiding discrimination?

100

Unit 9

Teaching Note

*Use this page to introduce the new
language in the unit. Whenever possible,
encourage peer teaching. Supply any
language the learners need.*

PREPARATION

1. To present or review new vocabulary,
draw or display a picture of a **wheelchair
ramp.** Role-play a job applicant taking
a **typing test.** Tell learners that many
workers **retire,** or stop working, when
they are 65 years of age.

2. Use picture cards of employees in
appropriate and **inappropriate** dress
to clarify the meanings of these words.

PRESENTATION

1. Have learners read and discuss
the Purpose Statement. See "Purpose
Statement," page viii.

2. Have teams read the Team Work
instructions. Remind the teams that they
are responsible for making sure that
each member understands the new
language. Then have teams complete

the activity. Have team reporters share
the teams' answers with the class. See
"Team Work," page viii.

3. Have learners read the Discussion
instructions and work in teams to talk
about their ideas. Have team reporters
share the ideas with the class.

4. Have teams read the Survey
instructions. Make sure everyone knows
what to do. Then have teams complete
the activity. The horizontal axis on
the graph should show the numbers 0
through 8; the vertical axis 0 through
the total number of learners in the class.
Have teams compare graphs. See
"Survey," page viii.

FOLLOW-UP

Questions: Have teams review the
Survey and write a list of questions

about avoiding discrimination that they
would like answered as they complete
the unit. Help the class make a master
list of all of the teams' questions.

◆ As a class, brainstorm more questions
to add to the list. Post the list for
learners to refer to as they work through
the unit.

WORKBOOK

Unit 9, Exercises 2A–2B

Talk About It ·· Resolving differences

 PRACTICE THE DIALOG

A Can I talk to you about your schedule?

B Sure, Claudia.

A Well, Sandra and Tony just asked for the weekend off, so I'd like you to work on Sunday morning. Can you do it?

B I'm sorry, but I can't. I asked for this weekend off a month ago for my sister's wedding.

A You're right. I forgot. I'll see if anyone else can come in on Sunday.

B Thanks.

PARTNER WORK

Discuss the following scenarios with your partner. Use the dialog above and the Useful Language.

1. Your partner at work always takes credit for work that you did together. You want to make sure your supervisor knows you did the work together.

2. You and your partner at work are supposed to go on break together. You want to go at 10:00. Your partner wants to go at 10:30.

Useful Language

I would like to talk about . . .

I think that's a good idea.

Maybe we can work something out.

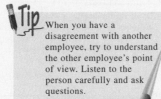

Tip When you have a disagreement with another employee, try to understand the other employee's point of view. Listen to the person carefully and ask questions.

ASAP
PROJECT

Work with a team. Make a list of rules for working together. Include rules for appropriate conduct, like being polite, and unacceptable conduct, such as improper jokes. Complete this project as you work through the unit.

Unit 9

`101`

WORKFORCE SKILLS (page 101)

Resolve differences

★   ★   ★   ★   ★

Language Note

Explain that using statements that start with "I," rather than "You," can be helpful in a conflict. Model examples, such as "I don't understand your directions," instead of "You don't make any sense," or "I hoped you'd be back by 10:30," instead of "You're late again." Have learners talk about how each statement would make them feel if directed at them.

ASAP
PROJECT

Have learners read the instructions. Discuss the project and its purpose with learners. Make sure that everyone understands. Help learners assign themselves to teams depending upon their skills, knowledge, interests, or other personal strengths. Have each team select a leader. Throughout the rest of the unit, allow time for learners to work on the project. Have the teams agree on a deadline when the project will be finished. For more information see "ASAP Project" on page vi.

PREPARATION

1. Use picture cards or realia to present or review **schedule** and **wedding.**

2. To present or review **takes credit for,** role-play an employee who doesn't help with a task but then accepts praise or claims to have done the work.

PRESENTATION

1. Have learners read and discuss the Purpose Statement. See "Purpose Statement," page viii.

 2. Have learners preview the dialog. Encourage them to say as much as they can about it. Then present the dialog. See "Presenting a Dialog" on page ix.

 3. Have partners read the Partner Work instructions. Focus attention on the Useful Language box. If necessary, model pronunciation of the phrases. Then have partners complete the activity. Have a few pairs present their dialogs to the class.

Tip Have learners read the Tip independently. Have them discuss how the advice will help them. See "Presenting a Tip," page ix.

FOLLOW-UP

Conflict Resolution: Write five common workplace conflicts on slips of paper, such as: You feel you do more work than your coworker; your coworker doesn't replace materials when they are used up; you both want the early shift;

your coworker leaves early every day without permission; your coworker doesn't tell you important information. Divide the class into five teams. Each team should select a slip and think of ways to resolve the conflict. Ask team reporters to share the teams' ideas with the class.

♦ Have teams role-play workers resolving the conflict. Have teams present their role-plays to the class.

WORKBOOK

Unit 9, Exercises 3A–3B

WORKFORCE SKILLS (page 102)

Respect cultural differences

Resolve differences

★　　★　　★　　★　　★

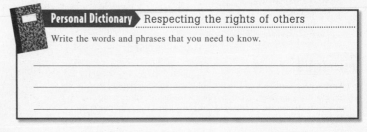

Personal Dictionary

Have learners add the words in their Personal Dictionary to their *Workforce Writing Dictionary*. For more information see "Workforce Writing Dictionary" on page v.

Keep Talking   Respecting cultural differences

TEAM WORK

Ed works at Friendly Used Cars. He always speaks very loudly to customers who look like they are from a different country. Sometimes, the customers seem angry and leave very quickly. What mistake is Ed making?

DISCUSSION

Ed doesn't understand why his customers sometimes leave very quickly. He's asked for your advice. What do you tell him? Use the Useful Language. Share your ideas with the class.

Useful Language

It bothers people when . . .

It might help if you . . .

Personal Dictionary   Respecting the rights of others

Write the words and phrases that you need to know.

_____

_____

_____

102   Unit 9

PREPARATION

To present or review **bother,** act out annoyance in reponse to music you don't like. Say, "That music bothers me."

PRESENTATION

1. Have learners read and discuss the Purpose Statement. See "Purpose Statement," page viii.

2. Focus attention on the illustration. Encourage learners to say as much as they can about it. Help them identify the occupation depicted. Have them say what they think the lesson is about.

3. Have teams read the Team Work instructions. Make sure everyone knows what to do. Then have teams complete the activity. Have teams present their ideas to the class.

4. Have learners read the Discussion instructions. Focus attention on the Useful Language box. If necessary, model pronunciation of the phrases. Make sure everyone knows what to do. Then have learners work in pairs to talk about their ideas. Have several pairs share their ideas with the class.

5. Have learners read the Personal Dictionary instructions. Then use the Personal Dictionary procedures on page ix. Remind learners to add words to their dictionaries throughout the unit.

FOLLOW-UP

Working It Out: Have learners work in teams. Ask them to think of behaviors in the workplace that bother them. Have team members discuss why the actions bother them and what they could say to

employees who act that way. Ask team reporters to share the ideas with the class.

♦ Have partners chose one of the behaviors their team discussed. Ask them to write a dialog in which one employee speaks to the other about his or her behavior. Have several pairs read their dialogs to the class.

WORKBOOK

Unit 9, Exercises 4A–4B

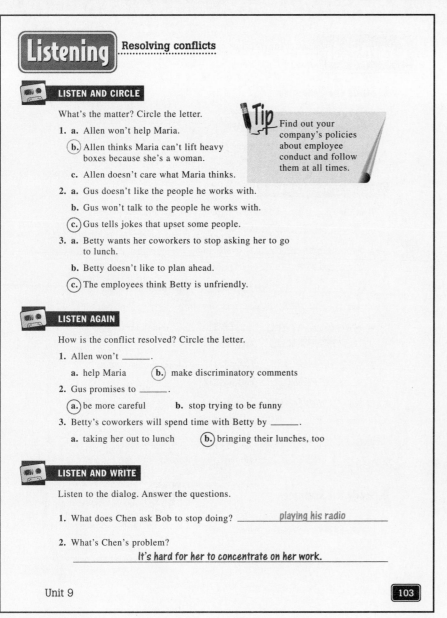

Listening · Resolving conflicts

LISTEN AND CIRCLE

What's the matter? Circle the letter.

1. **a.** Allen won't help Maria.

   b. Allen thinks Maria can't lift heavy boxes because she's a woman. *(circled)*

   c. Allen doesn't care what Maria thinks.

2. **a.** Gus doesn't like the people he works with.

   b. Gus won't talk to the people he works with.

   c. Gus tells jokes that upset some people. *(circled)*

3. **a.** Betty wants her coworkers to stop asking her to go to lunch.

   b. Betty doesn't like to plan ahead.

   c. The employees think Betty is unfriendly. *(circled)*

> **Tip** Find out your company's policies about employee conduct and follow them at all times.

LISTEN AGAIN

How is the conflict resolved? Circle the letter.

1. Allen won't _____.

   a. help Maria   **b.** make discriminatory comments *(circled)*

2. Gus promises to _____.

   a. be more careful *(circled)*   **b.** stop trying to be funny

3. Betty's coworkers will spend time with Betty by _____.

   a. taking her out to lunch   **b.** bringing their lunches, too *(circled)*

LISTEN AND WRITE

Listen to the dialog. Answer the questions.

1. What does Chen ask Bob to stop doing? _____ *playing his radio*

2. What's Chen's problem?

   It's hard for her to concentrate on her work.

Unit 9   `103`

SCANS Note

Suggest that learners make sure they understand a coworker's concerns before they respond. Explain that if they are in doubt about what a coworker said, they should restate the concern in their own words and ask if they've understood correctly. Role-play this strategy with several learners.

PREPARATION

1. To review or present **inappropriate,** follow the suggestions in Preparation on page 100.

2. Explain that **discriminatory language** describes negative words and phrases directed against specific groups of people.

PRESENTATION

1. Have learners read and discuss the Purpose Statement. For more information see "Purpose Statement" on page viii.

 2. Have learners read the Listen and Circle instructions. Then have them read the items. Make sure that everyone understands the instructions. If necessary, model the first item. Then play the tape or read the Listening Transcript aloud two or more times as learners complete the activity. Check learners' work. For more information see "Presenting a Listening Activity" on page ix.

 3. Have learners read the Listen Again instructions. Then follow the procedures in 2.

 4. Have learners read the Listen and Write instructions. Then follow the procedures in 2.

Tip Have learners read the Tip independently. Have them discuss how the advice will help them. For more information, see "Presenting a Tip" on page ix.

FOLLOW-UP

Making a Suggestion: Have learners work in pairs. Have partners take turns telling each other about conflicts they've had with coworkers and suggesting ways to resolve the conflicts. Have several pairs present their dialogs to the class.

♦ Have learners change partners and repeat the activity two times. Have learners decide which of the different suggestions they received they would try first. Have several learners present situations and solutions to the class.

WORKBOOK

Unit 9, Exercise 5

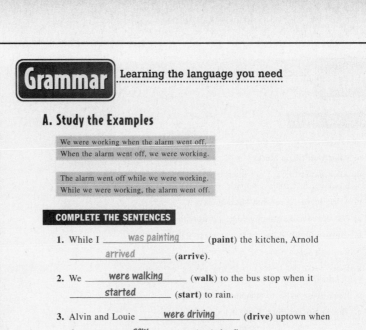

PREPARATION

Review the language in the grammar boxes with learners before they open their books, if necessary.

PRESENTATION

1. Have learners read and discuss the Purpose Statement. For more information see "Purpose Statement" on page viii.

2. Have learners read the grammar boxes in A. Have learners use the language in the boxes to say as many sentences as possible. Tell learners that they can use the grammar boxes throughout the unit to review or check sentence structures.

3. Focus attention on the Complete the Sentences activity. Make sure learners know what to do. If necessary, model the first item. Allow learners to complete

the activity. Have learners check each other's work in pairs. Ask several learners to read their answers aloud while the rest of the class checks their work.

4. Focus attention on the grammar boxes in B. Follow the procedures in 2.

Tip Have learners read the Tip independently. Have learners discuss how the advice will help them. For more information, see "Presenting a Tip" on page ix.

COMPLETE THE SENTENCES

Write about your workplace or school. Use the language in B.

1. After I arrived at work, _____ *I put on my uniform* _____.

2. After I spoke with my boss, _____ **Answers will vary.** _____.

3. I took a break before _____.

4. I checked my work after _____.

5. Before we left, _____.

6. I went to lunch after _____.

C. Study the Examples

Paul's workspace	is	as	large	as	John's workspace.
	isn't		small		
			nice		

COMPLETE THE SENTENCES

Use the language in C.

1. Andrea's work is _____ *as good as* _____ (**good**) Ali's work.

2. Is this mower _____ *as powerful as* _____ (**powerful**) the other one?

3. The back elevator is *n't as fast as* _____ (**not fast**) the front one.

4. The scissors are _____ *as expensive as* _____ (**expensive**) the stapler.

5. Is your new uniform _____ *as comfortable as* _____ (**comfortable**) your old one?

6. Today I'm _____ *not as busy as* _____ (**not busy**) Roy, so I'm going to help him with his work.

7. The blue pants are _____ *as long as* _____ (**long**) the brown pants.

 TEAM WORK

Talk about your workplace or school. Use the language in C.

Unit 9 — 105

---

 5. Have learners read the instructions for Complete the Sentences. Then follow the procedures in 3.

6. Focus attention on the grammar box in C and follow the procedures in 2.

7. Have learners read the instructions for Complete the Sentences. Then follow the procedures in 3.

8. Have teams read the Team Work instructions. Make sure each team knows what to do. If necessary, model the activity. Then have teams complete the activity. Ask team reporters to summarize the discussions for the class.

FOLLOW-UP

Sentences: Go around the room and have each learner state a task he or she did at work at the same time a coworker did a different task, such as: "While Tranh was sweeping the sidewalk, I mowed the lawn."

♦ Place a number of familiar classroom objects on display, for example, pencils, books, ruler, stapler, scissors, and chalk. Ask teams to compare the objects by writing as many sentences as they can, using the language in C. Provide examples such as: "The red book isn't as big as the blue book," and "The yellow pencil is as long as the ruler." Have teams compare sentences.

WORKBOOK

Unit 9, Exercises 6A–6C

BLACKLINE MASTERS

Blackline Master: Unit 9

READ THE POLICY AGAINST HARASSMENT

★ STAR MANUFACTURING　*Policy Against Harassment*

Employees and customers have a right to be in an environment without the fear of physical, psychological, or verbal harassment. To protect our employees and customers, the following types of actions are prohibited:

★ insulting language or gestures.

★ inappropriate jokes; especially jokes that refer to gender, race, religion, nationality, or disability.

★ unwanted physical contact.

★ other offensive behavior that is not mentioned in this list.

If you have any questions, call Human Resources.

WRITE

Are the people's actions OK? Write *yes* or *no*.

__yes__ 1. Maria waves goodbye when she leaves work at the end of the day.

__no__ 2. Ed likes to tell jokes about people of different religions.

__no__ 3. Rick always says that he thinks people from other countries are stupid.

__yes__ 4. Salespeople usually shake hands with new customers.

__no__ 5. Todd always tells jokes about people from foreign countries.

__yes__ 6. Julie enjoys working with people from other countries because she can learn about their cultures.

__yes__ 7. Veronica helped a visitor find the wheelchair entrance.

__yes__ 8. Shirley helps coworkers who don't understand English very well.

106　　　　　　　　　　　　　　　　　　Unit 9

Culture Note

Explain that the law requires all companies to protect employees from discrimination and harassment. Many companies display their policies so employees can read them. Ask learners if they know their company's policies.

PREPARATION

1. Clarify the meaning of **harassment** by saying that telling jokes about people from other cultures is a form of harassment.

2. Explain that **unions** are organizations of workers that work to protect workers' rights. Find out if any learners are members of unions.

3. Give examples of conditions that qualify as **disabilities,** such as the need to use a wheelchair or difficulty seeing or hearing.

PRESENTATION

1. Have learners read and discuss the Purpose Statement. For more information see "Purpose Statement" on page viii.

2. Have learners preview the Policy Against Harassment before they read.

For more information, see "Prereading" on page x. Encourage learners to say everything they can about it. Write their ideas on the board and/or restate them in acceptable English. Then have learners read the policy independently.

3. Have learners read the instructions for Write. Make sure everyone knows what to do. If necessary, model the first item. Then have learners complete the activity. Ask several learners to share their answers with the class while the rest of the class checks their work.

READ

Labor Laws Protect You

Many federal laws protect the rights of employees. The National Labor Relations Act lets employees start and belong to unions. The law stops companies from discriminating against employees who are in unions. Two Civil Rights Acts say that hiring and promotion cannot be based upon age, gender, race, religion, or national background. In addition, the Americans with Disabilities Act prevents discrimination against employees who have disabilities.

MATCH

Which law protects the people? Write the letter.

a. **National Labor Relations Act**

b. **Civil Rights Act**

c. **Americans with Disabilities Act**

___b___ 1. Tom is a Native American.

___a___ 2. The workers at Lisa's company are in a union.

___b___ 3. Manuel was born in a foreign country.

___c___ 4. Mark uses a wheelchair.

___b___ 5. Christine is a twenty-year-old woman.

DISCUSSION

Which of these laws will help you? Why do you think so? What do you think happens to companies that break these laws?

Unit 9

---

4. Focus attention on the article and follow the procedures in 2.

5. Have learners read the Match instructions. Make sure everyone knows what to do. Then have learners complete the activity. Check learners' work.

6. Have learners read the Discussion instructions and talk about the questions in pairs. Have several pairs share their ideas with the class.

FOLLOW-UP

Using Available Resources: Have teams discuss resources they can use when resolving conflicts at work. Can they talk with their supervisors or Human Resources managers? Have team reporters share their teams' ideas with the class.

♦ Have learners work in pairs to create dialogs in which employees who believe they are being harassed talk to their supervisors or Human Resources managers. Ask several pairs to present their dialogs to the class.

WORKBOOK

Unit 9, Exercises 7A–7B

WORKFORCE SKILLS (page 108)

Resolve differences

Understand policies

★   ★   ★   ★   ★

Language Note

*Suggest that learners look for answers to the questions **who, what, when, where, why,** and **how** as they read news articles. Ask learners to find answers to these questions in the article on the Student Book page.*

Extension | Dealing with discrimination

READ THE NEWS ARTICLE

★★★★★
FEATURES SECTION 2 | The City Tribune | **FORECAST** HIGH 72 LOW 56

Navajo Woman Files a Discrimination Suit

Luci Yava is a Navajo woman who filed a discrimination suit. She claims that in her five years of employment at Capital Corporation she was not given a promotion. The Equal Employment Opportunity Commission (EEOC) is taking her case to court.

While Ms. Yava worked for five years without a promotion, other employees with less experience were promoted. None of the workers who received promotions was from a minority background.

When Ms. Yava's supervisor refused to discuss the issue, Ms. Yava called the Human Rights Commission. The Human Rights Commission referred her case to the EEOC. The EEOC was established by the Civil Rights Act of 1964. This law prohibits discrimination based on a person's color, race, national origin, or gender.

While her case is being decided, Luci Yava continues to work at Capital Corporation.

ANSWER THE QUESTIONS

1. Who is taking Luci Yava's case to court? ___the EEOC___

2. What is the EEOC? ___the Equal Employment Opportunity Commission___

3. Who did Luci Yava contact after she spoke with her supervisor?
___the Human Rights Commission___

4. Why is Luci Yava filing a lawsuit? ___She feels she was not promoted because of racial discrimination.___

 **Culture Notes**

At your workplace, the boss asks Martha to work overtime every weekend. He says it's because Martha doesn't have children. All the other employees have children. Martha doesn't like to work overtime every weekend. What should she do?

108   Unit 9

PREPARATION

Explain that the **Human Rights Commission** protects basic rights and freedoms in the U.S.; the **Civil Rights Act** prohibits discrimination; and the **Equal Employment Opportunity Commission (EEOC)** handles discrimination cases.

PRESENTATION

1. Have learners read and discuss the Purpose Statement. See "Purpose Statement," page viii.

2. Have learners preview the article. For more information, see "Prereading" on page x. Encourage them to say everything they can about it. Write their ideas on the board and/or restate them in acceptable English. Then have learners read the article independently.

3. Focus attention on the Answer the Questions activity. If necessary, model the first item. Then have learners complete the activity. Have learners review each other's work in pairs. Have several learners read their answers aloud while the rest of the class checks their work.

 4. Have learners read Culture Notes and talk over their ideas in teams. Have team reporters share the ideas with the class. See "Culture Notes," page vii.

FOLLOW-UP

What to Do: Have team members discuss times they have had to deal with discriminatory situations at work. How did they handle the situations? Have team reporters summarize the discussions for the class.

♦ Have partners reread the news article. Ask them to discuss whether or not they think Ms. Yava's supervisor acted appropriately. What else might he or she have done? Why might a supervisor refuse to discuss an issue? Have several pairs present their conversations to the class.

WORKBOOK

Unit 9, Exercise 8

Performance Check
How well can you use the skills in this unit?

Complete the activities. Go over your work with a partner or your teacher. Then complete the Performance Review on page 110.

SKILL 1 **AVOID DISCRIMINATORY LANGUAGE**

Read the statements below. Write *yes* if the statement is appropriate in the workplace. Write *no* if the statement is inappropriate.

_no_ 1. Let me help you lift those boxes. A woman could get hurt doing that.

_no_ 2. We only hire Spanish speakers to work in the factory.

yes 3. We want to hire someone who can type.

_no_ 4. We gave the promotion to Josephine because she's younger.

SKILL 2 **RESPECT CULTURAL DIFFERENCES**

Linda is the plant manager. She uses gestures instead of words to communicate with employees who look like they are from another country. She notices that some employees seem to avoid her and don't ask her questions. What advice can you give her? Tell a partner or your teacher.

SKILL 3 **RESOLVE DIFFERENCES**

Discuss one of the following scenarios with your partner or teacher. Tell your partner or teacher what you will say to your coworker.

1. Your coworker tells jokes about people from other countries. You don't like the jokes, and you think other people also feel uncomfortable.

2. Your partner at work always takes the best jobs. You have to do the other jobs. Talk to your partner about making a plan to share the best jobs.

Unit 9

109

PRESENTATION

Use any of the procedures in "Evaluation," page x, with pages 109 and 110. Record individuals' results on the Unit 9 Individual Competency Chart. Record the class's results on the Class Cumulative Competency Chart.

BEST INDUSTRIES
Policy Against Harassment

To protect our employees and customers from physical, psychological, or verbal harassment, the following types of behavior are prohibited:

- Insulting gestures or language.
- Inappropriate jokes, especially jokes that refer to gender or culture.
- Unwanted physical contact.
- Other offensive behavior that may not be mentioned in this list.

If you feel that you are being harassed, please file a complaint report with the director of Human Resources. All reported incidents will be investigated promptly and may result in disciplinary action and/or dismissal.

Are the people's actions OK? Write *yes* or *no*.

__yes__ **1.** Manuel waves hello to everyone when he arrives for work.

__no__ **2.** Bob always tells jokes about different religions.

__yes__ **3.** Mark likes to meet workers from other countries.

Performance Review

I can...

❏ **1.** avoid discriminatory language.

❏ **2.** respect cultural differences.

❏ **3.** resolve differences.

❏ **4.** understand policies.

DISCUSSION

Work with a team. How will the skills help you? Make a list. Share the list with your class.

110

Unit 9

PRESENTATION

Follow the instructions on page 109.

INFORMAL WORKPLACE-SPECIFIC ASSESSMENT

Ask learners to discuss what they would do to resolve a conflict with someone at work.

WORKBOOK

Unit 9, Exercise 9

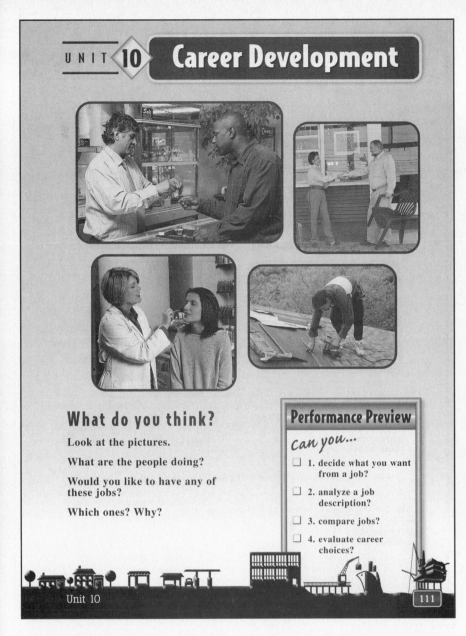

- Interpret and communicate information
- Acquire and evaluate data
- Organize and maintain files
- Understand social systems

Workforce Skills

- Decide what you want from a job
- Analyze a job description
- Compare jobs
- Evaluate career choices

Materials

- A sample job description; help wanted ads
- Picture cards of a dog groomer, veterinary assistant, florist, flower arrangement, factory, and warehouse

Unit Warm-Up

To stimulate discussion about the unit topic (jobs and careers), act out looking at and circling help-wanted ads. Read a few to the class and think aloud about whether or not the jobs are right for you. Ask learners how they decide if a job in an ad might be a job they'd like.

★　　★　　★　　★　　★

WORKFORCE SKILLS (page 111)

Decide what you want from a job

★　　★　　★　　★　　★

PREPARATION

1. Display and identify a **job description.** Ask learners to talk about the kind of information in it.

2. Ask learners to name jobs they consider good. What makes a job good? How can they get one of these jobs?

PRESENTATION

1. Focus attention on the photographs. Ask learners to say what the unit might be about. Write their ideas on the board and/or restate them in acceptable English.

2. Have learners talk about the photos. Ask them to describe what is going on

in each picture and help them identify the people's occupations. Ask which jobs appeal to them and why.

3. Help learners read the questions. Discuss the questions with the class.

4. You may want to use the Performance Preview to provide learners with an overview of the skills in the unit. Have learners read the list of skills and discuss what they will learn in this unit.

FOLLOW-UP

The Kind of Job You Want: Have partners ask each other these two questions:

1. What do you want in a job?

2. What jobs do you think might give you what you want?

Ask several pairs to present their dialogs to the class.

♦ Have partners write their dialogs. Check their work.

WORKBOOK

Unit 10, Exercises 1A–1B

WORKFORCE SKILLS (page 112)

Decide what you want from a job

Analyze a job description

Compare jobs

★　　★　　★　　★　　★

Teaching Note

Use this page to introduce the new language in the unit. Whenever possible, encourage peer teaching. Supply any language learners need.

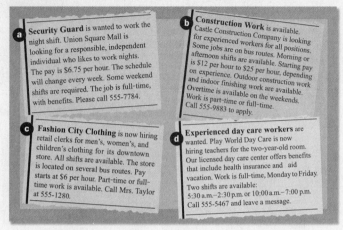

Getting Started — Talking about different jobs

TEAM WORK

Read the help wanted ads. Write the letter of the jobs that would be good for each person. Think of other jobs that would be good for them.

a **Security Guard** is wanted to work the night shift. Union Square Mall is looking for a responsible, independent individual who likes to work nights. The pay is $6.75 per hour. The schedule will change every week. Some weekend shifts are required. The job is full-time, with benefits. Please call 555-7784.

b **Construction Work** is available. Castle Construction Company is looking for experienced workers for all positions. Some jobs are on bus routes. Morning or afternoon shifts are available. Starting pay is $12 per hour to $25 per hour, depending on experience. Outdoor construction work and indoor finishing work are available. Overtime is available on the weekends. Work is part-time or full-time. Call 555-9883 to apply.

c **Fashion City Clothing** is now hiring retail clerks for men's, women's, and children's clothing for its downtown store. All shifts are available. The store is located on several bus routes. Pay starts at $6 per hour. Part-time or full-time work is available. Call Mrs. Taylor at 555-1280.

d **Experienced day care workers** are wanted. Play World Day Care is now hiring teachers for the two-year-old room. Our licensed day care center offers benefits that include health insurance and aid vacation. Work is full-time, Monday to Friday. Two shifts are available: 5:30 a.m.–2:30 p.m. or 10:00 a.m.–7:00 p.m. Call 555-5467 and leave a message.

_b, c_ **1.** Chang needs a job that he can get to on the bus.

_b_ **3.** Ben is looking for a job where he can work outside.

_b, c, d_ **2.** Janey likes to work with other people.

_c_ **4.** Maria wants to work downtown.

PARTNER WORK

Student A describes a kind of job he or she wants. Student B suggests a job. Talk about the companies in the ads or other companies.

A I like working outdoors.

B You should apply to Castle Construction Company.

 SURVEY

As a team, make a list of ten things people look for in a job, such as daytime hours or a location on a bus route. Talk to other learners. Find out who wants each job. Report to the class.

112　　　　　　　　　　　　　　　　　　Unit 10

PREPARATION

Display the help wanted ads and help learners identify key phrases used in the ads, such as **experienced, shift, part-time, full-time,** and **overtime.** Ask learners familiar with these concepts to explain them to the class.

PRESENTATION

1. Have learners read and discuss the Purpose Statement. See "Purpose Statement," page viii.

2. Focus attention on the help wanted ads. Encourage learners to say as much as they can about them. Write their ideas on the board.

3. Have teams read the Team Work instructions. Remind the teams that they are responsible for making sure that each member understands the new

language. Then have teams complete the activity. Have teams compare ideas.

4. Have partners read the Partner Work instructions. Make sure each pair knows what to do. If necessary, model the activity. Then have partners complete the activity. Have learners switch partners and repeat the activity. Have several pairs present their dialogs to the class. See "Partner Work," page viii.

5. Have teams read the Survey instructions. Then have teams complete the activity. Have team reporters share the lists with the class. See "Survey," page viii.

FOLLOW-UP

Bar Graph: Help the class use the information from the Survey to create a master list of qualities learners look for

in a job. Write the list on the board. Poll learners and write the number who look for each one.

◆ Have teams create bar graphs to show the information on the board. The horizontal axis should show the different qualities. The vertical axis should show the number of learners who look for each. Post the graphs in the classroom.

WORKBOOK

Unit 10, Exercises 2A–2B

Talk About It · Comparing jobs

Veterinary Assistant

Successful candidate will:
- have at least two years' experience working with animals
- be able to work full time Monday to Friday, 6:30 A.M. to 3:30 P.M.
- have a professional attitude and positive outlook
- be able to work well with customers and pets in a busy office
- be able to work without supervision
- be able to lift at least 50 pounds

Pay is $7.50 per hour plus health insurance

Dog Groomer

We are looking for an experienced dog groomer who:
- has at least one year's experience in a professional grooming shop
- can work Tuesday to Friday, 11:00 A.M. to 8:00 P.M. and Saturday, 9:00 A.M. to 5:00 P.M.
- has a cheerful disposition and works well with customers and dogs
- can schedule time and meet deadlines
- is relaxed and comfortable with animals

Pay is $8.50 per hour.

 PRACTICE THE DIALOG

A I can't believe it. Today I got two job offers: one as a veterinary assistant, the other as a dog groomer.

B That's great news. Which one are you going to take?

A I'm not sure. They both sound good. I have to decide what hours I want to work. The veterinary assistant job starts early in the morning. The dog grooming job begins later, but I'd have to work Saturdays.

B Is the pay the same?

A It's about the same. The assistant job pays a little less, but the benefits are better. Choosing between the two jobs won't be easy.

Now compare the two jobs. Talk about how she can decide which job to take. Use the dialog above and the Useful Language.

Useful Language

This job has better . . .

Both jobs offer . . .

That job doesn't provide . . .

ASAP PROJECT

Make a job search portfolio. Include a list of your job skills and a list of your previous employers' names, addresses, and phone numbers, supervisors' names, job duties, and dates of employment. Include samples of projects and assignments from this class. Complete the project as you work through the unit.

Unit 10

`113`

PREPARATION

1. If necessary, review what a **job description** is. Follow the procedures in Preparation on page 111.

2. Use pantomime to review or present the new language in the job descriptions: **professional attitude, cheerful disposition,** and **relaxed.** Use picture cards and/or explanation to present or review **veterinary assistant** and **dog groomer.**

PRESENTATION

1. Have learners read and discuss the Purpose Statement. For more information see "Purpose Statement" on page viii.

 2. Focus attention on the job postings. Encourage learners to say as much as they can about them. Write learners' ideas on the board and/or restate them in acceptable English. Then present the dialog. See "Presenting a Dialog" on page ix.

3. Have partners read the instructions that follow the dialog. Focus attention on the Useful Language box. If necessary, model pronunciation. Make sure each pair knows what to do. Then have learners complete the activity. Have learners switch partners and repeat the activity. Have one or two pairs present their dialogs to the class.

FOLLOW-UP

Making Decisions: Have pairs role-play situations in which one individual is trying to choose between two different job offers and the other asks questions about the jobs. If one partner has been in this situation, encourage the pair to use the experience as the basis of the role-play. Have several pairs present their role-plays to the class.

♦ Have teams brainstorm resources for information about jobs. Who can they ask for information? Where can they find information? What are some questions they can ask? Have teams share ideas.

WORKBOOK

Unit 10, Exercises 3A–3B

ASAP PROJECT

Have learners read the instructions. Discuss the project and its purpose with learners. Make sure that everyone understands. Help learners assign themselves to teams for help and advice preparing their individual portfolios. Throughout the rest of the unit, allow time for learners to work on the project. Have the teams agree on a deadline when all learners will finish their portfolios. For more information see "ASAP Project" on page vi.

WORKFORCE SKILLS (page 114)

Decide what you want from a job

★   ★   ★   ★   ★

Keep Talking

Deciding what you want from a job

 PRACTICE THE DIALOG

A What's important to you in a job, Ernesto?

B I'd like a job that has evening hours. That way I can take care of my children while my wife is at work.

A Would you be interested in a job as a delivery truck driver?

B I don't think so. I'd like a job working with people.

A Maybe you should think about being a waiter. You'd work with people and make good money waiting on tables.

B That's a good idea. Do you have any openings listed?

 PARTNER WORK

Student A describes a job. Student B tells whether he or she wants the job. Use the dialog above.

 Personal Dictionary ▶ Building Your Career

Write the words and phrases that you need to know.

_____

_____

114   Unit 10

Personal Dictionary

Have learners add the words in their Personal Dictionary to their *Workforce Writing Dictionary*. For more information see "Workforce Writing Dictionary" on page v.

PREPARATION

Explain that a **job counselor** is someone who helps people decide what kinds of jobs and careers they want to pursue. Ask learners who have worked with job counselors to describe their experiences.

PRESENTATION

1. Have learners read and discuss the Purpose Statement. For more information see "Purpose Statement" on page viii.

 2. Focus attention on the photograph. Encourage learners to say as much as they can about it. Have them identify the people and say what they think they are talking about. Write learners' ideas on the board and/or restate them in acceptable English. Then present the

dialog. See "Presenting a Dialog" on page ix.

3. Have partners read the Partner Work instructions. Make sure each pair knows what to do. If necessary, model the activity. Then have partners complete the activity. Have learners switch partners and repeat the activity. Have one or two pairs present their dialogs to the class.

4. Have learners read the Personal Dictionary instructions. Then use the Personal Dictionary procedures on page ix. Remind learners to continue to add words to their dictionaries throughout the unit.

FOLLOW-UP

Role-Play: Have learners work in pairs to create role-plays in which one learner is a job counselor and the other describes the kind of job he or she would like. Have several pairs present their role-plays to the class.

◆ Divide the class into teams. Ask team members to discuss what they like about their current jobs and what they would like in their next jobs. Have team reporters summarize the discussions for the class.

WORKBOOK

Unit 10, Exercises 4A–4B

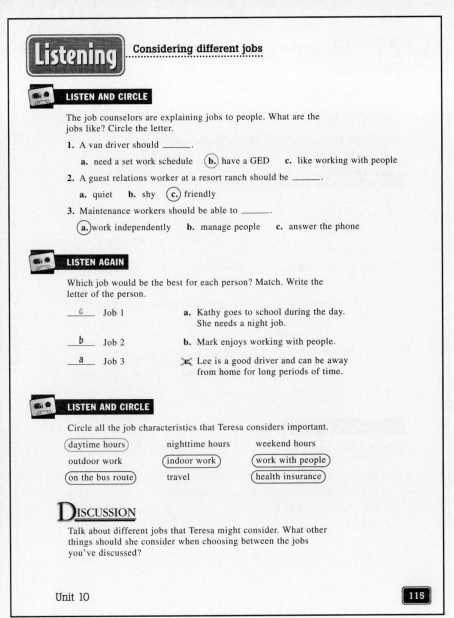

Listening
Considering different jobs

LISTEN AND CIRCLE

The job counselors are explaining jobs to people. What are the jobs like? Circle the letter.

1. A van driver should _____.

   a. need a set work schedule   **(b.)** have a GED   **c.** like working with people

2. A guest relations worker at a resort ranch should be _____.

   a. quiet   **b.** shy   **(c.)** friendly

3. Maintenance workers should be able to _____.

   (a.) work independently   **b.** manage people   **c.** answer the phone

LISTEN AGAIN

Which job would be the best for each person? Match. Write the letter of the person.

  _c_ Job 1   **a.** Kathy goes to school during the day. She needs a night job.

  _b_ Job 2   **b.** Mark enjoys working with people.

  _a_ Job 3   ~~**c.**~~ Lee is a good driver and can be away from home for long periods of time.

LISTEN AND CIRCLE

Circle all the job characteristics that Teresa considers important.

(daytime hours)   nighttime hours   weekend hours

outdoor work   (indoor work)   (work with people)

(on the bus route)   travel   (health insurance)

Discussion

Talk about different jobs that Teresa might consider. What other things should she consider when choosing between the jobs you've discussed?

Unit 10   **115**

WORKFORCE SKILLS (page 115)

Compare jobs

★   ★   ★   ★   ★

PREPARATION

1. To present or review **job counselor,** follow the procedures in Preparation on page 114.

2. Have learners brainstorm phrases that describe jobs, such as "daytime hours" and "regular schedule." Write the phrases on the board and clarify meanings, if necessary.

PRESENTATION

1. Have learners read and discuss the Purpose Statement. See "Purpose Statement," page viii.

 2. Have learners read the Listen and Circle instructions and the items. Use peer-teaching to clarify any unfamiliar vocabulary. Then play the tape or read the Listening Transcript aloud two or

more times as learners complete the activity. Have learners check their work as you read the answers aloud.

 3. Have learners read the Listen Again instructions. Then follow the procedures in 2.

 4. Have learners read the Listen and Circle instructions. Then follow the procedures in 2.

5. Have teams read the Discussion instructions. Make sure everyone knows what to do. Then have teams complete the activity. Have team reporters share their teams' ideas with the class.

FOLLOW-UP

The Ideal Employee: Give each pair of learners a slip of paper with a job on it. Ask them to write a list of characteristics

an ideal employee in that job ought to have. Have partners read their lists to the class.

♦ Have learners tell the class one thing they'd really like in a job, such as "talk on the phone," or "work with computers." As each learner identifies what he or she would like, have the class brainstorm possible jobs.

WORKBOOK

Unit 10, Exercise 5

Unit 10   115

WORKFORCE SKILLS
(pages 116–117)

Compare jobs

Evaluate career choices

★   ★   ★   ★   ★

Language Note

*Help learners understand words and phrases that appear in ads or job descriptions, such as **entry-level**, **salaried**, and **advancement opportunities**. Start a list on the board. Ask learners to add other words.*

Grammar — Learning the language you need

A. Study the Examples

Have you ever worked in a restaurant?

Yes, I have. I worked for Antonio's Restaurant from 1998 to 1999.
No, I haven't. I've never worked in a restaurant.

COMPLETE THE SENTENCES

Use the language in A.

1. Alana *'s never driven* (drive, never) a delivery van.

2. *Have* you *ever given* (give, ever) a dog a bath?

    Yes, I *have* (have).

3. Millie *'s never written* (write, never) a resume.

4. *Have* the bakers *ever made* (make, ever) a large wedding cake?

    No, they *haven't* (have, not).

    They *'ve never made* (make, never) a wedding cake.

5. *Have* you *ever driven* (drive, ever) a bus?

    Yes, I *have* (have).

ANSWER THE QUESTIONS

Write about yourself. Use the language in A. Write the answers on a sheet of paper.

1. Have you ever used a computer?
2. Have you ever worked as an electronics assembler?
3. Have you ever repaired a copier?
4. Have you ever been a cashier?
5. Have you ever arrived late to work?
6. Have you ever worked in a factory?
7. Have you ever worked in a warehouse?

116

Unit 10

PREPARATION

1. Review the language in the grammar boxes with learners before they open their books, if necessary.

2. Use picture cards to present or review **factory** and **warehouse**.

PRESENTATION

1. Have learners read and discuss the Purpose Statement. For more information see "Purpose Statement" on page viii.

2. Have learners read the grammar boxes in A. Have learners use the language in the boxes to say as many sentences as possible. Tell learners that they can use the grammar boxes throughout the unit to review or check sentence structures.

3. Have learners read the instructions for Complete the Sentences. Make sure learners know what to do. If necessary, model the first item. Allow learners to complete the activity. Have learners check each other's work in pairs. Ask several learners to read their completed sentences aloud while the rest of the class checks their work.

4. Have learners read the instructions for Answer the Questions. Make sure everyone knows what to do. If necessary, model the first item. Then have learners complete the activity. Ask several learners to read their sentences to the class.

B. Study the Examples

It's	going to	take four hours to fix your car.
I'm		learn how to drive a city bus.
There's		be a change in next week's schedule.

COMPLETE THE SENTENCES

Use *going to*.

1. I'm really hungry. I *'m going to eat lunch now* _____ .

2. Pablo just arrived at the hotel. He _____ *Answers will vary.* _____ .

3. I don't know how to use a computer. I _____ .

4. We looked up his phone number. We _____ .

5. It's cool and cloudy. I think _____ .

C. Study the Example

If I have time this year, I'll take a computer class.

WRITE

Give the correct form of the verb.

1. If you _____ *ask* _____ (**ask**) him,

   Alan *'ll show* _____ (**show**) you how to use the dishwasher.

2. If they _____ *paint* _____ (**paint**) the living room,

   they *'ll move* _____ (**move**) the furniture.

3. I *'ll cut* _____ (**cut**) your hair if Leticia

   _____ *washes* _____ (**wash**) it first.

4. We *'ll work* _____ (**work**) indoors if it

   _____ *rains* _____ (**rain**).

5. She *'ll make* _____ (**make**) donuts if you

   _____ *start* _____ (**start**) a pot of coffee.

6. If we _____ *close* _____ (**close**) the restaurant early,

   customers _____ *will be* _____ (**be**) upset.

Unit 10   117

---

5. Focus attention on the grammar box in B. Follow the procedures in 2.

6. Have learners read the instructions for Complete the Sentences. Then follow the procedures in 3.

7. Focus attention on the grammar box in C. Follow the procedures in 2.

8. Have partners read the instructions for Write. Then follow the procedures in 3.

FOLLOW-UP

I'm going to. . .: Have learners take turns using the phrase, "I'm going to," in a sentence that tells their next career step, for example, "I'm going to take a word-processing class."

♦ Have partners create dialogs in which they ask and answer "Have you ever...?" questions about their work histories.

("Have you ever pruned a tree?" "Have you ever delivered a pizza?") Then have each learner tell the class things his or her partner has and has not done. ("Lisa has planted trees, but she's never pruned a tree.")

WORKBOOK

Unit 10, Exercises 6A–6C

BLACKLINE MASTERS

Blackline Master: Unit 10

★　　★　　★　　★　　★

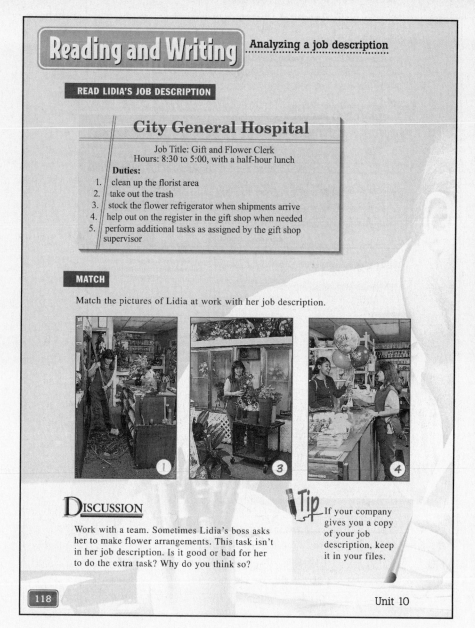

City General Hospital

Job Title: Gift and Flower Clerk
Hours: 8:30 to 5:00, with a half-hour lunch

Duties:
1. clean up the florist area
2. take out the trash
3. stock the flower refrigerator when shipments arrive
4. help out on the register in the gift shop when needed
5. perform additional tasks as assigned by the gift shop supervisor

MATCH

Match the pictures of Lidia at work with her job description.

DISCUSSION

Work with a team. Sometimes Lidia's boss asks her to make flower arrangements. This task isn't in her job description. Is it good or bad for her to do the extra task? Why do you think so?

Tip If your company gives you a copy of your job description, keep it in your files.

118

Unit 10

SCANS Note

Tell learners that it is generally easier to find a job when you already have a job. Suggest that someone who is unhappy with their job might want to line up another job before they quit the one they have. Ask learners why they think employers might prefer to hire people who already have jobs.

PREPARATION

Use picture cards, realia, or pantomime to present the words **flower arrangement** and **florist.** Have learners say what they think the job duties of a florist are.

PRESENTATION

1. Have learners read and discuss the Purpose Statement. For more information see "Purpose Statement" on page viii.

2. Have learners preview the job description before they read. See "Prereading" on page x. Encourage learners to say everything they can about it. Write their ideas on the board and/or restate them in acceptable English. Then have learners read the job description independently.

3. Focus attention on the illustrations. Encourage learners to say everything they can about them. Then have learners read the Match instructions and complete the activity. Ask several learners to share their answers with the class while the rest of the class checks their work.

4. Have learners read the Discussion questions. Make sure everyone knows what to do. Then have learners work in teams to discuss their ideas. Have team reporters share their teams' ideas with the class.

Tip Have learners read the Tip independently. Have learners discuss how the advice will help them. For more information, see "Presenting a Tip" on page ix.

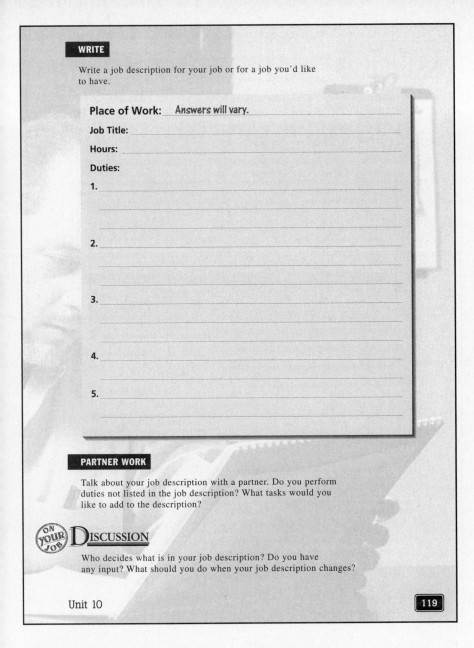

WRITE

Write a job description for your job or for a job you'd like to have.

Place of Work: _Answers will vary._____

Job Title: _____

Hours: _____

Duties:

1. _____
   _____
   _____

2. _____
   _____

3. _____
   _____

4. _____
   _____

5. _____

PARTNER WORK

Talk about your job description with a partner. Do you perform duties not listed in the job description? What tasks would you like to add to the description?

 DISCUSSION

Who decides what is in your job description? Do you have any input? What should you do when your job description changes?

Unit 10
119

---

5. Have learners read the Write instructions. Make sure everyone knows what to do. Then have learners complete the activity independently. Ask several learners to read their job descriptions to the class. Check learners' work.

6. Have learners read the Partner Work instructions. Make sure everyone knows what to do. Then have partners complete the activity. Have learners switch partners and repeat the activity. Ask several pairs to share their dialogs with the class.

7. Have learners read the Discussion instructions. Then have learners work in teams to discuss their ideas. Have team reporters share the ideas with the class.

FOLLOW-UP

Looking for Work: Have teams discuss ways they look for jobs. Have they worked with employment agencies? Do they use help wanted ads? Where else are jobs advertised? Have team reporters present the lists to the class.

♦ Have learners write short descriptions of each job they've had. Suggest they can use these descriptions when they fill out job applications. Review each learner's work.

WORKBOOK

Unit 10, Exercises 7A–7C

Extension   Evaluating career choices

READ AND WRITE

The Jobs To Watch

In the United States, experts predict there will be almost 20 million new jobs by the year 2005. People who prepare for jobs in the fastest-growing fields are going to have a lot of opportunities in the future. However, some occupations are declining. In these fields, there will be fewer and fewer jobs available as time goes on. It is important for workers to plan their careers based on their interests and on the jobs that will be available. People who are qualified to do jobs that are in high demand will be able to find work easily. In addition, many of the fastest-growing jobs pay more than other jobs. This is especially true of jobs that require special training.

According to the U.S. Department of Labor, most of the fast-growing jobs are in the service, retail trade, or government industries. These areas will provide many new jobs in the next few years.

Growing Jobs	Declining Jobs
• cashiers	• farmers
• janitors and cleaners	• sewing machine operators
• heat & air conditioning mechanics	• electrical assemblers
• nurses	• office machine operators
• home health aides	• gas station attendants
• retail salespeople	• bank tellers
• truck drivers	• electronic assemblers

1. Why is it important to prepare for growing jobs? _____ Answers will vary. _____

_____

2. Which of these jobs would you like to get? Why? _____

_____

3. Do you need additional skills or training to get one of these jobs? What kind

of skills or training? _____

 Culture Notes

People have different reasons for changing jobs. What are some reasons that people change jobs at your workplace? Do you think some of the reasons are better than others? Talk about when it is good to change jobs and when it is good to stay at the same job.

120   Unit 10

PREPARATION

If necessary, review or present the occupations in the table. Ask learners to speculate about which of the jobs are growing the most.

PRESENTATION

1. Have learners read and discuss the Purpose Statement. For more information see "Purpose Statement" on page viii.

2. Have learners preview the article. Encourage them to say everything they can about it. Write learners' ideas on the board and/or restate them in acceptable English. Use peer teaching to clarify unfamiliar words. See "Prereading" on page x. Then have learners read the article individually.

3. Have learners answer the questions under the article. Have several learners read their answers aloud as the rest of the class checks their work.

 4. Have learners read the Culture Notes and talk over their ideas in teams. Have team reporters share the ideas with the class. For more information see "Culture Notes" on page vii.

FOLLOW-UP

Top Ten: Have teams come up with a list of ten jobs team members most desire. Ask team reporters to share the lists with the class.

♦ Have teams discuss how team members' skills can qualify them for one or more of the jobs on the list of growing jobs. Have team reporters summarize the ideas for the class.

WORKBOOK

Unit 10, Exercise 8

Performance Check

How well can you use the skills in this unit?

Complete the activities. Go over your work with a partner or your teacher.
Then complete the Performance Review on page 122.

SKILL 1 **DECIDE WHAT YOU WANT FROM A JOB**

Tell your partner or teacher what things are important to you in a job.
Then talk about what jobs might offer what you want.

SKILL 2 **ANALYZE A JOB DESCRIPTION**

Match the pictures of Isabel at work with her job description.
Write the number.

Downtown Coffee Shop

Job Title: Kitchen Assistant

Hours: Tuesday through Saturday, 5:00 a.m. – 1:30 p.m.,
with a 30–minute lunch break

Duties: 1. keep the kitchen organized
2. chop fruits and vegetables
3. prepare salads
4. wash the counters and clean pots and pans
5. help the chef with minor cooking and do
additional tasks as assigned

Unit 10

121

PRESENTATION

Use any of the procedures in
"Evaluation," page x, with pages 121
and 122. Record individuals' results
on the Unit 10 Individual Competency
Chart. Record the class's results on the
Class Cumulative Competency Chart.

Read the ads below and compare the two jobs. Tell your partner or teacher how they are similar and how they are different. Would you like either of them? Tell why.

Elementary School Custodian

is needed. The hours are Monday to Friday, 7:30 a.m. to 3:30 p.m. The pay is $12.50 per hour. Applicants must enjoy children and be able to lift and push up to 25 pounds. Duties include cleaning and minor building maintenance. Health insurance is provided. Call 555-0099.

Baggage Handlers

are wanted. City Airport seeks individuals who like to work outdoors. The pay is $8.00 per hour. Schedule varies weekly. Some evening and weekend shifts are required. Duties include loading and unloading baggage to and from airplanes. Applicants must be able to lift at least 50 pounds. Call 555-7789.

SKILL 4   **EVALUATE CAREER CHOICES**

This table shows jobs that are expected to grow in the next few years. Are you interested in any of these jobs? Tell your teacher or partner which job you are interested in. Talk about any training you would need to qualify for the job.

Fast-Growing Jobs
- cashiers
- janitors and cleaners
- heat and air conditioning mechanics
- nurses
- home health aides
- retail salespeople
- truck drivers

Performance Review

I can...

- ☐ 1. decide what I want from a job.
- ☐ 2. analyze a job description.
- ☐ 3. compare jobs.
- ☐ 4. evaluate career choices.

Discussion

Work with a team. How will the skills help you? Make a list. Share the list with your class.

PRESENTATION

Follow the instructions on page 121.

INFORMAL WORKPLACE-SPECIFIC ASSESSMENT

Ask learners to describe a current job or a job they would like to have and explain how it provides what they are looking for in their work.

WORKBOOK

Unit 10, Exercise 9

Listening Transcript

Listening (page 7)

LISTEN AND CIRCLE

Listen to the messages. When did the people call? Circle the letter.

1.

A: Hi, this is Sylvia Carrington. I'm either on the phone or away from my desk. Please leave a message after the beep, and I'll call you back later today.

B: Hello, Ms. Carrington. This is Kevin Cho from KC Exterminators. It's 11:25 on Tuesday morning, and I'm calling to schedule next month's service call to exterminate Building 2. I know I just sprayed last week, but I'm going out of town soon. I'd like to set up the service call so I can get you on the calendar. Page me at 555-3320 later today when you have time. Thank you.

2.

A: You have reached Underwood Camera Repair. Our store hours are 8 A.M. to 6 P.M., Monday through Saturday. Please leave a message with the time you called, and we'll call you back.

B: My name is Lilia Silver. I'm calling at 6:20 on Monday evening. I guess I just missed you. I hear that you rent camera equipment. I need to rent a 35-millimeter camera for a photo shoot tomorrow morning. This is urgent because our camera doesn't work. Could you return my call tomorrow morning? Maybe I can pick up the camera in the morning. Please call me on my mobile phone. The number is 555-7781. Thank you.

3.

A: You've reached Candle Designs. We're out of the office until June 1, but please leave us a message and we'll call you back as soon as we can.

B: Hi, Amanda, this is Joe Ramos from JJ's Gift Shop again. Today is May 27, and I'm calling with some good news. I'd like to increase our usual order of candles. Our customers really love them, and I'd like to get more candles in stock as soon as possible. Please give me a call when you get back on June 1. I look forward to speaking with you then.

4.

A: Hi, this is Marilyn Wong. I can't come to the phone right now, so please leave a message and I'll call you right back.

B: Hi, Marilyn, this is Nancy Drake, Dr. Franca's nurse. It's now Monday at about 10:00 in the morning. I want to remind you about your appointment with Dr. Franca on Tuesday at 3:00. Please bring your health insurance information. There's no need to return this call. Thanks, Marilyn. See you on Tuesday at 3:00.

LISTEN AGAIN

Finish the sentences. Circle the letter. *(Play the tape or read the transcript of Listen and Circle aloud again.)*

LISTEN ONCE MORE

When will the callers probably get an answer? Write the letter. *(Play the tape or read the transcript of Listen and Circle aloud again.)*

Performance Check (page 14)

SKILL 4   USE VOICE MAIL

Listen to the voice mail messages. Circle the reasons the people are calling.

1.

A: Hi, this is Nancy Garret. I'm either on the phone or away from my desk. Please leave a message after the beep, and I'll call you back later today.

B: Hello, Ms. Garrett, this is Al Perez from Art's Auto Repair. It's 3:00 on Friday. I'm calling to schedule an appointment for your car's 45,000-mile service. Please call me at 555-7774 so we can set up an appointment at your earliest convenience.

2.

A: Hello, this is the Computer Connection. We're open from 10:00 to 10:00 seven days a week. Please leave a message and someone will call you back.

B: Hi, this is Gabe Harrison from Emmet's Grill. I'm calling to ask a question about the computer system you installed in our restaurant last week. Please call me back at 555-3317. Thanks.

Listening (page 19)

LISTEN AND CIRCLE

What type of feedback is the employee asking for? Circle the letter.

1.

A: I always feel as if I'm behind in my work. Then I have to catch up by working late or on the weekends. Do you have any suggestions about how I can get better organized?

B: What if you made a list of all the tasks you need to complete for the day? That's always helped me to be more organized and focused.

A: That's a good idea. I'll try making a list every day. I hope it works.

B: Well, let me know. I'd be interested in hearing if it does.

2.

A: How was your first day of work?

B: I'm not sure. I think I must be doing something wrong when I take customer orders. Several customers seemed kind of upset today when I told them that their cleaning would be ready in three days. Any suggestions?

A: Did you ask the customers when they needed their cleaning back? That would have let them know their needs are important to us.

B: But what if a customer tells me he needs his clothes back the next day?

A: In that case, tell him about our express service. It costs a little more, but we guarantee his cleaning will be ready the next morning.

B: I see. What you're saying is if I ask the customers what they need, I can give them the information they want.

A: Exactly.

3.

A: The customers in my checkout lane have been complaining that I'm too slow. I think I'm doing a good job, but I'm just not as fast as the other checkers. How can I work faster?

B: One thing to consider is that you sometimes talk to the customers in your line. It's good to be friendly, but it may be that you stop scanning the groceries when you're talking.

A: But they taught us in training that it's important to talk to our customers.

B: You're right. But you don't have to talk to the customer the whole time you're checking them out. Smile and greet the customer. After that, you should be paying attention to their groceries. You'll find that you're working faster.

A: Thanks. That makes a lot of sense.

LISTEN AGAIN

What does the supervisor recommend? Circle the letter. *(Play the tape or read the transcript of Listen and Circle aloud again.)*

Performance Check (page 25)

SKILL 2

ASK FOR AND UNDERSTAND FEEDBACK

The employees are asking for feedback. What problems are they asking about? Listen and circle the letter.

1.

A: I can't seem to get to a landscape job without forgetting something. Sometimes I forget the shovel, sometimes my gloves. One time, I even forgot the plants. What can I do to remember everything?

B: Why don't you make a list of all the supplies that you need to do a job and put it on your dashboard?

A: Thanks. A list should help me remember.

2.

A: Why do you think it takes me so long to stock my section?

B: You're very neat. That's good, but it can slow you down sometimes. Your aisle looks great, but you spend too much time lining up the cans.

A: I thought you wanted neat shelves.

B: Well, we do. But you can stock the shelves neatly and still work fast. You just need to line up the cans in the front rows. This way you can move on to your other responsibilities more quickly.

A: OK, I'll do it.

What feedback does the supervisor give? Listen again and circle the letter. *(Play the tape or read the transcript for Skill 2 aloud again.)*

 **U N I T 3**

Listening (page 31)

LISTEN AND CIRCLE

What are the employees troubleshooting? Circle the answer in column A.

1.

A: Bill, can you help me? I'm having a problem with this soldering iron.

B: What's the matter?

A: It starts OK, but it doesn't ever heat up.

B: There's no heat at all?

A: None. What do you want me to do?

B: You know, I've been thinking about replacing that soldering iron for a long time. I'm just about ready to call Kerry at Brace Hardware and check out how much it'll cost to get a new one.

2.

A: You're here early, Bradley.

B: Yes, I am. I wanted to set up the TV and the VCR in this meeting room for the 10:00 training session. And it's a good thing, too. I already have a problem.

A: What's wrong?

B: The TV screen stays blank even when I press the PLAY button on the VCR. Should we call a technician? We need a working TV and VCR by 10:00.

A: The screen's blank? Hmm. Tell me everything you've tried so far.

B: Let me see. First I turned on the TV. Then I turned on the VCR and put in the tape.

A: Did you rewind the tape before you pressed PLAY?

B: Yes. And then I pressed the video button on the remote control.

A: Did you set the TV to channel 3?

B: Oh, no. It's on channel 13, not channel 3. Well, that was an easy fix. All I needed to do was change the TV channel.

3.

A: I'm having problems with this scale. Can you help me?

B: Sure, what's wrong?

A: Well, the display shows the weight and price, but the scale won't print a ticket.

B: Let's see… Is there paper in the printer?

A: Yes, there is. I checked that first thing.

B: What about the print button? What happens when you push it?

A: Nothing.

B: Well, if the print button isn't working, I guess we'll have to call a repair person.

A: I can do that. The repair person's phone number is on the wall in the office, right?

B: Yes, that's right.

LISTEN AGAIN

How do the employees solve the problem? Circle the solution in column B. (*Play the tape or read the transcript of Listen and Circle aloud again.*)

LISTEN AND CIRCLE

Listen to the problem. Circle the questions that the employee asked.

A: Dependable Auto Repair, Thomas speaking. May I help you?

B: Hi, this is David Chow. River City Towing Service towed my car to your garage last night. Do you have time to take a look at it?

A: Oh, so that's your car. I saw it in the lot when I got to work. What's the matter with it?

B: Well, it stalled and wouldn't start again. Luckily, I could just pull over onto the shoulder and call a tow truck. The tow truck driver couldn't start it either, so I had him tow it to your garage.

A: It was running fine, and then when it stalled you couldn't start it again?

B: That's right.

A: Was the car warmed up, or had you just started driving?

B: It was warmed up. I'd been driving for about twenty minutes.

A: When you tried to start the car, did the engine turn over at all?

B: No, it was completely dead.

A: It could be the battery. Did your lights still work?

B: Yes, the lights worked fine.

A: It doesn't sound like the battery, then. Was there gas in the tank?

B: Yes, there was. I'd just filled it.

A: Hmm. It could be the gas line. I'll have to get out and look at it. Give me your phone number and I'll call you back as soon as I know something more.

B: Sure, it's 555-4801.

UNIT 4

Listening (page 43)

LISTEN AND MATCH

When does each task need to be completed? Write the letter of the deadline next to the assignment.

1.

A: This piano has to be delivered to Mrs. Taylor by 11:00 this morning. Can you make sure that happens?

B: I don't know. We've got three other deliveries scheduled for this morning. I'm afraid we might not make it downtown by 11:00.

A: Any way you can rearrange your schedule? Mrs. Taylor can't be home in the afternoon, and we promised we'd deliver her piano today.

B: Let me see... I can rearrange some of my other deliveries and get the piano to Mrs. Taylor before 11:00.

2.

A: Assad, did you know we need to finish painting this building on Friday?

B: Friday's just three days from now. Are you sure they said Friday?

A: Yeah well, everyone's schedule got pushed back because of the weather. Now we've got to get back on schedule and catch up. I figure I'll be putting in some overtime.

B: I can work extra hours.

A: I knew I could count on you. I'll tell Jack that we'll be done painting on Friday.

3.

A: Vicky, tonight's the first night of the new employee training. Can you help get the room ready?

B: Sure, what can I do?

A: According to the list from Human Resources, there are twenty new employees. We need to be sure there are enough employee handbooks and that the overhead projector in the training room is up and working.

B: I should be able to get those things together by tonight, but I'll have to stop doing this filing. Is that all right?

A: Of course. The filing can wait until tomorrow.

LISTEN AGAIN

What do the people change to meet their deadlines? Circle the letter. *(Play the tape or read the transcript of Listen and Match aloud again.)*

LISTEN AND WRITE

What is the company's deadline for each task? Write the day of the week.

A: Do you have a minute, Ernie? We need to go over our schedule for next week.

B: OK, let's look at the calendar. I see three projects set up for next week. The Smiths' driveway is due to be finished by Tuesday. Is that right?

A: That's right. I don't see any problems getting that done by Tuesday. It's a relatively simple job.

B: What about the tennis courts over at Buena Vista Resorts? My notes say we promised to finish them by Friday. How are things looking?

A: Quite good, actually. I don't think we'll have any trouble finishing the courts by Friday. In fact we've already started work out there. To tell you the truth, my big concern is the city job putting the sidewalk around the park. You know they've pushed the due date up by a week and now they want everything finished by Thursday.

B: Yeah, and that's a big job. I was thinking maybe I could call Lee and see if he'd bring in his crew. With their help I bet we can get the sidewalk finished by Thursday.

Performance Check (page 50)

SKILL 3 MEET DEADLINES

Listen to the dialog. What's the deadline for each task? Write the letter of the deadline next to the assignment.

1.

A: Alberto, can you come in early Thursday morning? We've got a special flower delivery.

B: Thursday? How early?

A: Well, it's got to be across town by 8:30.

B: That's not too bad. Sure, I'll come in a little early.

2.

A: Have you started the tile work at the Landry's?

B: Not yet. Why? Is there a rush?

A: Kind of. We need to have the tile job done by 3:00 on Tuesday afternoon. Do you think you can do it?

B: Tuesday at 3:00? It can be done, but I'll need some help.

A: No problem. I'll line someone up to work with you.

3.

A: We just got a last-minute order for a wedding cake for this Saturday.

B: Do you think we can do it?

C: Depends. What time's the wedding?

A: 4:00. It'll be our last order on Saturday.

B: What about the cookies we were supposed to decorate?

C: I think those can wait. We were just making them to sell in the bakery.

B: Well, if we don't have to worry about the cookies, we should have no trouble getting a cake ready by 4:00.

U N I T ◆5◆

Listening (page 55)

LISTEN AND WRITE

What is the customer calling about? Complete the sentence.

1.

A: Thank you for calling the Grand Hotel. This is Maria Prado. How may I help you?

B: My name is Min Chu. I'd like to reserve a room for Saturday, April 4.

A: Smoking or nonsmoking?

B: A nonsmoking room with a king-sized bed.

A: I'm sorry, Ms. Chu. We don't have any nonsmoking rooms with king-sized beds available on April 4. I can give you a room with two double beds on the nonsmoking floor.

B: That'll be fine. Thank you.

2.

A: Good morning. Long Last Tires. Stephen speaking. May I help you?

B: Yes, my name's Angela Wells. Your shop recently put two new tires on my car, but I think there's something wrong with them. I've noticed that whenever I drive over 55 miles an hour, the car pulls slightly to the right. What should I do?

A: It sounds like there's something wrong with the alignment. Why don't you bring your car in so we can check it out for you? If the alignment's the problem, we'll fix it free of charge.

B: Thanks, that would be great. I'll bring the car by later today.

A: See you then.

3.

A: Daily Donuts, this is Richard. How can I help you?

B: Hi, this is Michael Cross from E & J Mechanics down the street. You guys deliver donuts every morning for our 10:00 break. I'd like to change our order for today. Is it too late?

A: It shouldn't be too late to change your order, Mr. Cross. But you need to talk to Alma. She coordinates the delivery orders. Can you hold one moment while I transfer your call to her?

B: Sure, I'll hold.

LISTEN AGAIN

How do the employees respond to their customers? Write the letter. *(Play the tape or read the transcript of Listen and Write aloud again.)*

LISTEN AND CIRCLE

What is the reason for each telephone guideline? Circle the letter.

A: Hi, Gary. My name is Phyllis. Welcome to the Home Catalog Company. It's my job to get you oriented and answer any questions you may have. We'll start by going over the company guidelines for answering the phone. They're on page 3 of your employee notebook.

B: I have that right here.

A: Great. Let's look at them together. The first guideline is to smile when you answer the phone.

B: Smile? Why should I smile? The customers can't see me, can they?

A: No, they can't see you, but they can hear your voice. When you smile, the tone of your voice sounds positive. This makes customers feel welcome.

B: I'll try, but it sounds a little hard.

A: Don't worry, it's something you have to practice. You need to practice the greeting as well. In fact, why don't you read the greeting right now? Where it says *name*, go ahead and introduce yourself by saying your own name.

B: Hello, you've reached the Home Catalog Company. Thank you for calling. This is Gary speaking. How may I help you?

A: Good. Always tell the customer your name. That way, if the customer calls back with a question, he or she can ask

for you.

B: Sure. That makes sense.

A: Now, when you take an order, the computer screen will show you what you should ask. Just follow the questions on the screen.

B: OK. Anything else?

A: Just remember to thank the customer for calling. Our business depends on keeping our customers happy. When you thank them, you let them know how important they are to us.

B: I see.

A: Now let's try...

UNIT 6

Listening (page 67)

LISTEN AND CIRCLE

What are the people talking about? Circle the problem in column A.

1.

A: According to the weather report, we're going to get a couple of inches of rain this afternoon.

B: Those small plants out front might get damaged by a really hard rain. I think we'd better put them inside. Can you get started? I'll be out to help you as soon as I finish what I'm doing here.

A: Sure, but I think we'll need help to get the job done before it starts to rain. The sky is getting really dark. Gabrielle, can you help us move these plants inside? We're trying to keep them from getting damaged by the rain.

C: I'll be right there.

B: OK, let's work this out together. Gabrielle, if you clear a space for the plants, Nick and I can start moving them. What do you think?

C: I'm sure we can do it. Let's get going.

2.

A: I've been concerned for some time now that our team meetings last too long. People are telling me that they don't have enough time to get their work done.

B: The meetings are important. But I agree, they have been lasting a little longer than usual. Do you have any ideas?

Listening Transcript

A: I was thinking that we could make the meetings shorter by sending out an agenda before each meeting. If everyone comes prepared, the meetings shouldn't take so long.

B: That's a good idea. Let's try it out at next week's meeting.

3.

A: You wanted to see me?

B: Well, yes. I'm afraid we've had a few complaints about some of the rooms recently. I've heard from several guests that their rooms aren't always clean. I know the hotel prides itself on customer service, so I wanted to discuss it with you.

A: Have you seen what the guests are complaining about?

B: Yes. Sometimes the tables and chairs aren't clean, and the beds aren't always made up neatly.

A: Have you given any thought to what we should do?

B: I was wondering if we should make a checklist of everything that needs to be done before we say a room is ready. Then we could go over the list with the housekeepers and make sure they all use the list.

A: Good idea. Let's discuss it at the staff meeting tomorrow. If everyone agrees, we can start working on that list right away.

LISTEN AGAIN

How do the people want to solve the problems? Circle the suggestion in column B. *(Play the tape or read the transcript of Listen and Circle aloud again.)*

LISTEN AND ANSWER

Circle the letter of the answer.

A: Good morning everybody. I hope you all had a nice weekend. As you know, starting next Monday, Black Fox Industries will be instituting flex-time hours. I've asked each member of this department to come to this meeting having already decided what schedule you'd like to work: 8:30 to 4:30, 9:00 to 5:00, or 9:30 to 5:30. If flex-time is

to work, remember that you can't switch back and forth between schedules. People in other departments need to know where you'll be and when, so once you choose a work schedule, you need to stay with it. Also, we have to ensure that someone is here to answer the phone starting at 8:30. If everyone is clear on all of that, I'd like to find out what hours you're requesting and work together to build a schedule. Lin, let's start with you since you've been with Black Fox the longest.

B: I've got school at night so I'd prefer to work from 9:30 to 5:30 if possible.

A: OK. What about you, James? You've been here almost as long as Lin. Which schedule works best for you?

C: 9:00 to 5:00.

A: All right, we've got Lin coming in at 9:30 and James at 9:00, but we don't have the morning phone calls covered yet. Marta?

D: Well, I know I haven't worked here long, but I'd really like to be on the 9:00 to 5:00 schedule, too. My brother and I share a car and sometimes it's hard for me to get here by 8:30.

A: How about you, Marcos?

E: I can come in at 8:30 to answer the phones. I don't mind. In fact, I like getting to work early. And getting home early, too.

D: Thanks, Marcos.

A: Thanks, everyone.

U N I T 7

Listening (page 79)

LISTEN AND CIRCLE

What is causing the budget problem? Circle the letter.

1.

A: Can we talk for a minute, Mr. Denton? I'm planning the menu for a luncheon next week, and right now I'm over budget because the client's added people to the guest list. He doesn't want to spend any more money, so I'm trying to find some ways to cut back on the costs.

B: OK, Tranh. Why don't you start by telling me about the menu?

A: The client wants roast beef, which is kind of expensive, so in order to cut costs I've changed the side dishes.

B: What else are you planning?

A: A green salad, mashed potatoes, and steamed carrots.

B: Those side dishes aren't very expensive. They shouldn't put you over budget. What about dessert?

A: For dessert I'm planning strawberry short cake.

B: That's one of the most expensive desserts we offer. What about chocolate cake? It's easier to serve, and it costs less to make.

A: That's a good idea. I bet that'll put me back on budget again. Thanks.

2.

A: What's up, Malika?

B: I'm making the costumes for the Community Players.

A: If I remember correctly, you were on this project last year as well. How did it go?

B: Well, last time I came in right on budget. I'm trying to keep the cost the same this year. But the price of some of the materials has gone up.

A: Have you figured out what you're going to do?

B: Actually, I do have a plan. I was thinking that I could save money if I used less trim. The trim's pretty expensive and last time I used a lot of it.

A: That should work. It'll save you money and time.

B: That's what I'm counting on.

3.

A: I'm working with a bride on the flowers for a wedding, but I'm a little concerned about the cost. The prices at Flower Town have gone up recently and now I think we might not be able to use all of the flowers the bride wants.

B: Let's see, Ramona, maybe we can adjust the order. What flowers are you trying to buy?

A: The bride wants white roses. She said it's very important to her to have white roses.

B: What about your supplier? Sometimes we can get a better price from a different supplier. Flower Town can be a little expensive. Let's call around and compare prices.

A: Why would the prices be so different?

B: Well, for example, Flower Town ships many of their flowers from Hawaii. They're beautiful, but the shipping costs make them more expensive. If you buy from a vendor like the Flower Pot, you can save on shipping and the flowers are often cheaper.

A: Oh, I didn't know that. Thanks for the advice.

LISTEN AGAIN

How will the employees adjust their spending? Match the people with their solutions. Write the letter. *(Play the tape or read the transcript of Listen and Circle aloud again.)*

LISTEN AND CIRCLE

How can the people stay on budget? Circle the letters.

A: I'm glad you could all come to the budget seminar tonight. Since this seminar is about helping you manage your money better, please feel free to interrupt to ask me questions at any time. I'm here to help. I'd like to start off tonight by talking about common problems that people have with staying on budgets. Does anyone have a problem they'd like to share?

B: I do. It seems to me that the projects my team works on always cost more than we budgeted for. Is that a common problem or are we doing something wrong?

A: I'm afraid it is a common problem and unfortunately, one that can't always be avoided. But the good news is that if you plan ahead, you can often avoid going over budget. By planning ahead and anticipating problems that might come up, you can usually create a budget that works. Another problem?

C: I guess I don't understand how you can plan ahead. Something always seems to

Listening Transcript

happen in the middle of a project that you can't control. Last month for example, I was working on a project, and the price of materials suddenly went up. It was no one's fault, but then we were over budget.

A: You're absolutely right. Sometimes you can't anticipate things such as unexpected price increases. And the best suggestion I have for you in a case like that is to adjust your budget. If materials suddenly cost more than you budgeted for, see if you can save money somewhere else. Maybe you can use another supplier. If your regular supplier has a cost increase, check with other suppliers in your area. Or substitute a different product. For example, if you're building a house…

Listening (page 91)

LISTEN AND MATCH

Match the employee to the situation. Write the letter.

1.
A: Marty, what's wrong? You look kind of pale.
B: I hurt my back while I was unloading that new shipment of boxes. I think I strained it.
A: You need to see a doctor. Let me find someone to take you to the emergency room.
B: Thanks Mr. King, but I'll be OK. I don't think I need to go to the doctor.
A: Sorry, but it's company policy. You've got to see a doctor right away.
B: Sure, if that's the policy, I'll go.

2.
A: Melissa, glad to see you back. How are you feeling?
B: Much better, thanks. The doctor said I had the flu. I'm sorry I missed so much work.
A: Don't worry about it. Everyone gets sick once in a while. That's why the factory has a sick-leave policy.
B: I know, but I feel terrible about being out for so long. And I've been worried

about my paycheck. Will I be paid for those days?
A: Of course you will. According to our sick-leave policy, you have five days of paid sick leave per year. You were out only three days, so your paycheck won't be affected.
B: That's good news. Well, I'd better get to work. See you later.

3.
A: Come on in Janda, and sit down. You wanted to speak to me?
B: Yes, I wanted to let you know that I'm four months pregnant.
A: Congratulations!
B: Thanks. Bill and I are very excited. Anyway, I've come to Human Resources because my supervisor recommended I talk to someone here about the company's maternity-leave plan.
A: Storage Services treats maternity leave like any other short-term disability. On our plan you're entitled to four weeks of paid time off. But by law, you can take up to twelve weeks. Unfortunately you won't be paid for the additional eight weeks.
B: Yes, I knew that. But I was wondering if my job will still be here when I come back to work.
A: Your job should be saved for you during the twelve weeks that you're gone. Any other questions?
B: No, that's about it for now. Thanks.

LISTEN AGAIN

Complete the sentences. Circle the letter.
(Play the tape or read the transcript for Listen and Match aloud again.)

LISTEN AND CIRCLE

Listen to the dialog. What happened? Circle the letter.

A: Good morning. Shipping. This is Scott.
B: Scott, it's Leo. I'm calling to tell you I'll be out sick again today. I went to the clinic yesterday afternoon. The doctor there ran some tests and gave me some medicine, but she said I shouldn't come back to work until my symptoms are gone.

A: That sounds like good advice.

B: I just hope I'll be out for only one or two more days.

A: Don't worry about it. You've still got five days of sick leave that you can take. Just be sure to call every morning and let us know you won't be in.

B: Will I need a note from my doctor when I come back?

A: Yes, bring one with you on your first day.

UNIT

Listening (page 103)

LISTEN AND CIRCLE

What's the matter? Circle the letter.

1.

A: Let me lift that for you, Maria. You could get hurt doing that.

B: Unloading boxes is my job. We work at a shipping company!

A: I know, but that box looks too heavy for a woman to lift. Why don't you let me get it for you?

B: Allen, I wish you wouldn't make comments like that. I can lift that box as well as you can. I wouldn't have been hired if I weren't capable of doing the work.

A: I'm sorry. I was just trying to be helpful.

2.

A: Hey, did you hear the joke about the guy who...

B: Gus, I think you should stop telling these jokes. They're starting to bother some of the people who work here.

A: I'm just trying to liven the place up. We work so hard all day, I thought people might appreciate some comic relief on our breaks. I'm not trying to make enemies.

B: I understand, Gus, but people interpret jokes differently. Lots of your jokes make fun of people. Sometimes people get upset.

A: I had no idea that my jokes upset people. I'd never hurt anyone's feelings on purpose. I'll be more careful from now on.

3.

A: Betty, some of us are going out for lunch. Do you want to come?

B: No, thanks. I can't.

A: You know, every time we ask you to lunch, you say *no*. Do you want us to stop asking?

B: I'd like to go, but I bring my lunch every day. You always go out.

A: Oh, I see. We thought you didn't want to eat with us.

B: That's not it. I'm just trying to save money by bringing lunch from home.

A: Well, maybe we could all bring our lunch one day next week and eat together in the break room.

B: Sounds like fun. Let's do it.

LISTEN AGAIN

How is the conflict resolved? Circle the letter.
(Play the tape or read the transcript of Listen and Circle aloud again.)

LISTEN AND WRITE

Listen to the dialog. Answer the questions.

A: Bob, I was wondering if you could stop playing your radio.

B: Is it bothering you?

A: Kind of. It's hard for me to concentrate on my work.

B: I'm sorry, Chen. I'll turn it off right away.

A: Thanks.

UNIT

Listening (page 115)

LISTEN AND CIRCLE

The job counselors are explaining jobs to people. What are the jobs like? Circle the letter.

1.

To become a van driver at Cross Country Movers, you need to have your GED and an excellent driving record. In addition, you must be able to stay away from home for days at a time. Your job may take you on the road for many days in a row as you travel from New York to California and back again.

Cross Country provides on-the-job training under the supervision of a trained instructor as well as a comprehensive benefits package.

2.

All guest relations workers at the Hill and Valley Resort need to be friendly and have excellent customer service skills. Whether you're a desk clerk, bellhop, pool attendant, or waiter, you need to have a relaxed, friendly attitude and the ability to solve problems. Our employees meet people from all over the world. Full time employees are eligible for benefits after six months, and there is opportunity for advancement.

3.

Capital City Bus is looking for maintenance people who want to work nights. The people on the night maintenance crew must be independent workers who can follow written work orders about cleaning and maintaining the overall appearance of the buses. Capital City offers all its employees medical insurance and a paid vacation.

LISTEN AGAIN

Which job would be the best for each person? Match. Write the letter of the person. *(Play the tape or read the transcript of Listen and Circle aloud again.)*

LISTEN AND CIRCLE

Circle all the job characteristics that Teresa considers important.

A: I'm not really sure what kind of job I'm looking for. Any suggestions?

B: We could start by making a list of things that are important to you. That might help you think of some jobs you'd like.

A: Well, for one thing, I know I want some kind of indoor work. In Florida I always worked outdoors, but now that I've moved to New York, I'd much rather work indoors. It gets so cold here.

B: What else?

A: It's really important to me to work days. I can't work nighttime hours with three kids. I need to work while they're in school.

B: I can understand that. Any other ideas?

A: It would really help if I could work somewhere on or near a bus route. And somewhere that offered pretty good health insurance.

B: And I think you'd be good at working with people. I'd guess that's important to you.

A: You're right. I do like working with people. Maybe a job as a receptionist…

Irregular Verbs

am, are, is	was, were	been
begin	began	begun
break	broke	broken
bring	brought	brought
build	built	built
buy	bought	bought
come	came	come
cut	cut	cut
do	did	done
drive	drove	driven
eat	ate	eaten
feed	fed	fed
feel	felt	felt
find	found	found
forget	forgot	forgotten
get	got	gotten
give	gave	given
go	went	went
have	had	had
keep	kept	kept
made	made	made
pay	paid	paid
put	put	put
read	read	read
ride	rode	ridden
see	saw	seen
sell	sold	sold
send	sent	sent
speak	spoke	spoken
spend	spent	spent
sweep	swept	swept
take	took	taken
tell	told	told
think	thought	thought
wear	wore	worn
write	wrote	written

Vocabulary

hold
transfer

message
phone log
voice mail
voice mail message
wrong number

feedback
problem
solution
status report
supervisor

go over

almost

battery
cash register
copier
fax machine
scale
scanner
VCR

troubleshooting

repair person

broken
not working
out of order

suggestion card

deal with

before
during
after

deadline
schedule

color
features
size
style

free
special
upgrade

customer service letter

help

team
together
team member

suggestion

strength
weakness

budget

expenses
actual expenses
labor
taxes

income

cheap
expensive

under budget
over budget
on budget

benefits
dental care
dental insurance
disability insurance
eye care
family leave
health care
medical insurance
sick leave
Workers' Compensation

copayment
deductible
salary deduction

appropriate
inappropriate
policy
discrimination
harassment

job offer

benefits
pay
job description

duties

Name _____

A. Complete the sentences. Follow the example.

1. Nico rides two buses to get home. He has to get a transfer downtown

   _____**but**_____ **(or, but)** doesn't need to buy another ticket.

2. He takes the bus downtown _____ **(or, and)** walks home from there.

3. He wants to buy a car _____ **(or, but)** likes riding the bus.

4. On the bus, Nico reads _____ **(or, but)** listens to music.

5. Nico meets nice people on the bus _____ **(and, but)** sees them every day.

6. When he needs to get to work early, he gets a ride from a friend

   _____ **(and, or)** takes the early bus.

B. Complete the sentences. Follow the example.

1. Mark plans _____**to clean**_____ **(clean)** the grill early in the morning.

2. Thomas enjoys _____**trying**_____ **(try)** new things.

3. Patty doesn't know how _____ **(open)** the store.

4. We stopped _____ **(call)** customers at 2:00.

5. Rick wants _____ **(get)** better safety goggles.

6. Georgia and Mike always spend time _____ **(plan)** their schedules every morning.

7. Lisa knows how _____ **(train)** new employees.

C. Complete the sentences. Use **to + verb** or **verb + ing.**

1. I like _____**using my new computer**_____.

2. Last year I began _____.

3. Next year I want to start _____.

4. I really like _____.

5. I love _____.

Name _____

A. Complete the sentences. Follow the example.

1. I just got my new name tag. Larry gave it to _____**me**_____ (me/them).

2. Joe and Sandy can't work at the same time. There aren't enough tools for

   _____ (them/you).

3. Mary asked for the extra shift, so the boss gave it to _____ (me/her).

4. Tim needed to talk to you. Since you weren't here, he left a message for

   _____ (him/you).

5. Are Tina and Joe here yet? I have an assignment for _____ (me/them).

B. Answer the questions. Use the words in the box. Follow the example.

> apply for a job at the animal hospital   ask for more help
> practice for the test   take a training class   call a repair person

1. Susan likes working with dogs and cats. What should she do?

   _____ **She should apply for a job at the animal hospital.** _____

2. Marco wants to learn to use a computer. What should he do?

   _____

3. Joseph's the only cashier, and there's a long line of customers. What should he do?

   _____

4. Brad and Pablo think the washing machine is broken. What should they do?

   _____

5. Chen has signed up to take a typing test. What should she do?

   _____

C. Complete the sentences. Write **do, does, make,** or **makes.**

1. The cooks _____**make**_____ breakfast before the guests are up.

2. After breakfast we _____ the dishes.

3. In the afternoon Jessica _____ the beds.

4. Felix _____ the shopping.

U N I T ◇3◇

A. Complete the sentences. Follow the example.

1. Jeff can finish the project _____**quickly**_____ (**quick**).

2. Always follow the safety rules and work _____ (**careful**).

3. Sylvia always behaves _____ (**professional**).

4. When Tania answers the phone, she listens to the customer
   _____ (**patient**).

5. Henry always lifts heavy boxes _____ (**slow**).

6. Brian never drives _____ (**careless**).

7. Pedro plans ahead so he can do his work _____ (**correct**)
   the first time.

8. When you fill out a form, answer the questions _____ (**complete**).

9. A watch repair person needs to work very _____ (**accurate**).

10. During an interview, answer all the questions _____ (**truthful**).

B. Complete the sentences. Use **going to.** Use the words in the box.
   Follow the example.

replace the light bulbs	deliver the bread	~~clean it up~~
dry them	buy more forms	leave soon
call the locksmith	call the repair service	rain

1. A bottle broke in aisle 3. I _**'m going to clean it up**_____.

2. Susan said that the oven is broken. She_____.

3. We're almost done with this job. We_____.

4. The sky is getting cloudy and dark. It_____.

5. I finished washing the towels. Next I_____.

6. Lisa ran out of forms. She_____.

7. We can't unlock the supply room. We_____.

8. I called the bakery. Later this morning they_____.

9. Jacob said the sign isn't lit up. He_____.

A. Read about Rosa Sandoval's work experience.

Work Experience   *List your current or most recent job first*

Job: shift supervisor   Department: housekeeping

Company: Old Town Hotel   Dates: January 1999 to present

Job: housekeeper   Department: housekeeping

Company: Old Town Hotel   Dates: September 1997 to January 1999

Job: laundry assistant   Department: laundry

Company: Excel Laundry & Dry Cleaning   Dates: September 1996 to September 1997

Complete the answers. Follow the example.

1. How long _____has_____ Rosa _____worked_____ (work) at Old Town Hotel?

   She__'s worked____ (work) there _____since_____ (for/since) 1997.

2. How long _____ she _____ (be) the shift supervisor?

   She_____ (be) the shift supervisor _____ (for/since)

   January 1999.

3. How many jobs _____ she _____ (have) in the last
   few years?

   She_____ (have) three jobs _____ (for/since) 1996.

B. Answer the questions. Use **for** or **since.**

   1. How long have you lived in the United States?

   _____

   2. How long have you had your present job?

   _____

   3. How long have you studied English?

   _____

   4. How long have you lived in this city?

   _____

Blackline Masters

C. Look at the picture. Answer the questions.

1. Has he washed the plates ?

   _____**Yes, he has.**_____

2. Has he put away the plates?

   _____

3. Has he washed the pots and pans?

   _____

4. Have they cut the cake?

   _____

5. Have they served the cake?

   _____

D. Read the dialog. Then write a summary. Follow the example.

1. **A** The supply clerk should move these boxes, Miguel.

   B I think so, too. The supply clerk should move the boxes.

   Miguel _____**thinks (that) the supply clerk should move the boxes**_____.

2. **A** Brenda, this chair is too low.

   B I agree. It's too low.

   Brenda _____.

3. **A** Marco, I think the store room is very cold.

   B I think so, too.

   Marco _____.

4. **A** Chris, the new knife sharpener works well.

   B I agree.

   Chris _____.

Name_____

A. Write the correct form of the word. Follow the examples.

1. The first shift workers are _____ **busier than** _____ (busy) and
   _____ **more organized than** _____ (organized) the second shift workers.

2. The third shift workers are _____ **the busiest** _____ (busy) and
   _____ **the most organized** _____ (organized).

3. Joe's new electric drill is _____ (powerful) my drill.

4. These stains are really difficult to remove, so we need to use
   _____ (strong) cleaning chemicals we have.

5. The new stocking inventory system is _____ (efficient)
   the old system.

6. These new floor mats are _____ (comfortable) the
   bare floor.

7. Downtown Paint Supply is _____ (good) paint
   store in the city. It has _____ (large) selection and
   _____ (low) prices.

8. Quality Supermarket just moved. The new store is
   _____ (nice) the old store. I think they have
   _____ (good) fruits and vegetables in town.

9. Friendly Bank is _____ (convenient) City Bank.

10. The big moving vans are _____ (comfortable) the
    old ones.

11. I think that the clerks at our store are _____ (friendly)
    clerks in the city.

12. A power sander is _____ (fast) sanding by hand.

13. Z Mart is _____ (expensive) store in town, and it's also
    _____ (big).

14. The limousine is _____ (clean) the taxicab.

15. Taking the bus is _____ (slow) driving your car.

A. Complete the sentences. Follow the example.

1. She **'ll go** _____ (**go**) to the break room if she

   _____ **needs** _____ (**need**) to make a phone call.

2. He _____ (**ask**) if anyone needs help if he

   _____ (**finish**) his work early.

3. If we _____ (**not have**) that size in stock,

   I_____ (**call**) another store to see if I can find it.

4. If Julie and Margaret _____ (**decide**) what shifts

   to work, they_____ (**make**) the schedule today.

5. Ahmed_____ (**get**) overtime pay if he

   _____ (**come**) in early.

6. Marco_____ (**call**) the company to check on the

   order if the shipment _____ (**not arrive**) today.

7. If the office supply store _____ (**not have**) the safety signs

   we need, we_____ (**order**) them from a mail-order catalog.

B. Look at the pictures. Complete the sentences. Use **feels, seems,** or **looks.**
Follow the example.

1. Maxine has a lot to do.

   She _____ **looks busy** _____.

2. George enjoys his new job.

   He _____.

3. Joe's bus is late.

   Joe probably _____.

4. Janice doesn't feel well today.

   She _____.

Name _____

A. Complete the sentences. Use the correct form of the verb. Follow the example.

1. Manuel _____**started**_____ (**start**) work four hours ago.

2. Maxine _____ (**go**) to lunch half an hour ago.

3. Yolanda _____ (**deliver**) the package a week ago.

4. Sam _____ (**mail**) the bills two days ago.

5. I _____ (**finish**) my work a few minutes ago.

6. They _____ (**make**) all the signs three days ago.

7. He _____ (**catch**) the bus a few minutes ago.

8. Mike _____ (**drive**) downtown about an hour ago.

9. You _____ (**finish**) that project a few weeks ago.

10. Teresa _____ (**help**) that customer a week ago.

B. Complete the dialogs. Use the correct form of the verb, and write **already** or **yet**.

1. A _____**Have**_____ you _____**finished**_____ (**finish**) feeding
   the dogs yet?

   B No, we _____ (**not feed**) them

   _____ (**already/yet**).

2. A _____ the painters _____ (**start**) on the back
   wall yet?

   B Yes, they _____ (**already/yet**) (**start**) it.

3. A _____ the first shift workers _____ (**put away**)
   the new tools yet?

   B No, they _____ (**not do**) that _____ (**already/yet**).

4. A _____ Tanya and Marco _____ (**leave**)

   _____ (**already/yet**)?

   B No, they're still working. They _____ (**not finish**) mopping

   the floor _____ (**already/yet**).

Blackline Masters

C. Look at the calendar.

JUNE   Nadia's Schedule

Sunday	Monday	Tuesday	Wednesday	Thursday	Friday	Saturday
	1	2	3 Order new cookware	4	5	6 Go to Cooking Job Fair
7	8	9 Teach cooking class	10	11 Interview new bakers	12 Shop for Nick Gomez's dinner party	13 Cater Nick Gomez's dinner party
14	(15)	16 Teach cooking class	17	18 Meet with Patty and Joe Johnson	19	20 Cater the Miller wedding

Today is June 15. Use the calendar to answer the questions. Follow the example.

1. A _____ **Has** _____ Nadia _____ **catered** _____ (**cater**) the Miller wedding yet?

   B _____ **No, she hasn't.** _____

2. A _____ she _____ (**interview**) new bakers yet?

   B _____

3. A _____ she _____ (**go**) to the Cooking Job Fair yet?

   B _____

4. A _____ she _____ (**meet**) with Patty and Joe Johnson yet?

   B _____

5. A _____ she _____ (**buy**) the food for Nick Gomez's dinner party yet?

   B _____

6. A _____ she _____ (**start**) her cooking class yet?

   B _____

7. A _____ she _____ (**order**) the new cookware yet?

   B _____

A. Complete the sentences. Follow the example.

himself	myself	herself	yourselves	~~themselves~~	herself

1. We should clean up this mess. People could fall and hurt _____themselves_____.

2. Tom just got his driver's license. He drove _____ to work today.

3. I burned _____. I didn't know that pan was hot.

4. Marta counted all the cooks, but she didn't count _____.

5. John and Mary, be careful with those meat cleavers! Don't cut _____.

6. She bought _____ a lovely new dress.

B. Complete the dialogs. Follow the example.

1. **A** Does this hotel offer special **prices** in the **summer?**

   B Yes, in July and August we have _____summer prices_____.

2. **A** I need some warm **shirts** for **winter.**

   B Our _____ are in the corner.

3. **A** I need some **training** to get a **job.**

   B We offer free _____.

4. **A** I need some **glasses** to wear while **reading.**

   B We have lots of _____.

C. Complete the descriptions. Follow the example.

1. Maxine needs a knife for chopping. The knife must be sharp and heavy.

   Maxine needs a _____sharp heavy chopping knife_____.

2. Tom needs pants for work. He makes sure they are long and heavy.

   Tom needs _____.

3. Teresa wears goggles for safety. Her goggles are thick and clear.

   Teresa wears _____.

4. Samantha wears gloves for gardening. Her gloves are green and made of cotton.

   Samantha wears _____.

Blackline Masters

Name _____

A. Complete the sentences. Follow the example.

1. While I _____ **was making** _____ (make) the schedule, Pablo

   _____ **asked** _____ (ask) for Saturday off.

2. When I _____ (stop) Mike in the hall, he

   _____ (walk) to the work room.

3. Joe _____ (rake) the leaves on the lawn when the rain

   _____ (start).

4. Sally _____ (see) a terrible accident while she

   _____ (drive) her cab on Main Street.

5. We _____ (carry) bags of trash to the curb when the

   garbage truck _____ (arrive).

6. The power _____ (go) out while they _____
   (develop) the customers' film.

B. Complete the sentences. Use the schedule. Follow the example.

Same-Day Delivery Service		Tuesday, April 27 — Jim	
8:30	Arrive at work	12:30 to 1:30	Lunch
8:30 to 9:00	Wash the truck	1:30 to 2:00	Load the truck
9:00 to 9:30	Load the truck	2:00 to 5:00	Make deliveries
9:30 to 12:30	Make deliveries	5:00 to 5:15	Check the truck

1. After Jim arrived at work, he _____ **washed the truck** _____.

2. Jim _____ before he made his morning
   deliveries.

3. After Jim made his morning deliveries, he _____.

4. Jim loaded the truck again before he _____

   _____.

5. After Jim _____, he checked the truck.

C. Complete the dialogs. Write **before** or **after**. Follow the example.

1. **A** Did Tom use to work for the city?

   B Yes, he worked for the city _____**before**_____ he started working here.

2. **A** Did you have to take a test to become a nurse's aide?

   B Yes, I became a nurse's aide _____ I passed the test.

3. **A** Did you see the new sweaters that we had on sale?

   B No, I didn't. The sweaters were all sold _____ I got here.

4. **A** Did Tom put away the dishes?

   B Yes, he put the dishes away _____ he washed them.

5. **A** Did Miguel install the new refrigerator?

   B Yes, he installed it _____ he unloaded it from the truck.

6. **A** Will you change that light bulb?

   B Yes, I'll change it _____ I get a new one from the supply room.

7. **A** You need to change the oil in the delivery van right away.

   B OK, I'll change it now _____ I go to the post office.

8. **A** Did you frost the cake?

   B Yes, I frosted it _____ it cooled down.

D. Complete the sentences. Follow the example.

1. Is the lunch shift _____**as busy as**_____ (**busy**) the dinner shift?

2. I think the day manager is _____ (**polite**) the night manager.

3. John is_____ (**not fast**) Michelle, but his work is

   always _____ (**good**) hers.

4. Lisa usually is_____ (**not early**) Darnell.

5. Are Teresa's tables _____ (**clean**) Donna's?

6. The new laundry detergent is_____ (**not strong**) the old detergent.

7. The cookies are_____ (**not fresh**) the cake.

Name _____

A. Complete the sentences. Follow the example.

1. I _**'ve**_____ never _____**worked**_____ (work) in this department before.

2. David_____ never _____ (**have**) a sales job before this one.

3. I_____ never _____ (**think**) about working outdoors. I think I'd like it.

4. _____ you ever _____ (**notice**) how busy we are on Fridays?

5. _____ Jenny ever _____ (**tell**) you about her last job?

6. _____ Debbie ever _____ (**work**) at the cash register before?

7. This company_____ never _____ (**raise**) its prices.

8. Mr. Johnson_____ never _____ (**own**) his own business before.

9. _____ the mechanics ever _____ (**see**) this problem before?

10. We_____ never _____ (**have**) a workplace accident in our department.

B. Complete the dialogs. Follow the example.

1. A _____**Have**_____ you ever _____**taken**_____ (take) the bus to work?

   B No, I _____**haven't**_____. I_**'ve**____ always _____**taken**_____ (take) the subway.

2. A _____ Sam ever _____ (**apply**) for a job with us?

   B Yes, he _____. I_____ (**interview**) him once before.

3. A _____ you ever _____ (**read**) your job description?

   B No, I _____. I_____ never _____ (**see**) it.

4. A _____ you and Mike ever _____ (**cook**) roast beef?

   B No, we _____. We_____ only

   _____ (**make**) salads and desserts.

UNIT 10

Name _____

C. Complete the sentences. Use **going to**. Follow the example.

1. Jason *'s going to write* _____ (**write**) a letter to that company tomorrow morning.

2. They _____ (**move**) the furniture next week.

3. They _____ (**lead**) the safety meeting later today.

4. My supervisor _____ (**teach**) me how to fill out an order form this afternoon.

5. We _____ (**drive**) to the construction site next week.

6. He _____ (**check**) the oil.

7. Our company _____ (**buy**) new tools for all the technicians next year.

8. I _____ (**learn**) how to use the new computer system this afternoon.

9. We _____ (**deliver**) the new chairs to the hotel by Friday.

10. They _____ (**leave**) this desk when they move their offices.

11. I _____ (**go**) on vacation in August.

D. Write the correct form of the word. Follow the example.

1. If I _____ *go* _____ (**go**) to the training class, I *'ll learn* _____ (**learn**) how to drive the forklift.

2. If you _____ (**tell**) John about the broken light,

   he _____ (**fix**) it.

3. We _____ (**not finish**) this job on time if we

   _____ (**not start**) now.

4. If he _____ (**pass**) the driving test, he _____ (**get**) his driver's license.

5. If he _____ (**have**) time this afternoon, he _____ (**start**) making signs for tomorrow's sale.

6. You _____ (**not be**) able to get the paperwork done if you

   _____ (**spend**) all day with customers.

7. They _____ (**repair**) your car today if the new windshield

   _____ (**arrive**) on time.

148

Blackline Masters

© Steck-Vaughn Company. *English ASAP Level 3.* Permission granted to reproduce for classroom use.

UNIT 1

A. 1. but
2. and
3. but
4. or
5. and
6. or

B. 1. to clean
2. trying
3. to open
4. calling
5. to get
6. planning
7. to train

C. *Answers will vary.*

UNIT 2

A. 1. me
2. them
3. her
4. you
5. them

B. 1. She should apply for a job at the animal hospital.
2. He should take a training class.
3. He should ask for more help.
4. They should call a repair person.
5. She should practice for the test.

C. 1. make
2. do
3. makes
4. does

UNIT 3

A. 1. quickly
2. carefully
3. professionally
4. patiently
5. slowly
6. carelessly
7. correctly
8. completely
9. accurately
10. truthfully

B. 1. 'm going to clean it up
2. 's going to call the repair service
3. 're going to leave soon
4. 's going to rain
5. 'm going to dry them
6. 's going to buy more forms
7. 're going to call the locksmith
8. 're going to deliver the bread
9. 's going to replace the light bulbs

UNIT 4

A. 1. has, worked
's worked, since
2. has, been
's been, since
3. has, had
's had, since

B. *Answers will vary.*

C. 1. Yes, he has.
2. No, he hasn't.
3. No, he hasn't.
4. Yes, they have.
5. No, they haven't.

D. 1. thinks (that) the supply clerk should move the boxes
2. agrees (that) this chair is too low
3. thinks (that) the store room is very cold
4. agrees (that) the new knife sharpener works well

UNIT 5

A. 1. busier than, more organized than
2. the busiest, the most organized
3. more powerful than
4. the strongest
5. more efficient than
6. more comfortable than
7. the best, the largest, the lowest
8. nicer than, the best
9. more convenient than
10. more comfortable than
11. the friendliest
12. faster than
13. the most expensive, the biggest
14. cleaner than
15. slower than

UNIT 6

A. 1. 'll go, needs
2. 'll ask, finishes
3. don't have, 'll call
4. decide, 'll make
5. 'll get, comes
6. 'll call, doesn't arrive
7. doesn't have, 'll order

B. *Accept all answers that make sense.*
1. looks busy
2. looks, seems, *or* feels happy
3. feels worried
4. looks *or* feels sick

U N I T 7

A.
1. started
2. went
3. delivered
4. mailed
5. finished
6. made
7. caught
8. drove
9. finished
10. helped

B.
1. Have, finished
   haven't fed, yet
2. Have, started
   've already started
3. Have, put away
   haven't done, yet
4. Have, left yet
   haven't finished, yet

C.
1. Has, catered
   No, she hasn't.
2. Has, interviewed
   Yes, she has.
3. Has, gone
   Yes, she has.
4. Has, met
   No, she hasn't.
5. Has, bought
   Yes, she has.
6. Has, started
   Yes, she has.
7. Has, ordered
   Yes, she has.

U N I T 8

A.
1. themselves
2. himself
3. myself
4. herself
5. yourselves
6. herself

B.
1. summer prices
2. winter shirts
3. job training
4. reading glasses

C.
1. sharp heavy chopping knife
2. long heavy work pants
3. thick clear safety goggles
4. green cotton gardening gloves

U N I T 9

A.
1. was making, asked
2. stopped, was walking
3. was raking, started

4. saw, was driving
5. were carrying, arrived
6. went, were developing

B.
1. washed the truck
2. loaded the truck
3. ate lunch
4. made his afternoon deliveries
5. made his afternoon deliveries

C.
1. before
2. after
3. before
4. after
5. after
6. after
7. before
8. after

D.
1. as busy as
2. as polite as
3. n't as fast as,
   as good as
4. n't as early as
5. as clean as
6. n't as strong as
7. n't as fresh as

U N I T 10

A.
1. 've, worked
2. 's, had
3. 've, thought
4. Have, noticed
5. Has, told
6. Has, worked
7. 's, raised
8. 's, owned
9. Have, seen
10. 've, had

B.
1. Have, taken
   haven't, 've, taken
2. Has, applied
   has, 've interviewed
3. Have, read
   haven't, 've, seen
4. Have, cooked
   haven't, 've, made

C.
1. 's going to write
2. 're going to move
3. 're going to lead
4. 's going to teach
5. 're going to drive
6. 's going to check
7. 's going to buy
8. 'm going to learn
9. 're going to deliver
10. 're going to leave
11. 'm going to go

D.
1. go, 'll learn
2. tell, 'll fix
3. won't finish, don't start
4. passes, 'll get
5. has, 'll start
6. won't be, spend
7. 'll repair, arrives

Learner _____

Class _____

Teacher _____

Individual Competency Chart

Unit 1

	Date Presented	Date Checked	Result (✔)	Comments
1. Transfer a call				
2. Deal with a wrong number				
3. Keep a phone log				
4. Use voice mail				

Unit 2

	Date Presented	Date Checked	Result (✔)	Comments
1. Report progress on work				
2. Ask for and understand feedback				
3. Report job completion				
4. Create a status report				

Unit 3

	Date Presented	Date Checked	Result (✔)	Comments
1. Report problems				
2. Create solutions				
3. Troubleshoot				
4. Make recommendations for improvement				

English ASAP — Level 3

Learner _____

Class _____

Teacher _____

Unit 4

	Date Presented	Date Checked	Result (✔)	Comments
1. Build a schedule				
2. Organize tasks efficiently				
3. Meet deadlines				

Unit 5

	Date Presented	Date Checked	Result (✔)	Comments
1. Understand your customers' needs				
2. Explain your product				
3. Use telephone skills for customer service				
4. Write a customer service letter				

Unit 6

	Date Presented	Date Checked	Result (✔)	Comments
1. Make suggestions				
2. Build on team members' strengths				
3. Ask for help				
4. Be an effective team member				

Individual Competency Chart

Individual Competency Chart

Learner _____

Class _____

Teacher _____

Unit 7

	Date Presented	Date Checked	Result (✔)	Comments
1. Understand a budget				
2. Use a budget				
3. Complete work on budget				
4. Keep budget records				

Unit 8

	Date Presented	Date Checked	Result (✔)	Comments
1. Understand health benefits				
2. Read and compare benefit plans				
3. Understand your rights				
4. Complete a claim form				

 **Level 3**

Individual Competency Chart

Learner _____

Class _____

Teacher _____

Unit 9

	Date Presented	Date Checked	Result (✔)	Comments
1. Avoid discriminatory language				
2. Respect cultural differences				
3. Resolve differences				
4. Understand policies				

Unit 10

	Date Presented	Date Checked	Result (✔)	Comments
1. Decide what you want from a job				
2. Analyze a job description				
3. Compare jobs				
4. Evaluate career choices				

Individual Competency Chart

Class Cumulative Competency Chart

Unit _____ Class _____

Teacher _____

Workforce Skills

Name									Comments

English ASAP:

Connecting English to the Workplace

Certificate of Completion

This is to certify that

_____

has successfully completed Level 3 of
Steck-Vaughn's English ASAP series

_____
Instructor

_____
Organization or Program

_____
City and State

_____
Date

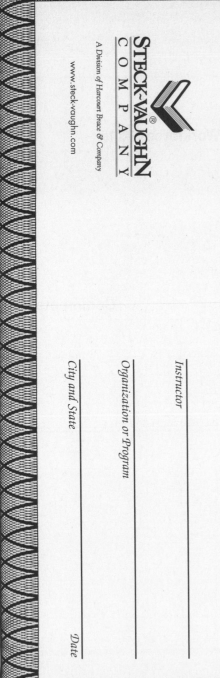

STECK-VAUGHN
C O M P A N Y

A Division of Harcourt Brace & Company

www.steck-vaughn.com